# a road called down on both sides: growing up in ethiopia and america

BY CAROLINE KURTZ

**CATALYST PRESS**
Livermore, California

In North America, this book is distributed by
Consortium Book Sales & Distribution, a division of Ingram.
Phone: 612/746-2600
cbsdinfo@ingramcontent.com
www.cbsd.com

In South Africa, Namibia, and Botswana,
this book is distributed by LAPA Publishers.
Phone: 012/401-0700
lapa@lapa.co.za
www.lapa.co.za

FIRST EDITION
10 9 8 7 6 5 4 3 2 1

Library of Congress Control Number 2018964622

*Dedicated to Mom, Dad, and Mark,*

*who took me on grand adventures*

*and have now embarked on adventures*

*beyond this earthly form.*

# a note of thanks

Before this book went to press, five generous Ethiopian readers gave me their feedback on how I had presented Ethiopian culture and history. The worth of their contribution is incalculable. They corrected my transliterated spelling of Amharic words, and in a few cases corrected my usage. They challenged me into deeper research about the tensions between ethnic groups that I had seen but not fully understood first as a child and later as a teacher in Ethiopia. They corrected misunderstandings that could have seemed embarrassingly ignorant or even hurtful to my Ethiopian friends. The process of working with them has been a new, exciting chapter of learning in my life as a participant in two cultures. Thank you, Dr. Woubeshet Ayenew, for reading my manuscript and passing it on to your mother Wzo. (Mrs.) Zemamnesh Adamu for her feedback as well. She created a chart of Amharic words I'd used, what pages they occurred on, and how they should be spelled! Thank you, Dr. Worku L. Mulat, Dr. Fethiya Mahmoud, and Wzo. Zenbaba Fikere for taking the time to read my manuscript and become my friends and teachers. All of you gave me feedback that was beyond invaluable, and made this book a richer, deeper story. Dr. Woubeshet said he was sorry our work together on the book is coming to an end, because our discussions have been so interesting. I totally agree! And as we go to press, I take full responsibility for any remaining mistakes.

Thank you also to Graham Abney, a history graduate student at Portland State University, who did a thorough fact-check of Ethiopian history for me. You saved this big-picture thinker and history lover from several careless mistakes, and from some sweeping statements that, again, might have embarrassed me later!

Caroline Kurtz
June 2019
Portland, Oregon

# CHAPTER 1

I grew up in Maji, on the edge of an Ethiopian escarpment that descends, one blue volcanic ridge at a time, to the lowlands of South Sudan. A dirt track ran through the middle of town. People walked to Maji from miles around on market days, and spread the extra their little farms had produced on mats in an open spot beside the track. The clay soil there had been pounded to an impenetrable surface. People used the coins they exchanged, or bills that had grown ragged and brown, to buy the soap, salt, sugar, and candles they couldn't grow. The market square was littered with bits of the leaves people used to wrap butter or *enset* root; chips off gourds that had held honey or milk; fragrant cow pies in the corner where cattle were sold; and strands of the pithy ribs of *enset* leaves that people used as twine.

We lived a mile from town, on a knoll overlooking the valley.

One morning over breakfast, when I was about eight, Dad said, "We're going on a hike today. I'm going to show you a surprise."

He beamed at the two aunties who had arrived the day before. Then he turned his smile on me and my younger sisters, Jane and Joy. "You're going to be amazed!"

Mom raised her eyebrows. "Amazed?" Her skepticism only made the surprise richer.

"Tell us, Daddy," Jane said. She was six.

"Eat your oatmeal. It'll stick to your ribs."

Above the table, morning light and fresh air came into our dining room between the top of thick mud-plaster walls and our *korkoro*, or corrugated iron roof. Dad had supervised the building of this home for us. When they poured the cement floor, he polished it to a pewter shine. Mom hung curtains at the windows, peacocks with red tails on a gold ground. Out the window stood the giant thatched roofs of the *gojos* where we'd first lived.

The aunties looked up, interested in this talk of surprises. They weren't our real aunties. They were single American women, nurses working in a hot lowland area, come to see the famous mountains of Maji.

A gong sounded to call the workmen—Dad's foreman hitting a battered Jeep wheel rim with a piece of iron pipe. Dad pushed his chair back. Wood scraping on cement echoed off the *korkoro*. "I'll get the men started. Meet me at the gate."

Dad had gone to seminary, but before that he'd been a farm boy in Eastern Oregon. Now his life revolved around a shop that smelled of oil, kerosene, and earth—with *korkoro* walls as well as roof.

Jane, Joy, and I ran out of the house, shoes on and tied. The aunties emerged from the guest-house *gojo* with walking sticks. They wore long skirts whose colors had faded in the tropical sun, white socks and white blouses, sturdy shoes, and sweaters that protected them against the mountain air we were so used to. Aunt Joan was solid and square and full of effervescent energy. Aunt Breezy had a smile as warm as the sunrise.

They sauntered, chatting, along the track that ran around our house, past the border of heavy-headed Shasta daisies. Jane and Joy each grabbed an auntie's hand. I was too big for hand holding. Dad came out of the shop, rubbing his hands together. His smile bunched his cheeks over high cheekbones.

As we descended the foot path outside the gate, I fell into line behind Jane, with her chopped-short hair. Short, because she'd screamed when Mom put it in a ponytail. Chopped, because she couldn't sit still while Dad cut it. We picked fern babies off the growing tips of waist-high ferns that grew beside the path. They smelled of chlorophyll and sunshine. Joy trotted ahead of us, the wispy tail on the back of her head bouncing with every step. The Maji air might be warm, with sun beaming down so direct, so near. Or it might be chill with valley fogs. At 8,500 feet, we could depend on the Maji air to always feel thin, always taste fresh. The aunties, from their lowland climate, immediately began to breathe hard.

Jane and I had named the clay outcropping against the opposite hillside Red Rock in a fit of poetic romance, though it was dull pink and smeared with cow pies. Where the two hills swooped together, a little stream threaded over a stone ledge, running to meet the river that fell in stages into the valley. Green moss waved in the faint current. The water trickled softly, and the hollow tonk of hand-carved wooden cow bells from the hillside above us drifted in the clear air.

Dad straddled the creek. "Step on my foot," he said to Joy. "Now jump!" Her ponytail flew and her little red t-shirt hitched up from her elastic-waist jeans as he levitated her to the other side. Jane, dancing with impatience, grabbed Dad's arm before he had even turned Joy loose. "Hold your horses," he said. She leapt so high that landing dropped her to her knees on the stone.

I stepped carefully past cow-splats, fresh and smelling of digested grass. "I can jump," I said. My toes landed on the very edge of the bank on the other side. I turned and squatted, then, to drop a fern-baby into the water. The current caught it. The baby bobbed and swayed. At my elbow, Jane said, "If I jumped in with her, I would be tiny and float down to the valley."

"We could breathe under water," I said. I had just read *The Water Babies*, and told her the story. We watched the fern-baby drift toward the watery adventures we were too big for in that little stream. Jane's brown bob was almost even with my ponytail. She threw a kiss and the fern eddied slowly around a sedge that had bowed over and dipped its salt-and-pepper flower into the water.

"Girls," Dad called. I jumped to my feet. I guided Joy onto the path, pulled at Jane's t-shirt. She shook my hand off and hissed. "You're not the boss of me!"

Only a few steps from the stream, a clay path swooped downward. Cut into the hillside by the passing of cattle and people, it looked as if it had been carved with a paring knife from the side of the mountain, the peel of sod and soil curling up and falling into the valley below. The hillside itself dropped away a thousand feet.

I put one foot in front of the other. My heart pounded, not from the effort of the descent, but from the effort not to imagine the endless tumble to the valley floor. I wanted to be Dad's brave and intrepid daughter, but my stomach lurched and prickles spread across my shoulders.

Joy skidded on a pebble and sat suddenly on the path, the width of her five-year-old hips. The aunties went on, keeping up with Dad in their own efforts to be brave and intrepid single women in Africa. "Girls," Dad shouted. All I could see was his hand waving over his head in his troops-onward gesture. "Keep up!"

Joy stood slowly. I dusted off her jeans. "You have to not fall," I said.

A buzzard swung over us and hung in the sunlight. Its body drifted effortlessly, wingtip pinions quivering in the air currents. Dad's voice came in erratic snippets in the breeze. He stopped and peered around at the train of daughters following like ducklings. The aunties breathed hard, leaning on their walking sticks. Aunt Breezy turned. Her smile looked a little trembly, as though her feelings on this cliff-side path were like mine.

"Listen," Dad said, as we reached him.

I held my breath and heard the tiniest whisper of falling water. Before we could ask, Dad turned back to the steep path. Even from behind he looked excited. A magician about to produce the rabbit.

As I took my next careful steps a strange smell filled my nose. It grew so strong, I gagged. An animal smell. Not the fresh compost of a forest, not grass or leaves or mud.

"Ee-yoo, Daddy, what is that?" Jane yelled.

Dad didn't turn. I clearly heard the white noise of a waterfall now, and I blinked droplets off my eyelashes. The path dropped even more steeply, rocky and slick. Jane hurried ahead to catch up with the aunties. Joy slipped, and whimpered.

"Keep up." I bossed Joy, although I was glad for the excuse to creep behind her. She lurched along, bent over and awkward, clinging to tufts of grass on the up-side of the hill.

When she disappeared around a rocky corner, I paused. The valley lay below, and opposite ran the ridge with the stony layers of a geologic story I couldn't read. Beyond, the golden low-lands where Sudan, Kenya and Ethiopia clicked together. The raptor soared. The fecund smell caught in my throat. The rush of falling water filled my ears and cool mist clung to my face.

I pulled myself back to business and stepped around the rock wall to a curtain of water. The basalt wall shone black as obsidian. Ferns and grasses growing from stony crevices hung with moisture and bobbed as drops collected and fell. I tipped my head back and looked up the dizzying wall. I got ready to look pleased and surprised. *Wow, Dad! Another waterfall!*

He was guiding Joy by the arm behind the curtain, into darkness. Jane lifted one finger from over her mouth and nose. "I can't breathe, Daddy," she shouted over the crashing of water on stone.

"Of course you can, Jane," Dad said, in the overly patient voice he and Mom used with Jane. He gripped her upper arm tightly, pushing her behind the crashing water. I didn't need to be guided. I didn't need to be pushed. I slipped by Dad, and looked up for some sign of appreciation for how I didn't need managing, how well I had negotiated the steep path, how I had helped him with my sisters. But he was busy maneuvering back to the head of his clustered subjects.

Only a few feet into the cave, darkness overcame the gray light flickering through the waterfall. Dad turned on his flashlight. He waved the yellow beam at the ceiling, where its circle played over a squirming mass. Red eyes glinted here and there like rubies on an ermine stole. "Look't that! You girls know what they are?" The mass writhed.

4

He moved the light slowly over it. "Bats!"

The bats pushed and crowded, shoving their neighbors, fighting for the best toe-hold in the rock ceiling. Dozens, black in the gray light, swooped past. There were thousands of bats. Maybe millions. Around me, Jane, Joy and the aunties were as silent as I was. Dad shifted his flashlight beam down onto a dun-colored hill that rose higher than our heads.

"Guano," Aunt Joan said. "Americans pay good money for guano. They put it on their gardens."

Dad laughed. "We could be rich!"

"What is it?" Jane said.

"It's from the bats," Dad said

"Yes, but what is it?"

In the dim light, Dad's eyes met Jane's and looked quickly away. He coughed. He looked down. "Bat BM," he said. His voice was so soft, I almost didn't hear.

Shame swept over me as though Dad's embarrassment had poured directly from his heart into mine. I jabbed Jane with my elbow. She hung her head. I didn't know yet that in her own, more defiant way, she had the same need I had, to protect Dad, to make him look good.

Dad recovered by launching into the tale of the bat cave: how it went for miles under the mountain, how local people had been coming for decades, maybe centuries, with primitive tools and tapers to mine salt from deep inside.

I barely listened. Dad was okay again and I was free to savor that delightful new word—*guano*. It was *guano* that had smelled so strongly back on the path. Overpowering out there, but magically, in with the bats, standing between the water and the mountain of guano, the air was sweet and clear.

Dad finished his tour guide lecture and led us deeper into the cave. Suddenly he turned off the flashlight. Darkness wrapped around me, tangible, weighty. I hadn't closed my eyes—or had I? I blinked, to check. Darkness surrounded me entirely. The rushing of water filled my ears. The restless bats squeaked and squealed.

"Caroline?" Jane said. Her voice came from in front of me. I stepped forward in faith, like Moses putting his foot into the Red Sea before the waters had even parted. Her hair felt rough under my fingers. I found her shoulder and held on.

# CHAPTER 2

When Mom was about twenty, working as a secretary for a tire company in Des Moines, Iowa (not the job of her bookish dreams), she thought about volunteering at a mission school in Egypt. But praying about it one day, she opened her Bible and pointed blindly to a verse. When she opened her eyes, she read: "Go ye not unto Egypt."

She went not.

Since God had closed the door to Egypt, Mom proceeded with her original plan—college. There, she met Dad. They married, and went off to seminary in Pittsburgh before she finished her English major. Mom's Bible-verse-pointing method of discerning the will of God was widely recommended when I was a child, but I don't remember hearing Mom talk any other time about reading her Bible and praying. Dad was the one with the dog-eared, much underlined Bible and margin notes in his spiky and unreadable handwriting. Mom seems to have decided, after she married a pastor, that Bible guidance was his territory.

When Dad finished seminary, he became a popular young pastor in Portland, Oregon, resuscitating a Presbyterian church that had threatened to die. There, when he was thirty and I was four, he got his call. Not directly from God, but pretty close: a letter, unbidden, from the Presbyterian Church headquarters.

*Missionary.* What a fraught word. It gives many people hives, including some of my siblings. I am not fond of it either. Even the Presbyterian Church got squeamish about *missionary*. For a while the church tried *Mission Co-worker*, emphasizing partnership. But no one heard anything beyond the M-word. The next try, *Fraternal Worker*— what does that even mean?

I went back to Ethiopia under the Presbyterian Church, but if I say *missionary*, people's eyes fog over with stereotypes. And if I keep my words simple and precise—I taught Ethiopian girls English, I lived in Kenya and promoted women's development in South Sudan, I organized a peace conference there—people brighten and ask, "Peace Corps?" As soon as I mention the church, they say, "Oh. A missionary."

Jane once posted some pictures of Dad on Facebook—in his Army

Air Corps cap; horsing around with his teenaged sister; standing beside the Cessna 180 he flew in Ethiopia for about five years. A friend posted, "I thought your dad was a missionary!" Jane studied the pictures. What about them said not-a-missionary? My sisters and I agreed he was lacking a pith helmet and big black Bible. That was the cheap answer, the answer that let us roll our eyes at people's annoying preconceptions. But it might have been the Air Force and the Cessna. Or worse, it might have been the evidence of his sense of humor.

Mom and Dad were not embarrassed to call themselves missionaries. They believed in a God who created the heavens and the earth. They believed in Jesus—that he taught what the gospels say he taught, that his death had redemptive significance, and that he rose after being crucified. Presbyterians are trinitarians, so the Holy Spirit fit in there as well, but the mystery of the Trinity washed over me like a downpour in the *kiremt* rains of Ethiopia in the summer.

It's reasonable to assume that Mom and Dad were perfectly clear about their faith and the benefits of it, so they could commend it to others. The full truth about their faith is more elusive. Dad could preach in two languages, but he didn't talk about what his faith meant in his daily life. When he was a young Army Air Corps pilot (*EIT: Exiled in Texas* is what he called it in a scrapbook at the time), he read *The Robe* and *The Shoes of the Fisherman*. Those novels by Lloyd C. Douglas, a pastor turned author, were about people who were deeply changed by meeting Jesus. They led Dad to become a pastor in spite of his college double major in physics and math.

But what did he actually use from those books? How did his faith sustain him? What did he pray for? Did God answer his prayers? When it came to talking about his personal faith, Dad was almost as mute about his as Mom was about hers.

By the time the letter inviting Dad to be a missionary arrived at the manse in Portland in 1954, three daughters had changed Mom's view of going to Africa. Dad loved a good story, and when he told this one, he threw his hands up and asked, "How do you discuss something with your wife if every time the subject comes up, she bursts into tears? For weeks, I didn't need to salt my eggs!"

One gloomy February morning in the middle of their impasse, Mom went out to hang the ubiquitous diapers on the line. A weak ray of February sunlight burst through the clouds. Mom thought, *If God can make the sun shine on me in February in Portland, He can make the sun shine on us in Ethiopia.* She went back inside and announced, "I'm ready to go."

And that is how they gave me the gift of a big, adventuresome life.

Before the photographer posed us for our first family passport picture, Mom sprayed her hair and applied her signature scarlet lipstick. Dad combed his hair back with water. They pulled my wiggly sisters' dark hair up into tails on top of their heads. Mom had curled my fine blond hair and now she fussed and sprayed it into a flip. In the photo, I look delighted with the toy the photographer waved at us, confident and solidly planted, as though I know well where I belong.

Dad crated up furniture. When a friend asked Mom how she could pack and get halfway around the world with three preschoolers, she breezily said, "We have a covenant with chaos." She packed five years' worth of clothes for three girls in fifty-gallon barrels. Dad sent everything off to the docks in New York, but their visa did not come. Chaos kept up its end of the deal: Mom got pregnant again.

Finally, after nine months of waiting, the visa gestated. Jane, Joy and I bounced along like tin cans rattling after a jalopy: to New York; onto the USS Elizabeth to London; in four-engine planes over the bulge toward the equator, refueling in Athens, Cairo and Eritrea.

Dad told stories about how all five of us had diarrhea at the same time as we adjusted to food and water in Ethiopia. How Mom put damp diapers on Joy because the small rains started and nothing dried on the clotheslines. I loved the taste of Kaopectate, and I told lies about having diarrhea at kindergarten. I was amazed that Mom didn't know. She held a serving spoon carefully to my lips and I slurped the pink, chalky liquid.

A brother was born in the middle of the chaos, two months after we arrived in Addis Ababa. Our big, analytical family has discussed why he failed to thrive, but really, no one knows. At four months, he died in the night.

The next morning, Dad gathered us on their big double bed. *I have something to tell you.* Mom was not around. Dad hollered at Jane for bouncing. Then he got his somber voice on again. He said Kenny had died, but we shouldn't cry, and I studied his face, because as he said this, he was crying. Jane, who'd felt special because Kenny shared her birthday, asked if we could get another baby. Joy, who was now two, walked around and around his bassinet saying, "Kenny went to Jesus."

I had taken care of my brother with Dad one day when Mom went into town. He'd cried, and we couldn't comfort him. Now, I said, "We tried so hard to keep him."

Our brother was buried immediately. That was the Ethiopian way. The next day, Mom and Dad woke to the sounds of soft conversation in our living room. Ethiopian men and women, still wrapped against the chill in thick, hand-woven cotton *gabis* half rose, bowing, as Mom and Dad came sleepily out of the bedroom. Our house worker introduced them, neighbors from the thatched *gojos* around our Italian style house.

"We know that morning is the hardest. You shouldn't be alone. We will sit with you," she said. Ethiopians knew death well. They often waited to name their children until they passed the critical second year.

The poignancy of this story always broke Dad up. Anything that touched his heart brushed across his tear ducts first. On furlough, preaching in churches from New York, where we landed, to Oregon, where we ended up, he talked about the people of Maji, without medical care, without education. "People die because they believe they are cursed by the evil eye," he said, and his voice broke. In the stillness, as Dad struggled to steady himself, my sinuses fizzed. I sat back on the pew cushions of prosperous Presbyterian churches. I stopped kicking my feet, which didn't reach to the plush carpets. Beside me, my sisters grew still. We hardly breathed until Dad's voice returned to normal. Mom passed Kleenex down the row so we wouldn't go on sniffing in church. She always had a supply that she had saved after blotting her scarlet lipstick. Blowing my nose, I felt relief, and smelled Mom's warm sticky kisses.

Chaos showed up again in Addis Ababa, and I got hepatitis. I passed it to Dad and Mom. Mine had been a light case; they were bedridden for weeks and a missionary auntie moved in to take care of us girls. A few months later, Cathy was born in Addis Ababa.

It's amazing to think that Mom and Dad were in Amharic language school during all this birthing, living and dying. When Mom's house worker, sweeping up crumbs one day, said, "You need a chicken," Mom laughed. She was equally delighted at the image of a hen under our table, and that she had understood.

This must have been when Mom and Dad began the habit of thinking of us as an unindividuated gaggle: The Kurtz Girls. There was surely no time for anything but group management. I still find myself saying *we* about my childhood, as though I had only shared experiences with my sisters, nothing of my own.

After he finished language study, Dad went along on a survey trip to Maji, the remotest station, five hundred miles from Addis Ababa, maybe fifty miles from the border with South Sudan—a week in and another week back out over a bone-jarring Italian-built road. One section, where the Jeep lurched over a rocky outcropping, they named

The Golden Staircase. Dad got malaria as they dipped through lowland valleys. During the fever and headache cycle, he hallucinated the neon Seven-Up sign in downtown Portland. When the fever switched to violent chills, he asked to drive. It was a typical, counterintuitive Dad-solution—using the steering wheel to stabilize himself.

Later, Dad had a relapse during the all-mission meeting they called Association, where they came together to set policy. The mission doctors wanted Dad to stay in bed, but compromised when he promised to stay prone on a couch at the back of the room. Old growth boards on the floor and wainscoting glowed, polished with bee's wax and kerosene. On the agenda was the report, and the question of Maji—had the Presbyterians over-reached?

Ethiopian Airlines didn't run regular air service that far, and a few years earlier, Fred Russell, who had opened Maji station, had rolled the Jeep down a steep embankment where shoulder-high *senbeliet* grass had camouflaged the edge of the road. Tents, food, and camp stove scattered. Aunt Daisy, a short woman with a halo of white hair, broke her hip. The nurse with them broke her collar bone. Uncle Fred was seeing double in the evening gloom as he crawled around, trying to gather things to shelter them before night fell completely.

They swallowed aspirin and lay through the night with the canvas tent draped over them. Animals prowled around them in the dark.

The next day, out where it seemed there was not a soul for miles, local people gathered in that uncanny way of Ethiopia. They helped Uncle Fred find the rest of their belongings and push the Jeep back up to the road. The only thing they never found in the grass was the gear-shift knob. Uncle Fred offered a reward of one Ethiopian *birr*, about twenty cents.

Men carried the women on makeshift stretchers several days into Maji. It was weeks before Uncle Fred could charter a plane and get them out. By that time, their bones had knitted where they lay. Now, Aunt Daisy wore a special shoe, its sole an inch thick on her left foot, and still she walked with a limp.

Two months after they returned to Maji, a boy jogged into the mission compound carrying the gear-shift knob, sweating and proud, to collect his reward.

Uncle Fred and Aunt Daisy were about to retire. Should the Maji mission station be closed?

"No!" Dad said, prone and feverish, from the back of the room. The stories people remember about Dad are legion and they are all dramatic. *No, no. The Kurtzes will keep Maji station open.*

# CHAPTER 3

There is some debate about whether Dad conferred with Mom before he volunteered them. Once he died and she disappeared into dementia, it became a question with no answer. All Mom would say was, "I married adventure!"

And once I had children, I was astounded that Dad even considered taking his little girls to so remote a place. Was the Russells' accident not a warning? Or did Dad hear in it not the danger, but God's protection from real harm? None of us ever questioned him about where he thought we would get medical care. I don't know, even now, whether Dad acted out of a deep faith that God would protect us because he was doing God's work, or if he was driven by heroic hubris. It was difficult to challenge Dad on anything, and if I did accuse him of endangering his family, the evidence would line up on his side. In the ten years we lived in Maji, our stitches and broken bones and Dad's kidney stones occurred on furloughs or in Addis Ababa.

But why would I want to accuse him, anyway? His choice gave me my wonderful Maji childhood.

To get us there, Dad chartered a plane. He ferried to the airport what was, by Ethiopian standards, a mountain of luxuries—by American standards, the basics. In Portland they had crated up a double bed and matching dresser, two rocking chairs (Mom had said, *I'm not having any more babies if I don't have a rocking chair*), and an odd green rug with loops of cording, like a rough prototype for shag. There were the barrels full of clothes, books and shoes. In Addis they bought cans of Kraft cheese, rolled oats and powdered milk to last six months; burlap sacks of flour and sugar; marshmallows in boxes for campfires; and a few luxuries like olives and maraschino cherries. However, no event was special enough for Mom to bring out the luxuries, until, in the months just before furlough, she served olives with every meal so they wouldn't go to waste.

Our family stood for a photo the morning of our departure for Maji: the mother in scarlet lipstick and a full red and white checked skirt,

11

the descending row of three girls who look solemn, and the father holding the baby. She wears a blue corduroy bonnet against the tropical sun. Behind them stands a C-47 troop carrier from the US Army Air Corps in Europe, donated to Ethiopia to start an airline. Its tail feathers glow with the green-yellow-red of the flag, and the royal lion rears up on the side.

The charter landed in the city of Jimma to refuel, and muscled laborers in torn shorts began off-loading our crates and boxes, and on-loading soap, kerosene, matches and salt for merchants to sell in the Maji market. Dad watched for a few seconds in shock, and then shouted at the laborers in his language-school Amharic. They just looked at him as they pounded past, sweating under their loads. Dad rushed over to the agent, outraged—*I chartered this flight!* But the merchants had bribed the agent, so he pretended not to understand. Finally, Dad violated his own standard of submission to the culture, and went to the American pilot.

The pilot shouted at the agent, the agent shouted back, and in a classically Ethiopian solution, they agreed to make a second rotation for the merchants, who were understandably eager to get their goods to Maji market by air in one day, instead of overland by pack mule over the following week.

I sat limp and airsick on the tarmac, in the shadow of the airplane wing. The air smelled of tar in the hot sun. As they refueled, white gas fumes rippled the air and stung my sinuses. Dad had been teaching us what he called the Maji hymn, "To the Hills I Lift Mine Eyes." We had moved so many times by then, I knew just this much: my daddy would get us to Maji, and there would be mountains.

Two hours later, our plane buzzed the airstrip to clear any grazing wildlife. It circled again and lumbered down. Ostriches fled through the golden grass of the airstrip. The propellers' whirlwind flattened the grass and blew their feathers toward their naked necks as they scattered. "Look, their panties are showing," I said to Jane. She was four, and had announced that we were secretly twins.

The flaps clattered. The propeller slowed. Lowland heat hit the plane like a blast furnace. With Dad's charisma to promote it, Maji was to become known among the Presbyterian missionaries for this hot, dry airstrip called Washa Wooha, and for the forty-kilometer drive back up the mountain. The trip took four hours with the best of mechanical and weather-related luck. It took twelve hours one memorable trip, the short wheelbase Jeep hauling ten of us and a trailer through the mud with brakes that gave out halfway home. You could walk the Washa Wooha road as fast as the Jeep could go. The mules could walk faster than the Jeep, but they took two days to make the trip because refueling mules involved hours of grazing.

I first experienced when I was five, the soaring blue mountains lined up into the distance, row upon row; the air cooling as we climbed; the heart-stopping cliffs we skirted; the welcome supper in Maji.

Uncle Fred drove the Jeep that day; Aunt Daisy, with her limp and her warm smile, welcomed us that evening. The next morning, I ran out of the thatch-roofed house with Jane and Joy to see the mountains we'd been promised. We discovered that we were *on* the mountains of Maji. Behind the gray thatched *gojo*, the knoll fell into a valley a thousand feet below. We stood enchanted in a mismatched row: Jane and Joy dark-haired, pink and freckled; me with my olive complexion and a blond ponytail.

Dad rushed away from the after-breakfast conversation to find us, thinking we might be lost and disoriented. Jane said, "We're lifting our eyes unto the hills."

Dad guffawed and beamed his full-hearted smile down on Jane. He must have told the story of Jane lifting her eyes a thousand times, and every time, I felt a pang. I was proud of my clever sister. I was equally sorry I wasn't the clever one.

"Don't fall," I said, and pulled her back from the edge. She was too happy to object.

From that moment of lifting our eyes unto the hills, Maji was Camelot, a brief shining moment in the Kurtz family mythology. We had moved six times. Added two members to the family. Lost one. Mom and Dad had survived the frigid shock-in-the-face of African culture eleven time zones from their home. Succumbed to tropical diseases. Learned a Semitic language with syntax inverted from English and sounds made in parts of the mouth they couldn't find. The mission station on the edge of the mountain became, in the deepest sense, home.

Maji had cedar trees that curved in a somber semi-circle away from our house and moaned in the night wind. Maji had eucalyptus trees by the gate, dropping fragrant acorns. Maji had the *korch* tree, which grew when you stuck it into the ground. Everyone in Maji used *korch* branches, with their thorn-studded bark, to make impenetrable fences around their compounds, avoiding the problem of termites while keeping sheep and cattle in, thieves and wild animals out.

Maji had the Gap, a divot in the ridge beyond the valley. Had God reached out with the hand James Weldon Johnson wrote about in the creation poem Dad played for us on a record—the hand, which gathered up the light "and flung it against the darkness/Spangling the night with the moon and stars"—had that hand lifted away a handful of rocks and earth when God made Maji?

Maji had the *gojos*, twin huts attached by back-to-back kitchens with *korkoro* tin roofs that stovepipes could safely reach through. Golden thatch had turned gray years before the Kurtzes arrived. Huge posts in the middle of each disappeared up into shadows and cobwebs, to hold up roof poles that reached down to the walls like spokes of a collapsed wheel. We lived in the right hand *gojo*. Its earthen floor ran unevenly from one edge of the circle to the other, covered by mats made of fibrous marsh reeds, which workers bought for Mom in the Maji market, and Dad nailed, through layer over worn out layer, into the ground.

Later, Grandpa and Grandma Kurtz came to visit us, and Grandpa helped Dad build us a new house in the middle of the compound— the house with corners, windows, and a cement floor.

"Someday we'll have a view of the valley, when the *gojos* fall down," Dad said to guests like our aunties.

"Hasten the day," Mom said.


Mom had stuffed the barrels with books, and she and Dad read aloud to us—in the living room, or around the dining room table, or as the four of us girls blew bubbles through washcloths and washed each other's backs in the bathtub during our weekly bath.

"One chapter," Mom said, when I was about nine and Jane and Joy just starting school. "Then it will be nap time."

"Wilbur!" Jane said, and we ran to the jute couch, pushing and squirming.

When she read, Mom put aside the school boys who worked for her in the kitchen, and the women's Bible study, and her job as station treasurer, she who had been an English major and had no mind for math.

I worried for Wilbur, who was shedding lonely tears in the corner of his pigpen. A voice came out of the darkness and comforted him. When morning dawned, he climbed to the top of his manure pile, stood as tall and proud as he could and asked, "Will the party who addressed me at bedtime please..."

"'The party who undressed me?'" I said.

Jane giggled. "What was he wearing?"

"A party undressed him," Joy said. We were shouting with laugher, and Cathy, beside me, wiggled with delight. Jane bounced her head against the foam cushion.

"Hush," Mom said. But Jane and I were gasping for breath.

"Party means a person," Mom said. "Ad-dressed him. Now settle down."

Jane put her hand over her mouth. My eyes watered with the effort. A snort escaped. Jane put her other hand over the first. Her body shook. Joy looked at us, her dimples deep. Mom read on, and the story quickly pulled us back in: the party who undressed the pig at bedtime was a spider. What magic.

Maji had *goom*, fog that spilled over the ridge and through the Gap like merengue, filling the valley and erasing the world behind it. We waited on the edge in ready-set-go crouches as it rolled toward us. Someday I would run faster than *goom*.

"Come on!" Jane said. She rubbed her goose bumps. We couldn't go until I said so.

"Go!" I said. We dashed toward the house, but *goom* rushed up and swirled around us. The kerosene lamplight behind Mom's homemade peacock-print curtains glowed through a world turned gray. I leapt over Shasta daisies, across the drainage ditch, across the dirt track and up the mound to our house. At the front door I turned to laugh at my sisters' hair, strung with glittering droplets of *goom*.

The people of Maji were proud that we had come to them. The men Dad hired watched over us as we played. They smiled as we ran in and out of the shed, collecting fragrant sawdust to cook for our teddy bears. They called our unpronounceable names as we crossed the compound. They spoke to us in the musical tones of the Dizi language, and laughed when we ran away, not understanding. Our safety was a matter of honor. In the way children have of knowing when they are safe and loved, we felt safe and loved. Maji morphed into a character in our family story, like a grandmother or a loving nanny who soothed the struggling parents and the anxious children and gave them the courage to go on.

Maybe it wasn't my inheritance from Dad that led me on, believing the world could be perfect if we all tried hard enough. Maybe it was Maji. Maji came so close.

And I wouldn't have grown up in Maji if it hadn't been for the Italians, who invaded Ethiopia in 1935. They believed in roads, like their predecessors, the Romans. The road from Addis Ababa to Maji still winds down into the Gibe River Gorge over Roman-style arched bridges the Italians built. They built culverts to channel away spring water that oozes out of the mountainsides. They cleared the Washa Wooha airstrip, down where they found enough level land to lay down a plane.

The presence of Italy in Ethiopia seeped into my childish consciousness like the tropical highland sun into my skin, like the smell of eucalyptus oil in the noonday sun on the hillsides around Addis Ababa, sitting high on the shoulder of another mountain.

The Italians planned to settle and farm Ethiopia as the British had settled Kenya and the Dutch had settled South Africa. But most of the Italian immigrants stayed in Addis Ababa because of guerrilla resistance throughout the countryside.

In Addis Ababa, a few blocks away from the mission headquarters stood the statue of martyred Abuna Petros, serene in cream colored marble, eternally chained to an Italian anti-aircraft gun, which I took as a child for a canon. By the time my memories of life in Ethiopia took shape, I already knew his story. The Archbishop of the Ethiopian Orthodox Church in 1935, he was told by the Italians to admonish the people to submit to their invaders. Instead, he urged them to fight on.

We came into Addis Ababa twice a year for mission meetings, vacations, and massive grocery shopping events. We shopped in the bakeries for Italian bread, and in an Italian-run import grocery in the *piassa*. I don't remember learning that *piassa* was an Italian word, I seem to have always known. Shops in the *piassa* sold imported shoes and lingerie. Jewelry stores displayed lavish spreads of intricately filigreed Ethiopian gold Orthodox crosses, rings with gold Lions of the Tribe of Judah set in black onyx.

On a red-letter day when I was a teenager, Mom suggested we stop in a *piassa* café to take a break from our shopping. We walked into a moist cloud smelling of coffee, cigarette smoke, and pastries baking. Mom sipped her coffee, which she wanted to burn all the way down. I concentrated on the joy of being so grown up, and ignored the Ethiopian men smoking and staring at us. I sprinkled my yogurt with large crystals of gray local sugar. Sweet bursts punctuated each mouth-puckering bite.

Wooden homes behind the café stood two stories high, with balconies, carved eves, veranda brackets, and wooden shutters. Undoubtedly, offspring of the thirty-five thousand Italians who immigrated to Ethiopia lived in those homes, but I never saw anyone looking out the windows or lounging on the balconies.

The rest of us, Ethiopians and foreigners, lived in mud stucco houses. Depending on our income and status, we lived in mud homes built square and roofed with *korkoro*, or in round, traditional, thatched *gojos*. Some of us cooked in kitchen huts over open fires, and some used cast-iron wood stoves that stood on black and red checkerboard tile floors. The smoke from all our fires united in the skies of Addis Ababa and turned dusk a fragrant blue-gray.

In Maji, everyone called Dad's *korkoro* shop the *me-GA-zen*, an Italian word. Dust mites floated in the light that entered through small windows. The dim interior of the *megazen* smelled of *benzin* (gas). Dad kept his tools on a deeply scarred workbench saturated with old motor oil. There he might fix the *goma*, tire. Or the *fren*, brakes. He would use his *pinsas*, pliers, to fix the *makina*, or vehicle. Italy had not only invaded the country, but the language.

Between Maji and the airstrip, the Italians had blasted a road into the side of the mountain, which rose up on one side and fell away on the other. In one spot they had blasted hollows into the rock walls.

"What are those cave-y things for?" I asked Dad one day. The air in the Jeep smelled of dust and exhaust.

He patted my knee. "They're for the enemy to hide. All tucked out of sight."

I didn't need to ask him, *Who are the enemy?* As the Jeep jolted over ruts and stones, I imagined creeping up the road, an Ethiopian partisan with my rifle. Adrenalin flooded my heart. An Italian soldier might be hiding in a cave, waiting for me.

# CHapter 4

I knew—the way children in America know that the Fourth of July means more than fireworks, sparklers and flags—that canons at the palace in the early morning of March second celebrated routing the Italians. For years I ran together the Italians' two attempts to colonize Ethiopia—their failure in 1896, and their temporary success in 1935.

But many years passed before I was curious enough to read Ethiopian history. How back in 1863, Emperor Tewodros (Theodore) asked Queen Victoria for military help, because the Muslims were threatening to invade from the southeast, the princes were nipping at his heels and his troops were defecting in droves. When the queen did not respond, how in a pique, Emperor Tewodros took two British missionaries and the British consul hostage. How Queen Victoria raised nine million pounds to punish a man she seems to have considered not an emperor, but an upstart barbarian potentate. How the British General Napier built seven hundred yards of pier out into the Red Sea and took a caravan of thirty thousand animals—including mules, camels, and elephants—into the mountains to lay siege to the emperor's fortress. And then, how the troubadour sang that, when he saw all was lost, Emperor Tewodros took a pistol and *drank a bullet*.

How, in spite of all that, England ceded Ethiopia to the Italian sphere of influence. (Italians complained they'd been squeezed out of their share, and since they were in Italian Somaliland to the south and Eritrea to the north, obviously Ethiopia should be theirs.) In 1889 Italy gave Emperor Menelik II a bilingual treaty which, in Amharic, offered consular services in Europe from an embassy in Italy. The Italian man who devised the treaties must have laughed over his grappa that night, since in Italian it made Ethiopia an Italian protectorate.

The Italians in 1896, determined to enforce their version of the treaty, planned a stealth attack at Adwa at nine on a Sunday morning. Devout Ethiopian soldiers, up early for worship, warned their commanders and the Ethiopian army dashed out at six a.m. in a ferocious defense. According to an Ethiopian historian of the time, *That day the servant did not find his master, the soldier did not find his chief, each*

*one marched straight to battle and into the canons like monkeys who have seen a sack of grain.*

The historians paint such an Ethiopian scene: Orthodox priests roaming the battlefields excommunicating soldiers who threaten to retreat; the queen and princesses setting up a water station; the wounded saying, *Let the throne be saved! I forbid you to touch me! Pick me up on your return!*

And the Italians suffered that day a more devastating defeat than any other army in a nineteenth century European battle—even Waterloo. Their five generals were killed, wounded or captured, and seventy percent of the army was destroyed. When word got back to Italy, people rioted and toppled the government. The defeat at Adwa postponed Italian adventuring in Ethiopia until Mussolini got the itch for expansion and revenge.

And after Adwa, Ethiopia's mountain peaks and high volcanic plateaux guarded Ethiopia, the only non-colonized African country. But Ethiopia welcomed other things Europe offered. A German immigrant introduced carrots and potatoes, and now we give our burning mouths relief from spicy *wat* sauces with a vegetable stew fragrant with clarified butter, and yellow with turmeric.

The British and the French, as in so many things, jockey for credit over who gave Emperor Menelik the eucalyptus tree, which Captain Cook had brought out of Australia. The eucalyptus, called *bahr-zaf*, ocean-tree, because it came from across the ocean, springs up after harvest from a root burl that can last for decades. Emperor Menelik planted eucalyptus to replace the junipers that had disappeared into the cooking fires of his nation-building army as it marched through the country, leaving the hillsides behind denuded.

When the royal entourage moved down into volcanic central Ethiopia, Empress Taitu discovered hot springs that bubbled from far underground and soaked her arthritic bones. She named the encampment Addis Ababa, New Flower, and Emperor Menelik, with the help of *bahr-zaf*, stayed. The French laid the railroad from Djibouti, and gave Arabic and Amharic the word for white folks—*ferenj.*

Meanwhile, Italy lay in wait in her colonies to the north and south. After World War I, Mussolini stirred up nationalistic fervor to distract his people from their economic woes. When France and Britain wooed him to help curb German ambitions, Mussolini tested their willingness to deal by building a fort fifty miles inside the Ethiopia he so coveted. France and Britain looked away. Ethiopia's new ally,

Japan, had imperialist ambitions of its own and stepped aside. The chess board stood wide open.

Here's how the contest lined up: Ethiopians enlisted with their spears and hippo hide shields and were issued rifles dating back to 1900. Over a million Italian troops massed on the borders with nine thousand machine guns, two thousand artillery pieces, and eight hundred tanks.

Each side had an air force: the Ethiopians had four pilots with a Frenchman in command, choosing on any given day among three ancient biplanes and ten other slightly more modern planes; the Italians had six hundred modern aircraft.

Pope Pius XI condemned the Nazis, but Italian bishops blessed the troops, who were going to *conquer new and fertile lands for the Italian genius.* That Italian genius used Royal Corps of Colonial Troops from Eritrea and Somalia as advance fighters, to take the greatest losses. But of course, the Ethiopian deaths ran highest—in one battle the Italians lost ten men and the Ethiopians eight thousand.

The Ethiopian army was quickly overwhelmed, the war was declared over, and Italy slotted Ethiopia into the gap between colonies, creating the new Africa Orientate Italiana. "The Italian people have created an empire with their blood!" Mussolini shouted in victory speeches. "Will you be worthy of it?" Jubilant crowds roared, *Yes!*

The Italians, to their credit, did not bomb the train that carried Emperor Haile Selassie to Djibouti in May 1936. He spoke on the floor of the League of Nations: "It is us today. It will be you tomorrow," he said. *Time* magazine chose him as Man of the Year. He spent the exile years in Bath, England, quietly supported by anonymous gifts.

Mexico was the only country to condemn Italy's invasion, and in appreciation, Ethiopia later built a traffic roundabout we called Mexico Square. I wondered as a child why Mexico? And I wondered if Mexico cared that its monument was overgrown with weeds, the cement chipped, and the fountain always dry.

In Ethiopia, the partisans, unbowed, fought a guerrilla war. Mussolini responded with *terror and extermination.* First, the Italian Air Force dropped bombs and grenades they had filled with a mixture of mustard and tear gasses. Then they simplified the operation and sprayed poison gas like insecticide over villages where resistance was high. People came to the Swedish Red Cross with blistered skin and suppurating sores, talking of a *terrible rain that burns and kills.*

When the opposition made an assassination attempt on Viceroy and Governor General Graziani, the Italians massacred thirty thousand Ethiopians, including about half of the educated elite. Many Italian soldiers had themselves photographed standing next to rebel bodies hanging from gallows, or beside chests full of detached heads. I wonder, as I write that, whether that is the measure of racism in Europe at the time, or whether an added measure of vengeance for their unique defeat at the hands of Africans had infected the Italians.

Britain gave His Majesty refuge for his six years of exile, but did not interfere with Italy's colony until Italy threatened to expand into the Anglo-Egyptian Sudan. At that, Britain sent colonial troops to join Ethiopian rebels. They drove the Italians out in 1941.

As Haile Selassie returned to the throne, he said, "Let not our rejoicing be in any other way but in the spirit of Christ...Take care not to spoil the good name of Ethiopia by acts which are worthy of the enemy." He gave amnesty to any Italian families who chose to stay.

This may be part of the reason we white foreigners were not resented. Ethiopians had retained the moral high ground. Their dignity was intact, and foreigners posed no threat. And it's no wonder that, to this day, I invariably cheer for the underdog. Ethiopians gave me a childhood home when my roots had been torn up by one move after another until I didn't know quite who I was.

As the Italian-Ethiopian history was unfolding, Dad was an Eastern Oregon farm boy. Mom's family was struggling through the depression, farming in Iowa. Neither of them imagined that their destiny would be impacted by those events so many time zones away.

When Dad was eighteen, he enlisted in the Army Air Corps. He'd had one year of ag school, and expected to go back to Oregon, take over the farm, and raise alfalfa seed (if he came back from the war at all). He was a crack pilot, the only student told to take off and land in formation with his instructors. They wanted him—that young, baby-faced man, hardly more than a boy—to be a flight instructor himself, but he was determined to get to the front. He purposely failed his instructor course's entry exam.

His superiors eventually offered him one path to the war in Europe—breaching German lines at the Northern Rhine River in Operation Varsity, history's largest glider drop. He was warned that only fifty percent of the glider pilots would make their way out of Germany alive. There were two thousand casualties. Dad didn't know, until he crossed the bridge back into France on foot, that he wouldn't be one of them.

He used to quote that cliché, *How can you keep them down on the farm after they've seen Paree?* He went up with Air Corps friends to celebrate Armistice, buzzing over Paris, swooping among the fireworks. Did he fly through the Arc de Triomphe? Or was that a daring and half-drunk friend of his? Or am I making that part up?

Mom graduated from high school while Dad was flying in Europe, and began her job at the tire company. Neither of them heard about the Italian slaughter of young, educated Ethiopians. No one yet knew how that would induce Emperor Haile Selassie to open Ethiopia to missionaries in the 1950s, taking a chance that Protestants wouldn't threaten the Ethiopian Orthodox Church too much, willing to let mission schools help Ethiopia catch back up. Mom and Dad didn't know the events that would string together and bring them, with a family, to Ethiopia, to work for twenty-three years. Even so, they never doubted their real home in the US.

Their children's identity confusion came as a surprise, and showed up as soon as we went to the States on furlough. We took a Dutch Freighter from Amsterdam, and docked in New York, where the Presbyterian Church shared the *God building* on Riverside Drive with other mainline denominations.

"This is a palace!" I whispered to Jane in the George Washington Hotel, as Mom and I kept the luggage and kids corralled and Dad checked us in. The heavy curtains, the maroon carpet, huge cushioned chairs—I was nine, and I'd read about these things in fairy tales.

The woman who ran the old-style elevator, with its accordion gate and ship's pilot wheel, chatted with us girls as we clustered on two days later, feeling brave. The Elevator Lady asked us the dread question of mish kids: *Where are you girls from?*

We knew exactly where we belonged: in Maji. But where were we *from*?

We held a whispered consultation, and appointed extroverted Joy to speak for us. Her dimples, inherited from Mom, punctuated her smile. "We're from America!"

Four years earlier, just after the Kurtz family arrived in Maji, two Land Rovers had appeared over the crest of the hill and roared down toward the mission compound. Usually the mission Jeep, the police Land Rover, and the governor's Land Rover were the only three vehicles within one hundred and fifty miles.

Six white men climbed stiffly out of the vehicles, men and machines encrusted with dust. The government of Ethiopia, believing minerals must lie just below the surface of the land waiting to make the country rich, had hired them, a team of geologists, to search. Hearing from local people there were other foreigners around, and with no way to communicate ahead of time, they'd shown up.

Ethiopia was desperate for foreign currency to buy goods on the world market—fuel, tar for road building, wires for electric lines. Back then everyone assumed it was a win-win for Africa to get foreign currency by supplying the raw materials for industries in the developed world.

That's how economics works for Africa in the modern era. Western observers complain: *why doesn't Africa develop, in spite of all the aid we pour in, in spite of the United Nations, in spite of the World Bank?* Some people imply that there is an African genetic flaw that makes this poverty intractable. They've forgotten what we learned in fifth-grade social studies—industry requires cheap labor and cheap raw materials. Africa was selected to supply both on the world market—free labor during the three hundred years when Africans were exported as slaves.

Mining Africa's resources for the industrial world to this day keeps Africa impoverished. African workers receive a poverty wage. Selling raw materials gives African countries a modest measure of foreign currency. And buying raw materials gives the wealthy world what it needs to feed factories and take products to market with huge added-value mark-ups. Picture the few cents paid to an Ethiopian farmer for two tablespoons of raw coffee beans vs the three-dollar cup of gourmet coffee those beans make. Imagine what's paid for a cacao bean versus the price of a chocolate bar. I have no idea what is paid for raw tantalum, but I know Central African miners aren't getting rich from the boom in cell phone use around the globe.

The geologists hadn't found anything worth mining. Worn out and discouraged, they quizzed Dad over supper, hoping they might still find some treasure in the lowlands toward Sudan or Kenya. Dad told them only foot trails and wild animal tracks lay beyond Maji. He offered to get them set up with mules. Before the evening was over, they had beguiled him to go along as their translator.

Loving adventure as he did, Dad must have jumped at the chance. *What better way for me to learn the lay of the land?* he would have said to Mom, in his Eastern Oregon cowboy way.

*Lie*, she would have corrected him.

# CHAPTER 5

Mom may not have been thrilled at being left with four little girls at the end of the earth as Dad went off on a treasure hunt. Besides the ongoing struggles with the wood stove, she now had to fill and light the kerosene pressure lamps every evening, run her toddlers to the latrine, and supervise workers with her completely inadequate Amharic. But this was the economy of Mom and Dad's covenant with chaos. He would have the big life, she would keep a home and bask in the reflected glow of his adventures.

Dad put word out. Muleteers arrived at the compound. The geologists produced tents, bedrolls, tools, food and Primus stoves, and began loading the next morning. We girls stood in our descending row watching, smelling dust swirl, mules fart and men sweat. Packing began with a big white mule, who stood docile as you please while the muleteers balanced the load and tightened the cinches. The minute they turned, the mule's joints loosened and he dropped to the ground. The geologists and Dad shouted, but the muleteers waved them away. *Leave him*, they told Dad.

The mule tried, load and all, to roll over. Dust flew. We girls laughed.

When the muleteers had the other dozen mules loaded and saddled, the muleteers gathered around the big white mule. They lifted him off the ground and onto his hoofs. They leaned their shoulders against him to keep him upright. They slapped. They kicked. They swore and shouted. Finally, Big White wobbled forward. The other mules fell in line, and off they went.

"Bye, Daddy, bye," we shouted. He turned in his saddle and waved. We wiped the dust out of the corners of our eyes.

Every morning, Dad told us later, the routine was the same: pack up Big White, cinch the load so he couldn't rub it off, let him lie down until everyone else was ready, then hoist him bodily to his feet and swear him into action. Finally, one of the geologists turned to Dad. "You came here to convert. Why don't you start by converting this mule?"

Dad loved a joke on himself. He would punch that punchline with delight, his face red from holding back his laughter.

The mules plodded quietly back into the compound one afternoon. Jane and I danced around. Dad hollered at us to stay clear of the backs of the mules. Joy jumped into his arms. The muleteers unloaded gear as fast as they could, and the geologists stood in a semi-circle smelling of mule sweat and looking dazed. Mom hurried to the kitchen to cook up a welcome supper. The aunties sent their workers with notes to say they would bring salad and a cake.

The dining room quickly filled with fragrant steam—hand kneaded rolls baking in the oven, pasta water, onions and oregano sautéing, and ground beef from hunks of maroon raw meat pushed through a by-hand meat-grinder.

Over supper the men told how one afternoon, in all that wilderness, the muleteers managed to choose a bee tree for the campsite. When the bees swarmed, mules, cooking pots, and men were scattered far and wide in the shoulder-high grass, and Dad lost his Swiss Army knife.

"Bees landed in our ears and on our necks. We were shouting and swatting and running in every direction," Dad said, and his hands flew around his head. "Our faces puffed up fat. Ed, here, his eyes swelled shut."

"Did it hurt, Daddy?" Jane asked. She leaned a little forward, and her short bob swung over her cheeks.

"Boy howdy, did it hurt." And then Dad's voice grew soft. He pointed to the young man across the table. "He's allergic. Deathly allergic. And you know what? He was only stung once."

Dad shook his head in wonder. The aunties and Mom murmured. The word miracle slipped out. The geologists smiled awkwardly, scientists among missionaries, not knowing how to credit it. Invoking Lady Luck would have sounded a little lame.

The men cleaned up every crumb of the home cooked meal. Mom brought the aluminum pot of coffee from the stove, and clinked cups and saucers onto the table. I leaned over to breathe the rich coffee steam as she poured. The adults moved to the living room, balancing cups. We girls trailed along and sat cross-legged on the floor.

One of the men said, "Okay, Harold." They all chuckled. That had to mean another story. The biggest story. The loops of the green rug dug into my legs. The kerosene lamps hissed, the fire in our Franklin stove crackled. Its heat smarted deliciously on my back and flickered light onto Dad's animated face.

The geologists had collected samples all the way from Maji to the wide, lazy Omo River, Dad said, but they hadn't found anything. There at the river, they convinced Dad to hire local men with dug-out canoes to ferry them across for one last search. They would leave Dad and the muleteers in camp, and return by nightfall. The six geologists set off in three canoes with tall, black Nilotic men, who dropped them off on the opposite shore. The geologists tramped off to explore. The men in the canoes disappeared. And never returned.

Dad paused for effect. Joy jumped up from the floor by Jane and squeezed between Mom and Dad on the couch. Mom and the aunties joined the hubbub—had the boatmen gone to the nearest town to celebrate on local beer? The first half of their payment may have been more money than they had ever seen before—why should they wait for a second installment? Or were they planning a divide-and-conquer attack that night? Dad waited out the interruption, his cheek-bunching smile shining.

"I couldn't leave the geology team on the other side of the river, without food or shelter overnight, now could I, Joy?" He tickled her.

Joy giggled. Her dimples drilled deep. "No, Daddy!"

I shook my head reflexively, and looked at Jane, who was doing the same, mouth open.

So he took two air mattresses and tied them in tandem, with twine through the corner grommets. He waded out, lay on his back on the lead mattress, and launched into the river for the rescue.

Dad went into detail about calculating for the current (using that math and physics major) and pulling right up at the feet of the men on the other side. They'd already drawn straws to see who would be his first passenger. Dad nodded at Ed, across the living room. Dad had been a thespian in college, and he knew every dramatic effect.

Ed lay down on his back on the second air mattress, and Dad pulled the contraption out to deep water. He counted out their strokes so they'd be in concert.

They'd gained the middle of the river when the muleteers on one side and the geologists on the other began to shout.

"Ed sat up. He had his feet hanging down into the water, and the air mattress doubled up around him when I lifted my head," Dad said. "I shouted at him to lie down."

"Why, Daddy?" Joy asked.

"Because there's nothing easier than dumping over an air mattress. And I didn't want to lose him in the Omo River!"

Ed raised his eyebrows. "I lay right back down," he said. I knew the voice Dad had used—when he sounded mad and you got scared, and oh yes, you obeyed.

Dad's voice got softer. My chest tightened. "I just kept up my back-stroke. Watched my angle from the shore."

They pulled into the shallows. If the word *crocodile* in Amharic had not been on Dad's language school vocabulary lists, he learned it now. *Azo.* Dad dashed out of the water. A croc can snatch and grab from shallow water as well as from deep. Ed stumbled up the bank and dropped, pale and shaken, to the ground.

There was no sign of the croc now. The opaque river rippled where currents pushed and crossed. The geologists on the far side shot into the river with their rifles. No ribbon of blood streamed out into the gray-green water.

"What else could I do?" Dad asked. A third of the way back across, the shouting began again. Jane and I sat shoulder to shoulder, wide eyed.

"I knew the croc had come back up and was following me," Dad said. "But the croc didn't know what I knew—what his teeth would do to an air mattress! So I figured I was safe as long as I kept going."

I could just see that old croc following Dad, his big eyes poking up, his big grin hidden under the water. I could just see him crunching down on the air mattress. Dad sliding into the water. Into the croc's teeth. I held my knees tight to my chest. The geologists sipped their coffee, silent as the rest of us.

Dad made six trips across the Omo River to rescue the geologists. What else could he do? He was the fourth in a family of six, and from a young age he'd made his place by being his mom's hard-working right-hand boy.

Every time Dad got out to the deep water of that wide, lazy river, the croc surfaced again and swam ten feet behind. After every trip, the geologists shot into the river. Then the next man, fearing he would be crocodile dish before the trip was over, climbed on the air mattress and set off with Dad. They concentrated on not tipping the air mattresses. They counted out their strokes.

And the croc followed. Back and forth.

By the time Dad had reunited the camp, his chest, legs, and face were so sunburned he couldn't sleep that night for the pain. He didn't say, but his thoughts just might have kept him awake, too.

Stories like that seemed to confirm to Dad that he was living a charmed life. He laughed with delight when a woman came up to him in the States years later and asked, "Were you born great, did you become great, or did you have greatness thrust upon you?" He liked to think God had thrust greatness upon him.

I think Dad would protest that he never courted drama. He showed up for the work God called him to, and then did what needed to be done. He wasn't all innocence, though. Given the option, Dad always chose the greatness angle.

And yes, I wanted to be the brave daughter that my great dad could be proud of. I pushed the terrifying images out of my mind that night, and clapped with everyone else at his success.

Dad chose to be a missionary pastor. But then, to transport a family of six in and out of Maji, he had to pull up his background as a farm-trained mechanic. Mission vehicles were imported and assigned from the office in Addis Ababa to various down-country stations. When a new Jeep came to Maji, the Washa Wooha road broke it in. Or just broke it. After a couple of years, it was retired to a station with easier roads, like a pair of down-at-the-heel shoes, and Maji got the next new one. Otherwise Dad would have spent all his time trying to keep his wheels running.

He admitted that driving the Washa Wooha road had turned his hair prematurely gray. All the way down the mountain, rock walls rose up on one side of the single lane and dropped away on the other.

Even a new Jeep was vulnerable to rocks that flipped up from the road and popped holes in gas tanks, or snapped brake lines. Even new Jeep axles broke when the Jeep high-centered in rainy season ruts. Even new Jeeps' canvas canopies tore tracking through acacia thorn forests. Dad had to be endlessly inventive. Once he nursed the Jeep up the steep climb to Maji by stopping every few miles to refill the brake fluid reservoir with what he had on hand from camping—dishwashing detergent. *It had just the right viscosity!*

When Dad embarked on a major building project in Maji, replacing the big old *gojos* with square, *korkoro*-roofed houses, the mission sent a Daimler-Benz Unimog truck to get building materials up from Washa Wooha. On family trips down the mountain in the truck, we older kids rode up on the load in back, or stood in the empty truck bed for hours, knees loose against the rolling and jolting of the truck. We sang, or told each other stories, or, glazed and tired, just tried to keep from bumping our chins on the top slat. And Dad drove worried, afraid that the truck's center of gravity was too high to be safe on the narrow Washa Wooha road.

On a trip when my only brother Chris was about three years old, our missionary auntie took charge of him on top of the load in the truck bed. Mom needed a break, because she was also holding the baby, my youngest sister Janice. It was dusk. Rains had washed out divots in the edge of the road. Dad took a corner too wide, and the front wheel dropped over the edge. The truck crashed down on its axle.

The truck, with that high center of gravity, tipped slowly toward the down-side. Everyone in the back scrambled to the high side. The missionary auntie held Chris over the slats. Ready to drop him clear of the truck if it went over. It was the only thing she could think of to do, she said later. Lacking wolves in the mountains of Maji, would hyenas have come to raise him?

# CHAPTER 6

As the truck teetered, Dad shouted for everyone to get out, *Get clear away!* He clambered up the bench seat and out after Mom.

Grabbing the tool box, he wiggled on his back under the precariously balanced chassis. He wedged a jack under the axle. In the cramped, darkening space, he maneuvered the jack handle. It popped out of its slot. He jammed it back in. Inch by inch the jack lifted the truck.

Dad climbed back into the cab. Slid carefully downhill to the driver's side. Rumbled the diesel engine back into life. Crimped the steering wheel toward the road. Let up on the brake. Pressed the gas pedal ever so slightly. Three wheels pulled. The jack tipped. The truck landed on all fours, back on the road.

Dad inched the truck away from the edge, and sat with his forehead on the steering wheel.

When Dad told that story, he said again that he didn't sleep that night. He replayed the moment over and over. The truck tipped. It swayed. It stopped, halfway over. It crawled forward. It rolled off the jack. It righted itself, rocking on its tires.

Also, when Dad told that story, Mom made a dismissive gesture. "Harold's exaggerating," she'd say. Guests would laugh: *How brave they both were!* Dad didn't fight Mom on it. He laughed with everyone. But his smile had a quavery look.

And my sister Cathy, in second grade and not yet in boarding school, remembers that moment: the stomach-knotting tip. The scramble to the high side. Her pounding heart. The discussion after they had all climbed clear. Arguing about whether the jack would even fit under there. Mom saying they should just pitch tents on the road and spend the night.

"It wasn't a cliff," Cathy says, "but the truck would have rolled a bunch of times before something stopped it."

And after that trip, Dad asked that the Unimog be reassigned to a station with safer roads. He quoted the story of Moses and the children of Israel in the wilderness without water. "Thou shalt not put the Lord your God to the test."

The people of Israel were not only thirsty, they were mad. *God promised to take care of us, and we don't even have water? We should have stayed in Egypt!* Moses struck the rock, and water flowed. And Moses named the place Massah and Meriba, Testing and Quarreling, because the people of Israel had quarreled with God and put God to the test, saying, "Is the Lord among us or not?" Dad wasn't going to quarrel with God. He wasn't going to find himself tempted to ask that question.

Mom had her limits, too. She had given up Portland to come to Ethiopia. She had given up electricity and running water to go to Maji. She was not going to give up her scarlet lipstick and look like another pale, washed-out missionary, and she was not going to send her six-year-old to boarding school.

"Caroline won't ever adjust if you don't do it now," the older missionaries warned Mom. But she set her face. She would teach me at home. Dad's elementary school principal brother sent workbooks, but Mom was allergic to routine of any kind, so morning in our house never looked much like school. Jane and Joy played in the living room. Cathy crawled around and then learned to walk on the lumpy dirt floor covered by mats. And Mom bustled in the kitchen, managing the logistics of keeping a family fed and clean without conveniences, but instead, a team of workers who didn't speak English.

And I raced my way through the workbooks at the table. I sniffed the musty smell of yeast softening in warm water for bread, as I sat on one leg, holding my pencil tight. I sounded out words, pulling in the coffee roasting smoke rising from a cast iron pan. I sniffed the burnt-toast smell of a worker toasting wheat for our next day's breakfast cereal, and wood smoke when he opened the firebox to put another stick in.

If Jane lost interest in her game with Joy, she hovered at the table beside me as I laboriously traced the dotted lines, obeyed the tiny arrows, and formed my letters. She leaned against my arm and I read to her, *Run, Spot! Run!*

Outside the house, Ethiopia was like the Middle Ages in Europe, with landlords and serfs, a monarchy, and an ancient church. Monastery schools taught boys the dead liturgical language so they could be priests. In Europe, that had been Latin. In Ethiopia, it was Ge'ez. Otherwise, my Irish, Dutch, Scottish and German ancestors, like the Ethiopian children, learned to be adults by doing child-sized versions of adult work.

But the modern world had come to the US, and so I was learning to read instead of lugging a sister on my hip or bundled on my back like Ethiopian girls my age. I didn't have to carry water from the river with a miniature of my mother's pot tied on with hand braided rope. Later, my brother Chris didn't watch the cattle or help our father plow with oxen, scatter the seed, scythe the grain or thresh it, cracking his hand-braided whip to manage the oxen that trampled it. My mother and sisters and I didn't loft the grain into the air on a windy day, and watch the chaff blow away.

Even now, most Ethiopians are subsistence farmers. They grow what they eat. They walk to the nearest town on market days to sell their surplus.

Or, by accident of birth they throw those pots, forge those plow and spear tips, weave the gossamer ceremonial *netellas* women wear gracefully wrapped around their shoulders. Or they weave a heavy cotton *gabi* to snuggle in against the evening cold.

In traditional Ethiopia, artisans are evil-eye. If they eat in the home of a neighbor, they use a fin of the flat, dark green *enset* leaf as a plate so they don't contaminate the family. They are not considered fully human. They are not allowed to own land.

Curiously, some people think that my 1850s ancestor Peter Kurtz, who is grafted onto our family tree from out of nowhere, came from Germany to the US because his people were blacksmiths and couldn't own land. Peter's great grandson was my Grandpa Kurtz, who smithed in Oregon. My dad set up a smith in Maji.

But traditions fall apart. In the 1950s, a few Ethiopian children defied their fate as farmers and went to school. When some of them later became my friends, they told me they had been incorrigible— the cattle went missing when they were in charge. The monkeys ate the corn. Beatings made no impression. Their parents said, *Let the missionaries see what they can make of these worthless children!* This was going on all over Africa, the outliers of a generation drifting into Western-style schools run by missions, poised to become leaders for their dawning Modern era. But our missionary aunties who ran the schools didn't suspect the seismic shifts they were generating.

Back then, not knowing just how historical it was for them to be there, several dozen Ethiopian children walked to that Maji mission school—the only school in one hundred and fifty miles. Around the flagpole in the morning they sang, *Ethiopia Hoy! Des ye-belish!* O Ethiopia, rejoice! As they sang outside the *korch* tree fence and down the swale, I joined in: *Ethiopia hoy!* I'd never sung the soaring, impossible, *Rockets' red glare.*

And then the school children chanted the two hundred and thirty-one letters of the Amharic *fidel* in sing-song with a lilt on the sixth form—*luh-loo-lee-lah-lay-**lih**-lo*. Remote Maji's tiny mission school produced three medical doctors, a double-master sociologist, and countless teachers and nurses in its thirty-year history.

The next September, when Mom called me in to start school again, Jane said, "Mommy, I'm going to school, too."

My second-grade workbooks in one arm, Mom cleared a spot at the table with the other.

"Mommy," Jane said in a stern voice.

"Okay, Jane. If you want to have school, you can."

"No, Mommy. Say I *have* to."

Mom set the workbooks down. She pushed at the almost black wave of hair on her forehead and sighed. "Find yourself a pencil, Caroline. Okay. Jane, you *have* to have school."

We went through that every morning for weeks. I didn't know why Mom took so long to figure out two things I already knew: Jane was determined to keep up with me. And you couldn't win an argument with her. Jane followed my example and learned to read as just one more form of play.

After the three years of chaos it had taken for our family to get from Portland to Maji, the storm finally died down. Later, on a camel trek into the deserts of central Egypt, when the wind that had blown all day stilled at dusk, I felt an intense relief. That's how I felt in Maji, when one day began to follow another in a pattern I could count on.

Besides, we belonged in Maji. Dad built us a house. Maji and the Kurtzes would be together forever. It was a world of goodwill on two sides of a huge cultural chasm. And a world of intense sister intimacy, because I seldom had friends other than Jane and Joy. There were only seven people I could talk to—my family and the aunties who ran the mission school and clinic. No one else in Maji spoke English.

Dad had suffered through Amharic language school and regularly failed his tests. But when he got out with the workmen, he picked up idiomatic Amharic. "The muleteers taught me many things I couldn't use in polite society," he said, but he used what he could. Ethiopians said he spoke "tasty" Amharic.

Mom was the opposite. She aced language school. But when she tried to talk, she analyzed the grammar in her head like a star pupil and her thoughts never flowed straight from her brain to her mouth. She also had an awkward accent.

"Mommy! Roll your r's! It's easy!" Joy said, dimples deep. We ran in circles around Mom like little lawn mowers, trilling. She tried, just to amuse us. Her tongue stuck to the roof of her mouth.

"No, like this," Joy said, and spouted another rapid-fire string.

"That's enough," Mom said. The moment was gone. We crowded out the door.

Accent or not, Mom worked at her role of missionary wife, teaching some women to sew on our treadle sewing machine, meeting with a few women for Bible study, teaching Engilsh to the sixth graders at the school. When Bible study met at our house, she had the strange green rug rolled up so the women's babies could pee on the cement floor and she could wipe it right up. But the language and culture gaps in Maji were too wide for any of us to bridge in an intimate way.

When an Ethiopian teacher's son came a few times to play, he didn't wear shoes. This worried me—I got spanked if I went outside barefoot. I knew no Amharic and he knew no English. I pointed to his feet and to my shoes and spread my hands wide to ask what happened to his shoes. He shook his head. He looked sad.

He didn't have shoes. This was a shock. I had three pairs—leather play shoes, which looked like Buster Brown advertisements; high-top Keds, with rubber circles over my ankle bones; and Sunday Mary Janes. I was wearing the Keds, my favorites. It was obvious what I had to do. I took them off and gave them to my friend. He ran off immediately. Halfway to the gate, he turned. We waved, smiling at each other.

Then I ran into the house, hoping stocking feet didn't count for a spanking.

# CHAPTER 7

"What happened to your shoes?" Mom asked. The frown wrinkles between her dark eyebrows gouged deeply.

I explained.

"No one has shoes," Mom said.

No one? I stood in my stocking feet, flushing shame all over.

Duke-tebar didn't have shoes. The school boys who came in the afternoon to work didn't. The workmen who gathered in the morning at Dad's shop, the man who drove the donkeys with water...I hadn't noticed. This was worse than a spanking. I had thought I was doing the right thing. The grown-up thing. What was the right thing?

The little boy came a few more times to play. I couldn't look him in the eyes anymore. I understand now that the people of Maji had survived for millennia without shoes, and could continue indefinitely. I understand that Mom felt burdened by the poverty around us, and maybe resentful at her guilt over an impossible chasm. All I understood then was how confusing it was to be the girl in the middle.

And of course, the chasm meant we didn't know the Dizi people believed evil spirits lived in the waterfalls. *Let the missionaries have that haunted land*, the Orthodox priests had said. *Let them wonder why no Dizi people will live out on the hill with them. Why no one will join their church.*

So we and the aunties picnicked down where white noise played its background music, spray drifted over to cool our cheeks, and wild begonias bloomed pink and red along the ledges where water hit and bounced and fell again.

Then someone told Dad that people were saying, *There goes the missionary with his wives and children, down to worship the spirits.*

Mom usually had a stubborn, *This is how we do things* attitude when American ways collided with Ethiopian ways. But in this case, the impression of our little outings was wrong on so many levels that picnics to the waterfalls had to stop.

"But Da-ad," we wailed in chorus on picnic night.

Instead, the missionary and his "wives" and children walked through the gate and along the growing fence that evening, and spread blankets on the western slope behind the *gojos*. Dad built a little fire with wood he'd brought from the wood box by our Franklin stove. Mom opened a can of hot dogs.

"Run, find sticks," Dad said. "Caroline, help Cathy."

I didn't run. I walked carefully, lop-sided on the hillside, and held Cathy's hand.

Dad whittled points onto our sticks, and carefully pierced the hot dogs so they wouldn't split. We roasted them, our faces turned away from the smoke that swirled in the evening breeze, stinging our eyes and burning our sinuses.

Mom spread a smear of precious imported ketchup onto round buns she'd baked in the wood stove's unpredictable oven. The hot dogs stuck out on each end, and I nibbled them before biting into the bread.

As the sun set, and the fire burned down to pulsing, flickering coals, Dad doled out square marshmallows, dug from the little box with blue words and a bright red flame. Jane immediately stuck hers too close to the coals. It burst into flames. She screamed and waved the flaming stick. Mom ducked. Dad grabbed Jane's arm and blew hard. She stared at blistered blackness that had been a marshmallow. Her face puckered.

"It's okay, Jane," Dad said. He pulled the crispy shell off and showed her the bubbly sweetness under it. She ate what was left on the stick, and stuck out her tongue to touch the blackened shell.

I kept my marshmallow above the coals, watching Dad. His face glowed in the firelight. His marshmallow puffed up and turned per-fectly, evenly golden brown. He turned to Mom with a beaming smile and offered it to her, like a knight after a joust. Mom smiled her dimply smile and accepted his gift, every bit the lady.

The sun set over the ridge and the Gap, gold-tipped magenta. The picnic blanket kept sliding downward, bunching and wrinkling. I buttoned my sweater against the damp evening air, then lay back and watched the bright sky, the wisps of pink that drifted across like kaleidoscope bits, reflecting the sun.

The sunset slowly faded. Dad started singing, "Day is dying in the west." The rest of us joined in softly, "Heaven is touching earth with rest."

On Sundays, the knobby eucalyptus flagpole stood empty. The rope on its pulley bumped softly. In the swale, the ground was littered with fibrous bits from the sugar cane school kids sucked sweetness out of for snacks. The grass was trampled.

In the dim school hall, with the door at one end and windows with shutters instead of glass at the other, I followed Joy down the packed-earth aisle. We always sat in the row near the front. Men sat behind us, women and children on the other side.

"Why do we sit on the men's side?" I whispered to Mom.

"Shhh." Mom flipped through the fat square hymnal. The smells of smoke and spicy food oils wafted up from pages stained by hands seldom washed, because water in people's homes came at such a physical price to women. Mom pointed to the words as she sang, but it went too fast. The only Amharic letter I could ever remember was *muh* መ, because it looked like a pair of glasses.

In the States, Mom would have had to manage kids while Dad managed the church service. But she would have had Sunday school to send us off to. In Maji, Mom counted on Dad to help keep the peace. They split us up on the wattle and mud bench. The reed mat covering smelled sweet, like dry hay, but its woven bumps dug and poked, and the mat rustled as we wiggled.

Mom passed out paper and crayons as the sermon scripture was read. Joy grabbed. Jane snatched. Mom whispered a fierce command. Dad passed Cathy off to her and stood to go up for the sermon.

My childhood was full of monastic-like disciplines: God invoked at every turn of the clock. We prayed before meals and before bed. We sang hymns. We recited psalms. We read the Bible stories of God and God's people. And we gathered for church. It didn't matter if I couldn't understand the hymns and prayers in other languages. They weren't for our edification. They were for God. I absorbed the sanctity of time and place, even though it was really just the school auditorium, all dust and chalky whitewashed walls and reed mats.

We were in church because that's where families should be on Sunday mornings. In church. We were there to be an example to the families in Maji: *Take your children to church. Men, help your wives with your children. This is the Christian way.*

A baby cried in the women's section, and his mother hauled her breast out the top of her dress and nursed him. When he sat up, satisfied, a drop of translucent milk quivered on the woman's nipple. Her breast, the same color as her neck and face, slipped slowly back into her dress. Mom had gone to the back bedroom to nurse Cathy, and pulled the sheet over her very naked looking, blue-veined breast if we came in.

A toddler crawled into the aisle, her bottom bare, and peed on the earthy floor. The acrid smell of urine rose up, with the smell of dust dampened after a long dry spell. The woman on the end of the bench scooped her up and passed her to her mother.

Since it was church, our pictures were supposed to be from Bible stories. With my tongue clamped between my teeth, I colored the Golden Calf with a yellow crayon, the calf the people of Israel danced around while Moses was up getting the Ten Commandments carved in stone by the Finger of God.

Dad was preaching in Amharic. It crackled with exploded consonants: P, T, Ch, Ts and K. The sermon translation in Dizin, the Dizi language, lilted musically, thick with a breathy D and variations of J like some people say in "garage." They use sounds we don't run together, like gn. Dizin is a tonal language. It sings from the Maji hills on market days, as people walk to town and home with bundles on their heads. It sings from tiny gourd flutes with little finger holes and a big hole in the top to blow across. People talk to each other with the flutes, with high and low notes: I'm on my way home; my wife is better; I sold the cow.

No one in our family could understand Dizin—no white people could understand Dizin, because missionaries were not allowed to study local languages. They were part of an imperial nation-building strategy begun by the emperors in the 1800s: Ethiopia was to be held together around one language, Amharic.

Ignorant of all that, charmed by the richness of sounds swirling around me, a few years later I flipped to the back of my precious spiral notebook, the size of a 3 x 5 card. I had written poems in the front of this notebook, and drawn pictures of flowers and horses. Now I wrote in big letters at the top of the back page: Dictionary.

I wrote the numbers to five in Dizin: koy, tagn, kudu, oogn, oocho. Sagu, one of the school boys who worked in the kitchen, had taught us to count.

I wrote Sagu—God. Next, Sagun kola—let us pray to God; Sagu tassa—God give to you, meaning thank you.

Ato Jimma, one of the teachers and a new church leader, was preaching that day. Love, he said. I knew that word: fikir. He said it three times, fikir, with the popping K. I listened for what the Dizi translator would say three times, so I could add it to my dictionary: love. I wanted to be the only white person in the world who could speak Dizin.

When we first got to Maji, our running water involved a Dizi worker with donkeys hauling water every few days from a hand dug well below the vegetable garden. Back up at the compound, he siphoned the water into fifty-gallon barrels outside the grass roofed *gojos*. Gravity fed the kitchen faucets. For our baths, Dad poured hot water into the tub with a huge kettle Mom always kept heating on the wood cook stove.

"Hot running water," Dad said. "See, I'm running to the bathroom with the water." Mom chuckled, but we didn't get the joke, because him carrying the heavy kettle herky-jerky to the bathroom was all we remembered.

By the tub sat a little potty chair for Cathy. We big girls were only allowed to use it at night. During the day, we had to use our outhouse overlooking the valley. We weren't allowed to use the aunties' outhouse. I won't say whether I snuck in there sometimes, when the need became urgent in the middle of a game. I'll just say, their outhouse didn't smell any better than ours.

And the holes in both were huge. I teetered on the edge and worried about falling in. I tried not to, but I always looked. Gross. I lifted the metal hook from its eye and burst back out the door. But if any of the teenaged school boys were nearby, cutting the grass a handful at a time with their half-circle scythes or chopping wood, they made comments in Dizin and laughed. I was sure they had listened to the tinkle of my pee hitting the pool of waste feet feet below. Or worse, ploppings.

After a few years in Maji, Dad ordered a hydraulic ram and hauled it up from Washa Wooha in the Jeep. He ran a pipe from the top of the small waterfall, a twenty-foot drop to the ram. It stood on the river bank like an iron dwarf with a bowler hat. It pounded inside, like a hammer striking metal, pounded the water up the hill into a new water tower, powered just by the water pressure. Dad explained it to us. *Physics*.

He put a screen in front of the intake pipe, but still it got blocked by leaves, or by frogs that slithered through. "Girls," he called, coming out of the *megazen*. "I'm going down to the ram." What an outcry there would be if we found out he went without us.

Dad set a businesslike pace. We followed, carrying our teddy bears. The bushes with white trumpet clusters were in bloom. By silent consensus, we stopped at each, to pick and suck the honey.

"Wait for us, Daddy," Joy shouted, but he didn't slow down. Mom believed in childrearing by benign neglect. Dad was too busy to fill in the gaps.

# CHAPTER 8

"Look," I said, pausing at the opening of the wild pig tunnel on the way to the waterfall. "Wanna crawl in?" Jane and I squatted, side by side. The rank scent of mulch and scat blew into our faces. We jumped up laughing and shivering.

The brushy path opened up to the river bank. The music of rushing water made my heart beat faster. Dad was already head-down at the top of the waterfall, working to free the frog. We threw stick boats into the cold river and leaned out to see around the brush as our boats bobbed in the current. Sunshine filtered warm through the trees.

*Ka-chunk. Ka-chunk.* Flowing again, water rushed against the ram. Jane and I ran over. "Me first," she said. She moved her hand around, searching for the jet of water, tiny and invisible, that shot out of the pressure release hole with every clang. She screamed when she found it.

I held my hand out and screwed up my eyes. *Ka-chunk.* Water zinged my palm, sharp as a needle. I laughed and rubbed the stinging red mark on my hand. "Try it, Joy."

Joy tucked her cheek into her shoulder and turned away.

"Come on, girls." Dad walked home like someone in a forced march, and again we stopped to play, then ran double-time to catch up. Our teddy bears kept up a constant chatter until we got to the compound gate, with the row of thirty-foot-high eucalyptus by the clinic. We fell quiet then, and clustered close to Dad to duck through the clinic crowd. Women with goat-skins tied over one shoulder sat, nursing babies. Men lounged, standing on one leg and leaning against their long, fat-polished walking sticks. All of them, I thought, were talking about us, in their four or five different languages. The clinic sat in a cloud of smells so strong it should be visible—eucalyptus oil, rubbing alcohol, sweat and wood smoke, ghee on people's hair and skin.

Dad veered off, back to the *megazen* without a word to us. We dashed back to privacy on the other side of our house.

Later, I lay on the prickly grass as the sun set, and put my ear on the iron pipe that ran across the yard. From down at the river, below the waterfall, the ram clanged. Moisture filtered up from the ground. The grass and earth smelled like old hay.

To this day, other Americans assume I must have noticed that my childhood in Ethiopia was exotic. But it was home.

After he put in the ram, Dad began another un-preacherly project He glowed with his signature self-deprecating pride about it: he ordered a pelton water wheel made in Addis Ababa. He ran a pipe down from the top of the big waterfall, through a ten-foot deep channel blasted by the Italians, who'd apparently had the same idea. River water shot from a shiny nozzle and slammed against brass cups on the wheel. It spun so fast the cups melted into a golden blur.

Dad hired Ato Kulkai to run a grist mill during the day, and men walked for miles with sacks of grain on their shoulders—corn, sorghum, highland teff. They walked down the hill to the mill, heels pounding into the path under the weight. Their wives and daughters didn't have to pound the grain in wooden mortars in front of their houses. What an elegant way that was, to shift some of the burden of women's work to the men.

Then Dad read a book on electricity and house wiring. He tied a hammer to the end of a roll of wire, inched out to the edge of the cliff below the mission compound, and flung it over. Dad showed Ato Kulkai how to switch the hydro power to a generator at the end of the day so we could put away the kerosene lanterns and turn on electric lights for a few hours at night.

The aunties inherited the finicky kerosene fridge. The new electric fridge (a *hallelujah* from Mom) ran at night and coasted through the day. Nothing would earn a spanking more quickly from Mom than opening the fridge during the day.

Wednesday afternoons, Mom had women's Bible study at some-one's house in town. "Hopefully they'll have sugar," she said to Dad as she gathered walking shoes, sweater, Bible. Even though Dad exhorted her that salt was more precious than sugar, so being served salt in coffee was a great honor, Mom made no secret about hating coffee with butter and salt.

After she left, we trooped through the kitchen, heading out to the cedars, to creep out along the branches, sure we could leap from tree to tree like the *guereza* monkeys with their cloaks of black and white sailing behind them; to fall between the ferny twigs with a thump instead; to pull off amber globs of pitch that would leave our fingers

41

sticky and pungent for days.

Sagu stood up from squatting behind a cupboard that had been pulled away from the wall. "Wanna box?" The school boys were enchanted by the word box, that it could mean two such different things.

"Not funny," Jane said.

"What are you doing?" I asked.

"Mama says there are Germans," he said.

"You mean germs."

"No," he said, his face serious. "Germans are here." But his eyes were laughing.

A couple of years before, Sagu had still been wearing a t-shirt, long as a tunic, over his only shorts—he hadn't had money to buy clothes he could wear to school. But he brought his father's sheep to graze on the hillside between the school and Dad's vegetable garden, and kept one eye on the sheep while he leaned in the school window, chanting the Amharic *fidel* with his friends inside, or listening to math lessons.

"Stand by the path to the garden," his friends told him. "When Mr. Kurr-tis goes by, he'll ask you why you're not in school."

Sagu did as they told him. Dad did as they said he would: *Why isn't a big boy like you in school?*

Sagu swore he was strong enough to work in the garden to earn money for clothes. After a few months, he was graduated to the kitchen, where after school he washed dishes, chopped onions, kneaded bread and tried to practice his English with us girls. Now he pulled a big knife out of the drawer.

"I'm going to cut your ears," he said. The Dizi notched their cattle's ears to brand them.

Joy screamed. Her pony tail trembled. Cathy hid her face at my knees. Sagu and I laughed. "He's just teasing. Don't tell Mommy," I said. Over my shoulder I said, "Wash the Germans and stop scaring the babies."

To the sound of Sagu shouting something at us in Dizin, we banged out the back door, past the screened *siga bait* where Mom kept vegetables and eggs cool on the shady side of the veranda. Past the sour smelling bunch of fat, starchy local bananas, bristling like stubby fingers all along the stem hanging from a eucalyptus rafter. Past the spiders that lived in the black debris that collected between the bananas.

"Why did his mother name Sagu *God*, anyway?" Jane asked. She squatted by an ant-lion's trap in the fine gray dust. She tickled a blade of grass on the bottom of its funnel. The little spider grabbed. She jumped to her feet and we ran out to the trees.

The next morning, Jane finished her second-grade workbooks and wandered off to the bedroom. Then back to the table.

"Hurry up," she said.

"Stop bothering me. Mine are harder. You'll see." I was practicing cursive writing. My letters were huge and round. It was laborious work. But I loved how letters strung together like beads on a necklace. Finally, I shut the workbook and we ran out.

Mom opened the door behind us. "Take Cathy with you," she said. It was my job to keep an eye on her, something I knew without Mom having to say. Cathy was two. She toddled with us, and sat down where we squatted by one of the flower beds.

"Who shall we be today?" I asked.

Jane always had good ideas. "Let's be the princess sisters who dance holes in their slippers every night."

We sucked out the honey and then slipped one petunia inside another inside another, shades of purple, pink, fuchsia, and white. No one ever had more gorgeous ballgowns.

Cathy, sitting on the grass beside us, let out a shrill scream. I leapt to my feet, yanked her corduroy overalls and puffy diaper down. There, in the tenderest folds of her body, was a shiny black army ant, its head half buried. That's what it always meant when Cathy screamed. I pinched the ant off. A tiny pink shred of flesh still hung between its pincers. I split it with my thumbnail and shook it off my fingers. The smell of warm, new urine steamed up from the diaper in the grass.

How did army ants know where to find our softest skin? They didn't bite our feet. They climbed all the way up our pant legs. Joy stamped her feet.

I hoisted Cathy up to my hip, stumbling a little with her weight. "Bring her things," I told Jane. She picked them up between thumb and finger, and marched behind me to the house, the diaper held at arm's length and her nose turned away. Joy ran ahead.

"Cathy had a *goon-don*," she shouted, and held the door for the sister parade.

"I'll be right there," Mom said from the kitchen.

Our bedroom floor was cluttered with toys. A big tin top, its two colorful halves crimped together in the middle, lay on its side.

"Lookie, Cathy," Joy said, and set it upright. She pressed down, but couldn't budge the top. Cathy was still whimpering.

"Let me." I leaned on the handle. The top creaked and turned. Faster and faster. The colors ran together and became a whirling rainbow. A breathy whistle began. *Whooo.* Cathy smiled. A drying tear ran a muddy track down her cheek and through her rust brown freckles. She reached for the top.

"Don't touch," I said, and blocked her hand. "Watch."

Too soon, the top began to wobble. The colors separated back out, the whistle faltered. The top fell over and rolled in a lopsided circle away from us, clattering on the cement floor.

"No more petunia ladies," Mom said at lunch.

"But Mom-my," Jane said. Her choppy hair made her face look fierce.

"Mom-my," Joy echoed, her voice dejected.

After lunch Jane suggested we sneak a few more petunias and run behind the *gojos* to go on with our game. But the magic had gone out of the princesses for me. "We'll just get in trouble." It wasn't easy being the oldest. No matter how much the others grew up, if we did something naughty, Mom told me, *You should have known better.* But Jane and Joy would never have to know better.

When Grandma Kurtz visited and I was almost nine, she wrote to my real aunts and uncles in Oregon, the ones I couldn't remember, that we girls had, *Remarkably good dispositions and so seldom ever have a set-to.* She shared Mom's standard for me: *Caroline has outgrown all her selfish ways and is very dependable to look after the others in such a grown-up way.*

On prayer meeting night, Mom gave me the job of clearing the sideboard between the living and dining rooms. As usual. The sideboard had collected enormous piles of clutter. As usual. I stormed from room to room distributing Cathy's pink sock; Joy's undershirt, inside out; three coloring books; broken crayons; the scissors we had spent an hour looking for the day before; torn envelopes with notes in Dad's scribble; *The Pokey Little Puppy*; the black Amharic New Testament with the *fidel* in gold on the front; mule syringes; Dad's hammer; and an empty cup with dried Ethiopian coffee grounds, still fragrant, in the bottom. I scowled and stomped, hoping Mom would get the hint. But she was disorganized and I was good at sorting. She must have thought the price of a few scowls well worth paying.

Eventually, Mom dangled the essentials from the sideboard drawer knobs on pieces of long, white cotton string: a pair of scissors, a role of tape, and a pen. A hairbrush would have had my vote if there had been another knob.

One day a *Highlights for Children* magazine with an article about crocodiles ended its six-month voyage and appeared in a box of mail off the EAL flight. Crocodiles. I had almost forgotten about Dad in the Omo River with the croc. Now I sat on my tailbone, heels braced against the jute-wrapped bar of the couch, knees in the air, smelling pulpy pages, musty from their voyage through the humidity of a Red Sea port.

Crocodiles take their prey to the bottom of rivers and wedge them there until their flesh becomes waterlogged and tender. Shiver.

# CHAPTER 9

I dreamed that night: the pool below the big waterfall was roiling with crocodiles. I leaned over to show Jane the biggest one of all. He reached up and pulled me in. He wedged me under a log and left me there. Fortunately, people can breathe under water, as long as they don't do it too much. I took tiny breaths. Just enough to stay alive. When the croc came back to eat me, I shouted for help. An Ethiopian boy beat the croc on the head with his walking stick and I woke.

My legs and the spot between my shoulders burned. I burst into tears and hid my face in my pillow, as though to blot out my own mind.

At night, the rustling of pages came over the wall with the lights from the living room. Mom's typing clattered—her weekly letter to the grandmas and close friends in the US. My sisters in the beds above and beside me breathed softly. Even without nightmares, getting to sleep was a project for me.

The cotton-stuffed mattress of my bottom bunk sagged cozily in the middle where the springs gave way under my weight. I pulled the sheet up and folded it over the rough Ethiopian wool blanket. I plumped up the pillow. Turned over. Flopped onto my back. Stared at the dark springs above me, and the places between them, where the upper bunk mattress bulged.

What if Mom and Dad died?

There was no question where they would die. On the Washa Wooha road. A wheel would pop off the Jeep. Dad would fight the steering wheel. His muscles would ripple under the black hair on his arms. But the Jeep would careen down a narrow place. And off the edge. And I knew just where.

Between two knolls, the Italians had built a land bridge the Ethiopians called Nifas Ber, Door of the Wind. It was true. There was nothing there to stop the wind. There was nothing to stop anything. You went out, unprotected, when you drove across Nifas Ber. We girls called it Down on Both Sides.

Down on Both Sides was eight feet across, the grass on either side of the tire tracks only as wide as the strip between them. Jane and Joy hid their faces as Dad steered the Jeep down onto the narrow track. I stared out the side, into the muted colors of the valley so many feet below—the yellow or dun brown patches that were fields, the smudges that were miniature trees in clumps or running along like a small green river.

That's where someone could die.

The Jeep would tip. Tumble over. The vision was as real as if I was watching, horrified, from up on the road. It tumbled until it was too small to see.

Now I would be alone. Forever. My eyes stung. It was good to know, no matter how mad I was at Mom, that I'd be sorry. I buried my face in my pillow so I wouldn't wake Jane. When I rolled back onto my side, the pillow against my cheek was damp and cool. My eyes felt scratchy. I closed them. I nuzzled deeper into the pillow, into delicious drifting sleep.

Some nights I counted faces in the eucalyptus rafters, dimly lit by living room light. Scars from bigger branches made mouths—surprised, mad, amused. Scars where twigs had been lopped off by machetes were eyes, walleyed, winking, or scowling like I did when I had to set the table and it wasn't my turn.

Why not stay awake until Mom and Dad went to bed? They'd be touched that someone was still awake to kiss them good night. An hour later, the light brightened and then dimmed, the hissing pressure with it, as Dad carried the lantern out of the living room and down the hall. I slipped out of bed. The polished cement floor chilled my feet; we weren't the slippers kind of family. I squeaked open the door to Mom and Dad's room, and winced in the direct light, so much brighter than that reflecting off the underside of the *korkoro* roof.

Mom was lifting the maroon comforter. Under her flannel nightgown, her breasts jiggled. "What are you doing, still up?"

I blinked until my eyes adjusted. The kerosene lamp gave off a faint smell of spent gas. If we bumped the lamp, the mantles fell apart, and Dad carefully tied a new nylon mantle on and burned it to ash, pure and delicate. This one shone pale and silver as the light of the moon, feeding fumes to the fire that had burned blue in the starter pool until it jumped up to the mantle and began to glow.

Dad, in a t-shirt on the other side of the bed, turned. Looked startled.

"I came to kiss you good night."

They chuckled. I gave my kisses. Their bed smelled warm and nest-like. "Why do grown-ups get to sleep together, and kids, who get scared, have to sleep alone?"

They laughed again. "You go to bed now," Mom said, and patted my bottom.

After a few late-night kisses from me, Dad brought two extra blankets and wrapped them around the frame of the bunk bed, tucking them under the edge of Jane's mattress above me. He overlapped them by my pillow, and showed me how I could pull one aside, and then the other, to climb into bed.

"That's better," he said. "Now the light won't keep you awake."

I lay, smelling the new blankets, the un-cozy chemicals that faded over time but never completely went away. No dim ceiling, no faces in the rafters. I couldn't see the springs or the puffs of the mattress above. The typewriter clacked away, but more muffled. The problem was my mind. It got too busy at night. But I hadn't told Dad that. I didn't want to disappoint him. To tell him his solution wasn't going to help me sleep.

But now I didn't get out of bed to get that last warm kiss, that last comforting scent of their solid bodies.

While workbooks and play defined my life in Maji, the mill, the ram, and the Washa Wooha road dominated Dad's. All supplies Mom could not send the school boys to buy in the Maji market on Saturdays came by plane and Dad hauled them up the hill in the Jeep and a trailer. When guests came, Dad went to meet them. He drove down the next week on plane-day to send them back out. It took a day to get the Jeep ready, a day to make the trip, and a day to make repairs. That went for the police and governor's Land Rovers as well, because Dad was the only mechanic in town. Is that possible? Maybe he was just the best— a farm boy turned missionary.

The shelf along the back of the workbench held broken alarm clocks, pots waiting to be soldered, a doll of Cathy's with the arm twisted off. It got more and more crowded. Fixing things for people was the role in the community Dad had figured out he could fill while he worked to nurture a church. But this was not how Dad had planned to spend his time. He wore a dogged, resigned look as he walked back and forth from the house to the *megazen* and down to the bottom of the waterfalls, fixing things. He was a master at being a responsible citizen. I learned that from him.

Dad shook me awake before dawn the day before our flight to the mission's Association meeting when I was nine. A day early, to give Dad time in case of car trouble. I squinted my eyes open just enough to grab the elastic waist jeans, t-shirt and sweater I'd laid on the bottom of my bed.

In the dim light, Mom's square black Amish trivet said, *No Matter Where I Serve My Guests, It Seems They Like My Kitchen Best.* I breathed deeply—coffee, roasted cracked-wheat cereal, a tinge of wood smoke. I sprinkled big gray crystals of Ethiopian sugar that popped under my teeth onto the *cinday*, and poured reconstituted powdered milk on, hoping there would be a few rich bits of powder that hadn't dissolved. Breakfast was quiet, everyone sleepy and hurrying. The *cinday* tasted of smoke and nuts.

I helped Mom clear our dishes into the dim kitchen. The black cast iron stove radiated heat against my palms. Jane's arm pressed against mine. The fire no longer crackled, but still smelled of fresh wood smoke.

"Load up," Dad said, and we big girls ran out in the dark to the Jeep that puffed exhaust into the foggy air on the track outside our house. We tucked our feet up onto the back bench, and shivered under a scratchy wool blanket. Dad carried three-year-old Cathy out, in her footsie pajamas. Her head bobbed loosely on his shoulder. He slipped her onto the towels jammed behind the gear shift post to make a third front seat. He propped her against Mom's arm, and tucked a blanket around them.

Good-bye *gojos*, huge in the gray light. Good-bye house, angular and dark. Good-bye daisies and roses and petunias.

After the sun came up, we pushed the blankets away. Cathy woke up, dark bangs stuck to her sweaty forehead. I asked Dad, "How long *is* it to Washa Wooha?"

Red ringed his white knuckles. The steering wheel fought, and his muscles, under his black hair, under his freckles, shifted and bulged. "At least four hours. More when it rains."

"But how *far*?" We'd started agitating for a mule trip to Washa Wooha. Dad wasn't making any promises.

"Here's a riddle for you. It's twenty-four miles going down, and twenty-eight miles coming home."

Joy leaned forward. "Of course. Going home is uphill."

I frowned. "That doesn't make it longer."

"Yes. Because going home is uphill." When Joy got stubborn, she said the same thing over and over.

"But Joy," I said, "whether you go up or down, the road—"

"Harold, please," Mom said. "Don't let them just go on and on." She pressed her fingers against her temples. The Jeep jerked her head back and forth on her white neck.

"Caroline's right," Jane said.

"Here's what happens," Dad said. "When we get stuck in the mud, the wheels spin around and the odometer thinks we're driving forward. Or sometimes we have to take more than one run at the steep places. So the odometer says we've gone further when we drive home."

"See, I told you it's because it's uphill," Joy said, freckles in the air, ponytail down her back.

"But it's not what you thought," Jane said.

"Girls," Mom said.

"Yes, it is," Joy whispered. Jane leaned toward her, fight on her face. Joy put her fingers in her ears. She pretended to look out on her side of the Jeep, through the dirty plastic window, cracked across the middle. Joy hadn't learned not to argue with Jane, either, but she had her own ways of winning. I felt like pinching her, but I didn't.

"Here we go, girls," Dad said, a few minutes later. "Nifas Ber." Down on Both Sides.

"Let me out!" Jane shouted. "I want to walk!" Sometimes Dad stopped the Jeep and let nervous guests walk across Nifas Ber.

"Sit still," Dad said. He eased the Jeep down and turned onto a road with no hillside up, no forest, no rail, nothing but down and down.

Joy whimpered. Jane hid her face against the back of Mom's seat. "I just can't look," she said. "It makes me want to throw up."

If we fell, I would die of the ache in my heart before I got to the bottom. I kept my eyes open just in case.

Safely across Nifas Ber, just before we got to Siski Chaka, the Siski Wilderness, where mud never dried, a rock jammed the right front wheel and the Jeep lurched to the left. Dad twisted the steering wheel sharply back. Snap. The wheel spun in Dad's hands. The Jeep kept going left. A bubble of adrenaline popped in my stomach. Dad stood on the brake.

# CHAPTER 10

The Jeep wedged between two rocks and came to a stop. "Well." Dad sat for a second with his hands in his lap.

Jane's eyebrows rose on her forehead. "Can you fix it?"

I jabbed her. "Of *course* he can."

Dad sighed and climbed out. Mom lifted Cathy onto the ground. Her little shirt was wrinkled and sweaty. I pushed the front seat up on its hinge, and followed Joy and Jane hunch-backed to the door and out. Dad scooted under on his back until all but his ankles and tan leather work boots disappeared. Jane peered under. "Can you fix it?"

Jane was such a worrywart. Dad wiggled out and stood up. "Steering coupling."

"Can you fix it?" Jane asked again. Mom sometimes said *ding-ding-ding* like the nap time timer, when Jane got like this.

Dad pulled the scratched and dimpled tool box out from under the back seat.

I asked, "Can we walk?"

"Stay on the road," Mom said, reflexively.

"We will, Mommy," we chorused. Of course we would. We would never dare push through the thick brush on either side, into the forest where the wild pigs ran, but Mom had to say it and we had to answer.

After the roaring and jarring of the Jeep, at first all I could feel was silence. Then insects buzzing and birds clucking in the bushes filled in. The forests around Maji aren't like tropical African forests, with a cacophony of birds singing, squawking, and calling. The mountain forests of southwestern Ethiopia are cold and startlingly silent. One history book claims that raptors only came into Kaffa Province with the imperial armies, which pillaged and killed the people who resisted empire-building Emperor Menelik. What a morbid piece of history, if that is true.

"What if we get to Siski Chaka before Dad comes?" Joy asked.

"What if?"

"There might be wild animals." She shivered.

"There's nothing but leopards. And they hunt at night."

Jane hopped over a rut and walked beside me in the grass. "We're Hansel and Gretel, and this is the road back to our house from the witch. Through the enchanted forest," she said. This Jane I liked better than the worrier.

Shrubs and vines spilled over the road, as though the forest couldn't wait to overrun all traces of human passage. A beetle buzzed out, circled around and dived back into the impenetrable green. *Lantana*, the flower Ethiopians call *yeh wof kolo*, bird snack, billowed up on green-black stems to our right. The flowers made our fingers smell like rosemary and cedar sap. We sucked the nectar out of clusters of tiny pink and yellow trumpet stars.

"We're following a trail of *yeh wof kolo* back to our home," I said, sprinkling flower stars behind us.

Twenty-five feet away, a bush shuddered. I put my arms out and stopped the other two. A baboon walked out. Jane stepped behind me and peered over my shoulder. Joy crowded close, ponytail quivering. My pulse beat in my temple. The baboon swung his head in either direction. He sat back on his haunches.

Jane's breath puffed warm on my neck. The baboon grunted. The bushes rattled and his troop straggled out onto the roadway, gray and brown, with puffy beards around their faces and their tails held up like flagpoles. The babies clung to their mothers. One baby turned his little old face to us. His eyes glittered. A teenage baboon sat down on the road and ate something between his knuckles.

Joy squeezed my hand. Her palm was sweaty against mine.

The baboon troop drifted across the road and disappeared into the bushes until Big Papa was the only one left. He looked at us once more, as curious as we were, and walked into the bushes on feet and knuckles. When the bushes stopped rustling, the road fell silent.

I stared deep in Jane's eyes. "No one else in all the world saw them."

I pulled back on Joy's hand when we got to where I thought the baboons had crossed. We looked hard at the grass. There was no trace of footprints. "Maybe we're asleep and we all had the same dream at the same time," Jane said.

We walked on. Then I turned my head. "I thought I heard the Jeep."

We sprinted up the road. "He'll never catch us," Jane shouted.

"We'll run clear through the Siski Chaka and all the way to Washa Wooha!"

We ran until Joy said, "I have a side ache," and drifted to a stop.

We braced our hands against our knees and heaved. When my heart settled down, I listened again. "It's coming."

I grabbed Jane's arm before she could go tearing off. "Just nice and steady, like this." We matched steps and swung our arms together. Joy's face was earnest, her freckles glowing on her pink face. I ran between the dark brown tracks. The Jeep's roaring got louder. Jane looked at me and grinned. Along the side of the road, bushes pressed in close. Up ahead the light dimmed. A tree loomed, its trunk bigger than our whole family could reach around, its high branches hung with stringy gray moss.

I looked over my shoulder just as the Jeep lurched into sight. The windshield flashed a flat, square wink. I couldn't see Dad or Mom, just the Jeep, a monster crusted with dust and splats of mud, lumbering from side to side.

Now was the time to race. I wanted to make it to where the forest closed over the top and from above, the road disappeared.

Behind me, Dad stopped the Jeep for Joy. I leapt over the track to run beside Jane. The monster came to life again, roaring at our heels, scaring me, even though I knew it was just the Jeep. Dad drove just behind us until we couldn't take another step. We were all laughing. Even Mom. I looked up to an arch of green with blue tangles of sky flashing and shifting between the leaves. The air had turned cool and dark all around. Jane pushed her hair off her forehead. It stood straight up. Her skin under her freckles was bright red. "You got it fixed!"

Dad patted the steering wheel. "Good as new."

In Adikas, palm trees appeared on the brushy hillsides, waving fingers in the sunny breeze. Dad stopped the Jeep and we ran behind the bushes. Then we gathered back around Mom, who held Cathy on one hip and a thermos of lime juice in the other hand. Dad was turning the little brass catches and rolling up the Jeep's canvas so we could stand in the back. In single file, Jane, Joy and I climbed between the front seats.

"I get the middle," Joy said. Her ponytail flicked as she jumped onto the seat.

Jane pushed her with her elbow. "What if I want the middle?"

"Caroline, you stand in the middle. Jane, over there. Joy, if you can't be happy you'll have to sit down." As much as Mom hated fighting, she hated whining even more.

On the level stretch out of Adikas, Dad revved the engine up, maybe fifteen, maybe twenty miles an hour. I leaned into the roll bar. My hair whipped around my face and I squinted against the bugs.

"Super highway-y-y-y-y!" The road jiggled our voices. Wind snatched my words away and puffed out my cheeks.

Too soon, rocks poked up through the dirt again, and Dad hit the brakes. My chest pressed hard into the bar. Red dust billowed around us. The Jeep went back to jostling and jouncing, but we stayed standing for a while in the wind and sun.

"Sing, Daddy," Joy said.

Dad lifted one hand off the steering wheel in a grand gesture. *Oh, a capital ship for an ocean trip was the Walloping Window Blind.*

We belted the chorus out with him: *So blow ye winds, heigh-ho, a-rovin' I will go!*

Then he sang "The Dream Girl of Theta Chi," which he and his fraternity brothers had sung to Mom. He looked across the front seat, over Cathy's head, and smiled. Mom's dimple flickered and she looked away, out the side of the Jeep, where the canvas door had come off long ago.

"Mommy, sing the one about the cow on the railroad track," Joy said.

We all sang along, *She was a good old cow, with eyes so fine, but you can't expect a cow to read a railroad sign.* Mom would sing a couple of silly songs with us but she said she was looking forward to heaven, and having a really good singing voice.

The sun beat onto our heads, hotter and hotter as we descended. My hair dull with dust felt stiff. Joy lay down. Her knee hung over the edge of the gray plastic seat and jiggled back and forth. Jane and I sat on the metal side bench and dangled our legs out. Where she had rubbed her face, dirty streaks swooned across her cheeks.

Finally, on the lowlands, 5,000 feet below Maji, the tilting road evened out. Dust changed to quartz-crystal sand, and crackled under the tires.

"Pull your legs into the car," Dad said. He turned the Jeep off the road toward a giant rock outcropping. The ground sparkled, and golden patches of grass grew between scattered acacia trees, whose delicate leaves camouflaged inch long thorns. As we brushed by, we could see ants crawling in and out of bolls the size of steelies.

"Caroline and Jane, you help me put up the tent," Dad said. "Joy, you gather wood for the fire. Take Cathy. If we hurry, the muleteers told me where the cave is, the *washa* that Washa Wooha's named for. Maybe we can find it." We all knew *wooha* meant water. It was one of the words we used in Amharic until we confused what was English and what was Amharic—water, bread, rain, kindling, corrugated iron.

"The *washa*!" Jane said, as though it might hold buried treasure.

"They stop for water when they drive their cattle from the Omo River to Gurfarda," Dad said. He pulled up and we piled out.

A black, whale-shaped rock loomed over the campsite, smooth as a river rock, left there by some gigantic alluvial event. We'd discovered that the roots of a big tree made a ramp up the back side. In the breeze, above the flat-topped trees, we'd laid out our collections of volcanic debris from eons ago: agates with fern shapes frozen inside, pink and white quartz pieces, and jasper pebbles that looked like extruded mud and shone dull red or green when we spit on them.

In the other direction, a bigger stone stood like an upside-down plug one hundred and fifty feet tall, flung by a violent explosion. Dad had taken us up to explore it once. A split down the middle, stomach-lurchingly deep, fluttered with bats like shadows in the darkness. A tree grew across the top. Its big root bridged the gap, and smaller roots snaked down both sides of the crevice. Dad jumped us across the crack. Remembering that dark crack, even fifty years later, my stomach turns over.

Cathy picked up a stone with mica glittering in the late afternoon sun. "Mommy, look't. Look, Mommy, look." Desert insects buzzed. Doves called softly.

Mom said, "Uh-huh," and went on digging through the food box. Dad dragged the tent out of the trailer, a bundle of heavy green canvas with a gummy, waxy finish. Jane grabbed a corner and unfolded it, raising a puff of dust.

"Girls! Think! Clear the rocks out. We have to sleep here."

We flung stones away from the tent site, then grabbed opposite corners with both hands and shook the tent into place. Dad laid wooden poles on the sand, squatted and started fitting them together. Jane's hair still stuck out funny in back. She bounced up and down on her toes. "Daddy, hurry," she said.

"Jane, I'm going as fast as I can." Dad was using his patient voice. I put my hand on Jane's arm.

She stamped her foot. "We're going to miss the *washa*!"

Dad rocked back on his tan work boots. "Jane, there's plenty of time. Go sit in the Jeep until we're done. Go on now. Caroline, hold that end for me."

If we had plenty of time, Dad should never have said anything about hurrying. It just got Jane all worried. He should know that. Jane's eyes looked wounded at me. I rolled mine up until I could see the ragged ends of my bangs. I'd tried to warn her. She could never just do something. It wasn't that hard. Her flip flops shuffled through the quartz sand to the Jeep. And I was stuck with all the work again. I wanted to yell at Dad. Or at Jane. Or at both of them. But I just yanked on the corner of the canvas.

Joy and Cathy marched back into camp holding bundles of sticks on their heads with both hands, their arms stretched up so tight, their bellies showed.

The sun turned golden, its rays coming at us from an angle, a little cooler. Jane was released from exile. We set off for the *washa,* and she crowded past Joy on the narrow trail that sparkled like sugar. I made a face to tell Jane I was sorry she'd had to sit in the Jeep. She lifted both shoulders up to the edges of her hair and smiled back, as though it was just her bad luck. I scowled all over again. Inside.

Around a corner, the path swooped down through the brush. Mom's Keds skidded on the sand and she caught herself with a jerk. The path led us into cool blue shadows. Brush stood high all around, leaning over us, making the sky a ragged circle of blue above. Ahead, black basalt columns stood in a curved wall fifteen feet high. At the base, a murky green pool, still as oil. This was the famous Washa Wooha?

"It's not a cave, Daddy," Jane said, her mouth drooping like the embroidered mouth of her bear.

It wasn't a cave. It felt like we were at the bottom of a well, half surrounded by the wall of basalt columns. Down there with the water, brush leaning in above us, the air felt cool on my cheek and smelled as green as a growing thing. The hot breeze, the warm sunlight, the clicks and buzzes of desert insects had all fallen away.

Dad swung Cathy off his shoulders. Her freckled fist grabbed his pant leg, and her toes disappeared into the fine sand that was now basalt black.

"Take off your pants and shirts," Mom said. She squatted to strip Cathy.

Our feet sank into the sand at the edge of the opaque water. I sat down. Cool seeped up to the band of my panties. Slowly I scooted deeper until my shins glowed tan under the water, and my toes just peeked out. The sides of my calves, flattened against the bottom, looked fuzzy in the murky green. Joy watched from the edge.

"Go clear in and cool off," Dad said. I looked over my shoulder at him. He always said, *When I say frog, you jump.* But that was only for serious obeying. Or for making guests laugh.

"I am cooled off," I said. There were secrets in that water I didn't want to know.

# CHapTer 11

Joy tiptoed to the edge of the *wooha*. "How deep is it?"

"Wade out and see," Dad said. He took off his work boots, shook them out, and sat down beside Mom in the sand. His feet, sticking out of his khaki work pants with the cuffs rolled up, were pasty white. Not like his red complexion and his sun-browned arms. Mom clasped her hands around her knees, around the edges of the pedal pushers she never wore in Maji. Her gold wedding band shone in the dimness.

"We can lie down," I said, and stretched out parallel to the edge. The water tickled, lapping around my middle. Jane and I lay head to head, washing the stones we'd picked up on the path. Joy squatted nearby.

"There's no such thing as water monsters," I told Joy. I knew Jane would keep a sharp eye out.

Back at camp, Dad built a fire and put water and rice in the dented aluminum pot with the dinky handle that arched over the top. At the last minute, he dumped in a can of peas and a can of tuna, opened with his new Swiss Army knife. He dished a pile onto each of our aluminum plates. It tasted like smoke. Dad smacked his lips. "Nothing tastes better than rice with peas and tuna cooked over a campfire, does it, girls?" The Kurtz girls agreed, gobbling down their rice. Mom hated the taste of smoke. She twisted her mouth into a kind of smile and looked at Dad, who was grinning at her, cheeks red.

Sunset streaked the sky gold and salmon over the tops of the low acacia trees. Back-lit, they turned to black lace. Tiny bits of quartz dug in through my shorts, and my face throbbed with heat from the dying campfire. For devotions we sang the Twenty-third Psalm. Then the Washa Wooha song, *The shadow of a mighty rock within a weary land.*

We settled for the night with sleeping bags under us and sheets over, in the warm, stuffy tent. It smelled of dust, wax, and engine oil.

Mom and Dad's voices murmured by the camp fire.

All the other kids my age in our mission had been sent off to boarding school in first grade. Parents had been assured that as they served

God, God would heal any pain inflicted on their children. They didn't actually look at what it did. Peer pressure kept them strong. For four years, Mom had defied this pressure, and let me rush through the workbooks, and run outside to the real heart of the family, my sisters.

Over the fifty years after that idyl in Maji, we girls scattered. We found eight husbands, and lost or mislaid six of them in the passage of time. And then we found each other again. All but Joy moved back to Portland. We are happiest living within walking distance of each other. We go to the same hairdresser, the same yoga class. Together for a reunion or holiday, when one of us needs to check something in the oven or a grandchild calls, we can't bear to miss a moment. "Stop talking until I get back!" we say. "Don't say anything interesting while I'm gone!"

But when we were finding those husbands and having our eighteen children, we assumed the time reserved for sister love had expired. We raised those children in Illinois, Minnesota, Kansas, Colorado, South Dakota, Oregon and Alaska—wherever those husbands took us.

The energy that flung us apart began when the time came for me to go to boarding school. We spent an unremarkable furlough year in Boise, Idaho, where I turned ten, and Mom and I spent the summer sewing name-tags on my clothes—twelve school dresses, not just one for Sunday. My own name on every sock and every pair of panties. All grown up, I could hardly contain my excitement.

We stayed in Boise long enough for baby Chris—*finally! a son!*—to be cleared for travel, and arrived in Addis just in time for the Mission Association meeting. Association was always timed so parents could drop their children off at school in Addis Ababa and kiss them good bye for the three months until Christmas.

Jane, Joy, and I were immediately cast into the pool of mission children, dressed by Dad in whatever he could find in the tumble of suitcases on the floor. Mom was strung out after the sleepless transatlantic flight. Groggy from sleeping pills in the morning, she was sharp and impatient. She couldn't put two-month-old Chris down on the floors of the two dingy rooms our family had been assigned to. Cathy was clingy—her mother had found a new love. And that mother's oldest daughter was all name-tagged for boarding school.

Mothers (those without babies) took turns leading us in daily Vacation Bible School while the adults held their meetings. We were herded in loose age groupings into rooms with stacks of pictures, bins of broken crayons, and plastic bits for mosaic craft projects. We rotated through the Bible story room. Aunt Esther played the piano with gusto for our devotions. Adults and children alike breathed free when the rainy season skies cleared and we could run and play outside.

I knew these kids from other mission meetings. Jeanie Haspels, a year older, lived on the mission station nearest Maji, only one hundred and fifty miles away. I'd stayed with her for a week, while the rest of the family visited other mission stations. Now finally I'd be at school with Jeanie. She would be my best friend. JR was also a year older than me, in sixth grade. I'd been in love with JR forever already—that shock of almost black hair that draped over his forehead and into his naughty blue eyes. His thin lips. His smile.

At noon, the dining hall of the school for Ethiopian girls where we were meeting echoed with voices and the clatter of silverware on blue melamine plates. I had no idea where any other member of my family was in the melee. *I'm a big girl now*, I thought. *I don't have to ask Mom where I can sit.*

"Where's your room?" I slid onto the bench beside Jeanie Haspels. Another sixth-grade girl flounced her wavy auburn hair and slipped in across the table. A redheaded girl I didn't know followed.

Jane appeared at the end of the table, tipping her tray dangerously. Looking at me with sad, puppy-dog eyes. I grabbed the edge of her tray and leveled it. I shook my head and frowned. She got the message, *Go find your own friends*, and wandered off.

"I'm in our room," Jeanie corrected me. "But right now, Helen is in your bed." The new girl smiled at me. I looked down at my meatloaf and potatoes.

*They'd moved in together? And not even told me? Why was Helen in my bed?*

"Mom!" I said after lunch. "I want to be up with the other kids. Ask for me!"

"We want you to stay with us," she said, and her eyes blinked fast. In the room that was dim and musty and smelled like dirty clothes? The room I couldn't walk in without walking on those clothes? The room where no one could find a hairbrush? And only I cared?

"Please!" I said. "They've moved in!"

Mom and I went to Jeanie Haspels's mother, Aunt Lois, who was going to be our dorm mother for the first month.

"You come on up this evening and we'll have a bed for you," Aunt Lois said, and gave my shoulders a warm, sideways squeeze.

Dad took everything out of a footlocker and gave it to me. A footlocker all my own. Unheard of. I gave him a big hug, glowing with the specialness.

Jane scowled, her head tipped down and her hair swinging forward. "What?" I said. "I don't want to take your underwear with me. Or Cathy's!" I pawed through the piles, looking for my things. Joy followed Dad out, whining for a suitcase of her own.

Jane sat on the edge of an unmade bed with her elbows on her knees and her cheeks all scrunched up by the heels of her hands. "Do you have to go?"

"Yes, I have to." I smoothed blouses, undershirts, panties and skirts into my footlocker. "You still have Joy to play with." After all, they were just a year apart and she was two years younger than me. "I'm too old for workbooks anymore."

Jane sat bolt upright. "I'm too old for workbooks, too!"

"I did workbooks for third grade. You have to."

Jane clenched her fists and made a growling sound. She was still recovering from the heartbreak of Boise, where she hadn't known what a number of things on her placement test were—a picket fence is one we remember—and the principal concluded she should be held back. The principal should have showed Jane a *korch* thorn post. She knew plenty about that kind of fence. Jane got fierce at any reminder that she was now trailing two years behind me again, even though she could read just as well.

After supper, Dad carried my footlocker up to a house that sat on one side of the Presbyterian mission compound. He hollered into the open door. Aunt Lois came out of the kitchen drying her hands on a faded floral apron. The screen door banged behind us. Aunt Lois gave me a hug. My head came just barely up to her soft breasts—her bosom, Mom would have called it. She smelled like flour and baby powder. "Here you are!" she said. "All ready to move in."

I nodded, with a tight little smile. My heart was pounding so hard, I was breathing fast. It felt so momentous, moving away from home.

"You know Helen Hays's dad died," she said. No, I didn't know anything about Helen, including her last name. "We thought it would be nice for her to have some time with her friends before school starts. After she leaves, that will be your bed."

Girl squeals came from the right, down the hall. Aunt Lois was guiding me the opposite way. She said, "Helen will move back to Bingham on Friday." We were in the living room now. Aunt Lois stood under the arch and pointed into the dining room. "Since you're so eager, we found a cot up in the Crow's Nest."

Along the wall between the dining room and kitchen. A camping cot all made up. The white sheet glowed in the dim light, neatly folded over an army green wool blanket.

"She'll be just fine here," Dad said. He gave my shoulder a stern squeeze. His voice echoed off the dining room table that would seat twelve. He plunked my footlocker down at the foot of the cot, fished a little key on a silver-beaded chain out of his chest pocket, opened the lock, and gave me the key. "Put that somewhere you can find it."

I gripped the warm key tightly. Dad took me by both shoulders and I obeyed his unspoken demand that I look him in the eyes. "Be a big helper."

Didn't he notice that I was always a big helper? What would they do without my big helping once they went home? I nodded and fought the stinging in my eyes. Dad hugged me and left.

I sat on the cot, in my blue flannel nightgown, one foot under me, one foot dangling down, clipping bright pink clips onto pokey rollers in my hair. The front door opened, the screen door bumped softly. Mom peeked around the corner of the archway.

I smiled at her with a closed mouth.

"You all moved in?" she asked. I nodded. My eyes stung.

"Here, I'll help you," she said. She must have known I wouldn't return to the family room no matter how roughly my fantasy had bumped to earth. "Turn." She'd been teaching me to put the rollers in my own hair. But the back was hard.

I turned and squeezed my eyes together. She brushed my chin length hair slowly. My hair that she'd put so many perms in, that she'd whipped up into a pony tail in a hurry so many mornings, that she'd marveled over—*How did two black haired parents give birth to this blond child?* She separated my hair into locks. Slowly rolled them up onto rollers. Clipped them. I wished she wouldn't stop.

I snuggled down between the cold sheets, under the army blanket. Mom kissed my lips. "Sleep tight." Her voice was a little wobbly. I nodded, not trusting mine.

Down the hall I could still hear murmured voices. Aunt Lois knocked. A burst of giggling quickly shushed.

After the next day's singing-crafts-Bible-story program, after the meals in the noisy dining hall, and a game of kick-the-can at dusk, Aunt Lois stood on the hostel porch and rang a tinkly silver bell. Eleven of us thundered through the door. A first grade boy. Two second grade girls. The rest of us straggling up the age ladder to Alice and Tommy in seventh grade.

Evening devotions over, Aunt Lois gave us a half hour to get ready for bed. I flew into my nightgown. I brushed and spit as fast as I could, and dropped my toothbrush into one of the plastic glasses lined up on the cabinet.

The big girls' door was closed. I knocked timidly. "It's me, Caroline," I said, quite a bit bolder than I felt. I sat on the end of one of the bottom bunks. I hugged my knees to my chest and tucked my nightie under my feet to make a tent. The auburn-haired girl was unbuttoning her shirt with her back to us. Her nightgown was draped over her neck and shoulders for privacy. With practiced movements she whipped off her shirt, slipped her arms into the sleeves of the nightie and pulled it down. Then she reached under, yanked off her panties and tossed them toward the woven bamboo laundry basket, standing as tall as my chest. The panties landed in a perfect circle on the floor. In the center of the circle, in the center of the crotch, was a jagged brown spot.

The room went silent as a vacuum tube. All the girls looked at me.

"Whoops." The auburn girl scooped up the stained undies.

Jeanie Haspels said, "Do you know about periods?"

"Mm-hmm," I lied.

Later I lay on my cot and stared at the fiberboard ceiling painted white. Well, I knew about periods and commas and question marks. I tested my conscience, like my tongue had tested the spot where a tooth had come out, where the flesh was surprisingly soft and a little raw, and tasted of blood. I found no guilt: I would even lie, not to be any more left out.

# CHAPTER 12

The dorms at Good Shepherd School were supposed to be finished that September, but of course construction had gone more slowly than hoped, and the dorm had only gotten as far as a maze of narrow foundation trenches dug into black soil. The missions had scrambled and made emergency housing arrangements for the forty students. Mennonites lived with the new principal and his wife. The rest of us were set up in hostels at our various mission headquarters in town.

School began on the Monday after Labor Day, just like schools half way around the world in Idaho or Kansas or Virginia. That way, we mish kids could come and go on furloughs without missing anything. And in Ethiopia, American Labor Day falls not at the end of summer, but at the worse-before-it-gets-better end of the rainy season, when mornings dawn bracing and cool, spring-like, crystalline with moist air. Afternoons, clouds pile up for a mountain downpour just after lunch.

On that first day, eleven of us in the Presbyterian VW Kombi van swung around Mexico Square, down the hill past the wine factory on the southwestern edge of the city. On the far side of the rickety Akaki River bridge, Demissie, the mission driver, shifted into a lower gear. The van lurched. We bumped onto an unpaved roadbed. Our nervous screams bounced off the metal and glass that dripped with condensation.

Half a mile later, Demissie stopped the van in the middle of the road and turned off the engine. We were startled into silence. He draped his elbow over the back of his seat. Some Ethiopian adults were cross with us—American kids who didn't sit quietly and avert their eyes like polite children should—but Demissie's face was always patient. "The road is not finished."

I scrubbed at the window. There was nothing to see but wet grass and eucalyptus trees. Demissie opened the van door and took my hand to help me down. When I stepped off the road, mud rolled over the toes of my new black boots like chocolate pudding.

Demissie pointed us along a short cut, maybe a quarter mile

through a eucalyptus grove that had been recently harvested. Out of wet, thickly gnarled stumps grew saplings with square turquoise stems and round leaves, a misty blue world standing as tall as our heads. In another seven years those whips would be spindly trees again, the Ethiopian equivalent of 2 x 4s. The owner of the forest would harvest, and women and girls would gather up the oil-laden leaves and twigs to make blazing hot fires for baking *injera*, the staple bread of Ethiopia.

But now, raindrops sat round on the oily leaves. As we brushed by, they rolled onto our hair, skin, and jackets. I picked a leaf and rubbed to find the green under its blue frosting. I sniffed the menthol on my fingers.

We straggled out of the eucalyptus grove. There sat a low cement block building, roofed in silvery wet *korkoro*. A few miles to the left stood the hill we later named Baldie, with plowed fields swooping up the sides the way a blanket covers wadded sheets. Behind the school building rose Crew Cut Hill, with a fringe of eucalyptus trees that grew from year to year and then got buzzed. Behind Crew Cut stood Mogle, a thumb-knuckle bumping out the side of a taller peak. The smell of eucalyptus, the chill of the wet forest, misty blue hills and bright yellow *Meskel* flowers in patches among fallow fields—welcome to Good Shepherd School.

Jeanie Haspels held up a strand of barbed wire and JR held down another so we could climb through. Some of the other big girls fussed at their little sisters, *Don't tear your dress!* As I bundled my skirt up and arched my back carefully, I gave thanks I didn't have sisters to look after.

On the granite veranda of the school building, one of the fourth-graders pulled on the sleeve of my raincoat. "You're in here with us." With the little kids? The third and fourth-graders? Jeanie was hugging a Mennonite girl in long braids. They walked arm and arm into the sixth, seventh and eighth grade room next door. My best friend had forgotten about me completely. Feeling tragic, I turned away.

My new classroom smelled of curing cement. Its metal window frames were empty of glass. The teacher, Miss Wilkins, gave me a rose-pink lipstick smile and introduced me to the only other fifth-grader, a boy named Benny. The classroom filled with about twelve third-graders and maybe seven fourth-graders, all chattering with high, excited voices. They knew each other from their years at Bingham. I glanced again at Benny, his unathletic posture, sandy brown hair and glasses. At the fourth grade girls. Who would be my friend?

At lunch, kids sat on the damp veranda stones. The big girls all sat together. I wasn't brave enough to join them. I sat at the end of the row of fourth grade girls, by a chubby Mennonite girl. I unwrapped waxed paper from a sandwich made with thick slices of homemade bread baked in the wood stove at the hostel and spread with peanut butter. In another packet, I found a few carrot sticks. A tangerine sprayed fragrant oil onto my fingers as I peeled it.

"Who is that?" I whispered, and pointed with my chin to the girl beside Jeanie.

"Jewel? Margaret? They're the Wenger girls. Jewel's in seventh grade. Margaret's the only eighth-grader."

Jewel Wenger. How could I hope to compete with a girl named Jewel? And she looked spunky, with glowing tan skin. To further seal my doom, she was the pitcher for our co-ed softball team. And there I was. New to boarding school. Barely over four feet tall, barely able with my thin arms to hit the heavy softball past the pitcher. And Jewel's braids hung down her back, clear to her waist. My hair fell about to my chin. And in spite of sleeping on those pokey rollers Mom insisted I use, the curls fell out by mid-afternoon, because my hair wanted to be itself—fine and straight.

When the principal rang the bell, we settled back in class with the scraping of desk and chair legs on red and black checkerboard cement tiles. Miss Wilkins walked back and forth in front of the blackboard— a patch of cement smoothed over block walls and painted black. The most beautiful woman I'd ever seen, her blond hair curled enthusiastically. Her lips glistened pink. Her full skirt swished. She was getting the third-graders started on a reading assignment. Beside me, Benny was bending over our arithmetic assignment, gripping his pencil so tightly his first finger bent back on itself.

Rain began to ping on the *korkoro* roof. Silver flashed out over the eucalyptus forest. The clap of thunder split open the heavens and rain pounded down. It sprayed in the open windows. Wet spots sprinkled my foolscap paper. Those of us in the window row jumped up and dragged our desks across the tile toward the middle of the room like an earsplitting herd of straight-legged animals.

By the end of the week, the windows had been glazed. The nutty fumes of curing putty greeted us every morning. Naughty third and fourth-grade boys pinched off bits and made fragrant pellets they blew like poison darts at us girls through ball point pens. The pellets made oily spots on the cement tiles when we stepped on them.

For a month we walked the final distance from the end of the road, wherever it had reached, through sucking mud and dripping eucalyptus shoots. The men who worked on the stone road crouched under pieces of plastic when the rain pounded down. When the sky cleared again, they tink-tink-tinked on chunks of granite with the sharp ends of little hammers, turning stones into blocks and laying them in rows for the roadbed. They pounded gravel with sledgehammers arcing over their heads. They pushed squeaky wheelbarrows with warped wheels through the mud and spread sharp bits over the blocks until the cracks filled up and the road was finished.

Over time, workmen planted the open courtyard of the school with arching purple salvia, calla lilies and a low-growing plant with shiny burgundy leaves veined in magenta. The workmen hand-leveled a dirt basketball court, constructed a backstop for our recess softball games, and poured cement into an old tire to anchor a tetherball pole. They welded pipes and erected the tallest swing set I have ever seen.

In those swings, I later hung my head back until the long straight ponytail I grew dragged on the ground in the downward swoop. I paired with a friend and pumped until the chains went slack at the zenith. I turned my head away in shame when one of the younger girls pumped high in a dress, laughing with the boys, who looked up at her panties.

A letter, addressed to me in Mom's precise classroom handwriting, lay on the desk just inside the hostel door one afternoon. I pictured Mom in the living room, typing away after the kids went to bed. Then the letter had been packed with others into a plastic bag and into a small box for the runner to take to Washa Wooha. I knew how the letter had bucked its way to Addis in the afternoon heat currents like I had. To my exile. From Mom and Dad. From Maji. From my sisters. They were playing without me. Grief washed through me like a fever.

# CHAPTER 13

I grabbed my letter and ran to my bed. I buried my face in my pillow. Jeanie Haspels burst into the room looking for me. She stopped inside the door. Tiptoed over to my top bunk. She laid her hand on my back. "Homesick?"

I didn't move. I was almost as much ashamed as I was grieved. Jeanie rustled around and then slipped something under my pillow. I wept. And slept. And woke up to remember and cry some more. When Aunt Lois rang the supper bell I checked—*Yes, I think I can do it.* I waited until it was quiet in the hall, then slipped down from the bed with a bump. I brushed my hair, stiff on the sides with dry tears. I splashed water on my face. I slipped into my chair at the table as Aunt Lois said amen.

Later I found that a treasure trove of hard candies, little notes, and even a stale home-baked peanut butter cookie had been slipped under my pillow. We did what we could for each other. No one was ever mean to someone who was homesick.

In choir, Mrs. Anderson played from the top of the piano to the bottom, and taught us the Good Shepherd hymn in harmony. Margaret Wenger and some of the older boys could hit tenor notes. Jeanie stood between Jewel and me, and I learned to sing alto by listening to them.

I signed up for piano lessons the minute they were announced. I ran to the piano after school and marched my way through practice— a diligent little pianist, but too worried about making mistakes to be an inspired one.

Another delight—Good Shepherd had a library. A wall of books! Floor to ceiling! Something I'd never seen or imagined. I dived in and read one hundred books my first year. I was pretty sure it was one hundred. Whenever I tried to count, I got lost among the gilt stars on my reading record. I became known as the tiny kid who was always reading. Always humming. Always talking about Maji.

I was glad I never had to make the choice between school and Maji. The choices we do have to make are hard enough.

I had no idea at the time that my American age mates had a president. I had a king. One whose mythology went as far back as King Solomon and the Queen of Sheba, and as far forward as modern Jamaica.

His dynasty felt most secure when they could link themselves to the Solomonic myth somewhere, no matter how tangentially. As one regent died, the Ethiopian princes and dukes, legitimate contenders through an ancestor somewhere, fought wars of attrition until one emerged victor. I didn't understand this then, but a sense of Haile Selassie's mythic stature, his reputation in the world, the regard he brought to Africa by way of his dignity and gravitas, penetrated my childish mind. If I could have found the words, I would have said, with millions of Ethiopian peasants, that Emperor Haile Selassie ruled Ethiopia by destiny. By divine decree.

As for the Queen of Sheba, with everyone else in Ethiopia, I knew her name was Makeda and she went from Axum, Ethiopia to Jerusalem to see King Solomon's wealth and glory for herself. I read a version of that story, taken from *Kebra Negast, The Glory of Kings*, written in the fourteenth century in Ge'ez. Including her cloven foot, and that Solomon tricked her into his bed. And that, when Makeda returned to Axum, she bore Solomon a son, Menelik the First.

That the prince went to Jerusalem as a young man, to be trained by his august father, then returned to Ethiopia to rule. That he and his retinue of young princes brought back the true Ark of the Covenant by sneaking it out of his father's temple in Jerusalem, leaving behind a facsimile. If you doubt this story, read the journalist Graham Hancock's book, *The Sign and the Seal*. He gets weird about the Knights Templar in Ethiopia, and the contents of the ark, but his research into all the oral myths about the ark's resting place is credible. He concluded that the true ark is indeed at rest in Axum, in St. Mary of Tsion Church, guarded by a priest who spends his days watching, praying, and lighting incense. And consider this: all reference to the ark in the Bible disappears after King Solomon's reign.

It was almost three millennia after Solomon, in 1913, when Emperor Menelik II of Ethiopia died and the scramble for power began. Ras Tafari won, becoming regent in 1916. When Empress Zewditu died, he became "The Conquering Lion of the Tribe of Judah, His Imperial Majesty Haile Selassie I, King of Kings of Ethiopia, Elect of God." For short, Ethiopians called him *Jan Hoy*, O Great One. For short, Mom and Dad and the aunties called him H-I-M, His Imperial Majesty. Never, as a child, would I have left out his title. I always said *His Majesty*. And only history nerds would remember his title, Ras, and his given name,

Tafari, if the Jamaicans had not declared him their African Messiah and themselves Rastafarian.

In the early fifties, Germame Neway, the younger son of a noble family, won a scholarship to the University of Wisconsin and went on to Columbia University for a master's degree. He returned to Ethiopia a radical Marxist. This was how the cold war played out in Ethiopia: Ethiopians who went to Russia for education saw the dysfunctions there and came back full of enthusiasm for the US; Ethiopians who went to the US ran into racism and radical professors, and returned to Ethiopia leaning left.

Germame Neway got back to Ethiopia around the time our family arrived. He became governor of a fertile but neglected sub-province to the south, where middlemen were taking larger and larger cuts of coffee and farm products, and corrupt government officials were forcing peasants off the land. Germame Neway tried to make reforms, but his wealthy neighbors had him recalled to Addis Ababa. There he explained to the emperor that he was only trying to end the suffering of the starving landless.

His Majesty reassigned Germame to the destitute Ogaden desert in Eastern Ethiopia. Surely he couldn't get into trouble there. He got clinics and schools built. He lived simply, eating only two meals a day in solidarity with the poor, becoming known as the Fasting Governor. When he was pulled again, for undermining the powerful, local people carried him in a sedan chair for a kilometer to send him on his way.

Maybe earning such love through his reforming zeal gave Germame his idealism. Certainly, he saw that change would not come to Ethiopia without radical intervention—too many oppressors had too many vested interests. Sidelined in Addis Ababa, he talked to his older brother Mengistu, commander of the emperor's elite Honor Guard. They recruited a few other conspirators.

Some historians say it wasn't idealism at all, but haste that precipitated Mengistu and Germame Neway's revolution. Maybe they got nervous their plans had leaked. For whatever reason, they put a coup into motion in the middle of December 1960, when His Majesty was gone on a diplomatic trip to Brazil. It is called The December *Girgir*. Chaos.

The *girgir* began for me like any other dry season Wednesday. Until Mr. Anderson popped open the metal and glass door to the classroom. He leaned in, dark eyebrows pinched together behind heavy black plastic glasses. Miss Wilkins, in her shirtdress, curled blond hair bobbing, walked quickly over. All eyes in the classroom turned to the kid in the closest corner. He mouthed, "Coo," his lips pursing as though for a long kiss. He raised his eyebrows to make it a question.

"Children! Math and spelling books into your bags. Your vans are waiting for you. Quickly. There's been a coup against His Majesty."

Out of school in the middle of the day, in the middle of the week— what I felt was excitement. I pushed through the cluster of sixth- and seventh-grade boys jostling each other, their energy bouncing off the *korkoro* ceiling of the veranda. My plaid book-bag bumped my legs. My heart beat in my tight chest. Jeanie Haspels came out with Jewel. I fell in behind them. I'd learned to be patient. I was Jeanie's after-school best friend.

Demissie stood by our van, its engine running. The three little Presbyterian kids ran down the steps, squabbling over whose turn it was for the window. As Demissie pulled out past the Mennonite van, they stood and waved. We bounced at high speed along the gravel. The grove steamed eucalyptus oils into the bright sunlight. The gritty cloud of another van's dust seeped into ours. My fingers turned chalky. When we got to the concrete, Demissie accelerated. Tires squealed. Little kids screamed.

I popped open my window and my strands of hair that had lost their curl whipped around my face. Demissie was a careful driver, he never drove fast, but today he could—there was no one in the streets: no cattle, long horned, with back humps; no donkeys piled to twice their height with teff straw for making adobe; no sheep trotting along with their fat tails swinging, followed by men with long, sweat-polished canes.

By the cotton factory, where workers usually sat, wrapped in ghostly white *gabis*, waiting for shift changes, bits of cotton pulled and quivered in the weeds. The only place where you could buy ice cream, there by Mexico Square, was closed. All along the street, *souks* were padlocked. Even Somali Tara, where Dad said you could get any car part if you didn't mind if it was fresh off someone else's car, looked littered, dirty, abandoned.

By the time we got to the mission compound, Jeanie and JR had cooked up a game—Pow, Gotcha.

I watched enviously as Jeanie filled her yellow plastic squirt gun under the bathroom spigot. She assured me she'd help me find a stick that looked like a gun. The screen door banged, and banged, and banged again as we ran out to choose up teams. My heart quickened as I looked at JR's lanky black hair, his pale skin and blue eyes, but I danced over, happy enough to join Jeanie when she chose me.

"Go!" JR shouted. I dived behind a geranium bush that reached up to the window sill. Sweet perfume surrounded me as I brushed the stems that were only too happy to sweat. Crispy fallen leaves crackled under my feet. But just hiding was cowardly. I crawled out and ran toward the corner of the house.

"Pow! Gotcha!" one of the younger kids shouted.

I flopped down and lay, staring up at the pale blue dry-season sky, smelling old smoke in the air, counting to twenty-five. The adrenalin tingle slowly washed out of my fingers and legs.

JR shouted. A first grader said, plaintively, "I'm already dead."

Uncle Don came out of the guest house. "John Russell, come here this minute!"

I slunk back to the geranium bush. There was nothing I hated more than getting in trouble. Uncle Don was leaning into JR's face. I couldn't hear what he was saying.

After Uncle Don marched back to the office, JR shouted, "Allie-allie-in-free!"

I joined the circle around him. *What-what-what* we all clamored. "We can't play. It's scaring the girls down at the school. Some of their dads are prisoners at the palace."

Jeanie and I drifted to the steps of the hostel, where the last of the afternoon sun shone solid against our faces. She pulled the shoestring out of her tennis shoe and made a harness for her left pointer finger. She galloped her three-legged horse along the granite step. I watched, mesmerized and half asleep, exhausted by all the excitement. Jeanie wanted us to give her a nickname: Horsespells. JR wanted us to call him Pole Cat. Silly. Everyone knows you can't choose your own nickname. It would be another year before I had a nickname, Core, because JR's sister said my brown eyes looked like a *kor-kay*, an antelope.

Over by the gate, the *zebenya* guarded the mission compound. He always stood there like a shadow, in his army greatcoat, whatever the weather. He always held his *dula* walking stick in his right hand. But maybe now that there had been a coup, maybe now he was hiding how jumpy he felt inside. Maybe he was holding his *dula* tighter, and grinding his teeth as he tried to look normal.

Years later, I would watch my sons slide-tackle in soccer games marveling like I did that day. It looked so innocuous, their bodies slipping easily along the grass. But they might come home with torn ligaments, sprains, or breaks. At the very least, with angry red abrasions. We seem robust, but our bodies and souls are easily wounded.

Mengistu told his Honor Guard that there had been a coup. He challenged them to defend His Majesty. They enthusiastically prepared for a fight. About what happened next, historians disagree. Did the brothers tell high officials that the empress was ill? Did they say His Majesty had taken ill traveling, and decisions must be made? Whatever they were told, as officials arrived at the palace, they were taken hostage.

The Honor Guard seized Radio Ethiopia, and the crown prince announced a new socialist government, one which would right the economic and social ills of the country. He would be the new titular monarch.

Downtown, university students flooded out of their dorms at this announcement. As we were dashing home with Demissie, they were filling downtown Addis Ababa, and marching in support of the revolt. By the time Jeanie and I sat, tense and drifting, on the front steps, the students had returned to their dormitories. Addis Ababa fell silent. We all waited to see what would happen.

# CHAPTER 14

Germame and Mengistu Neway waited as well. They waited for the Air Force to back them. They waited for the military to swing into line. They waited for the broad masses to rise up in ecstasy. They hadn't bothered to arrest the Commander in Chief of the army. They certainly hadn't counted on his immediately seizing the main ammunition depot. And the Neway brothers underestimated the bitterness between the arrogant Honor Guard and the poorly paid army.

They had also hoped for support from the Orthodox Church, but the church quickly printed leaflets excommunicating them. As for the common people, who had not read their Marx and did not understand their part in the drama, they were horrified that anyone would oppose the *elect of God*.

I whispered with my roommates for a long time that night after lights-out. Aunt Esther, our hostel-mother for the month of December, opened the door suddenly. A bar of light shot into the room. I buried my face in my pillow, afraid of trouble as always. "Girls, quiet down," she said. But we couldn't. Not for a long, long time.

In the wee hours, I opened my eyes. The fluorescent light on the corner of the house shone dimly through the curtains. Beds and dressers hulked against the walls.

Pop. Pop-pop. Pop-pop-pop-pop.

I lay flat, feet pointed, hands straight by my sides, face looking up at the ceiling. My wool blanket still smelled faintly of that chemical. Every toe and finger felt cold, even though the blanket lay heavy. Sheets rustled in the bed below. I whispered without turning my head. "Jeanie? Are you awake?"

"Yeah. Is that shooting?"

"I'm awake, too," JR's sister said, from across the room.

"Can I come in bed with you?" I asked. We all crept through black and gray to the safe darkness of Jeanie's bottom bunk.

Pop. Pop-pop-pop.

The sound was muffled, far away. But still I shivered and tucked

73

my toes further under Jeanie. "I read that if you point a gun at a snake, it will stare right into the round black hole and you can kill it without aiming," I whispered. Are people like snakes? Or can they duck and run away? My roommates' skin smelled of sleep, warm and comforting. Jeanie's hair tickled against my cheek. Her blanket scratched my chin. Light finally crept up behind the curtains.

With morning, Addis Ababa expelled its breath and the shooting began in earnest. Bursts of muffled gunfire interrupted our breakfast oatmeal.

"No," Aunt Esther said when Jeanie asked, "you certainly cannot go outside and play."

The hall was full of shadows as we came out of our room with jacks and a ball. "We're on His Majesty's side, aren't we?" I asked. His Majesty's picture hung in every office and store, looking out over businesses with a calm and dignified face. His face was on all the money and the stamps. I knew his face as well as I knew Dad's. Ethiopia didn't feel the same without him.

"I think so," Jeanie said. The red ball thunked on the wood plank floor and back into her hand.

Ahead of us, Aunt Esther's back filled the front doorway, her shoulder holding the screen door open. "...get their bags down from the Crow's Nest and have them pack," Uncle Don was saying. Over her shoulder, he looked at me. He turned away. Aunt Esther followed. The screen door banged.

Jeanie and I went back to our room. My teeth tore at bits of the inside of my mouth. Jeanie dug with her thumb at the jack's ball. She leaned her hip against the window sill and looked out. I lay on her bottom bunk and stared up at the underside of my top bunk, at the maze of chains and metal pieces bent into huge staples holding up my mattress.

"How can they send us home?" I asked. Home, of course, being Maji.

If Jeanie was home, she'd have two grownups. If I was at home there'd be two grownups and five kids, and if I helped with the little kids, there'd still only be three of us for four of them. I pulled a thread hanging from the mattress. Here, there were Aunt Esther and eleven kids. Uncle Don and his wife would help. Four of us were big kids. Was that better or worse than at home? I couldn't do the fractions in my head. I wanted to ask Jeanie if she was scared, but maybe boarding school kids didn't talk about being scared any more than they talked about being homesick.

Springs held the big staples to the green-painted angle iron of the bed frame. I followed a chain with my eyes. What if we had to go to some strange country in Europe where we didn't speak the language? I didn't speak Amharic either, but Ethiopians would take care of us. One staple pulled the chain this way, another staple pulled it that way, back and forth from the top to the bottom of the bed.

Or maybe they'd send Jeanie to Kansas and me to Oregon and we'd never see each other again. The chains were pulled apart. Then together. Back and forth. How would my family get out of Maji? How would we find each other again? The whole diamond pattern of the bedsprings was an illusion. The chains just looked like they made diamonds because of how the staples pulled at them every six inches.

Aunt Esther called us to the dining room: the US embassy wanted us ready in case we had to evacuate. One carry-on bag per person. We could pack a change of clothes, a couple pairs of underwear, something precious, if it was small.

When we had finished packing evacuation bags, when we'd pushed them under our beds, where dust lay in a dull layer over the waxed floor, we big girls started a game of Monopoly in the living room. The jute rug scratched our legs and rumpled the money tucked under the edge of the board. A slash of sunlight lay across it.

Jeanie had just drawn a Community Chest card when two little kids came chasing through and slipped on the corner of the rug. The silver shoe, car, and top hat scattered. Big sisters hollered. I was glad again I didn't have anyone I was responsible for. I sorted money back into piles, pink and blue and white. Jeanie folded the board and tossed the shoe and car and top hat into the box.

The little girls set up house under the dining room table. For the rest of the morning, the babies were naughty and the moms spanked them and they cried. We big kids sat on our spines on the couch. Rectangles of sunlight coming through the windows draped over my legs, hot and still. Dust mites drifted toward the floor. But we couldn't play in our rooms. Not with the just-in-case bags there.

We'd been in the house for three days when the shooting pretty much stopped. Jeanie and I begged to go outside. Aunt Esther said okay, if we didn't play where the little kids could see us and start up a clamor. We ran down by the Ethiopian girls' school, abandoned and silent. The whole city sounded eerie, a few birds calling softly, but the humans holed up in their houses.

Jeanie and I found a faucet that had dripped a small marsh. In the quiet of the empty school yard, we mixed grass chaff with mud, just like Ethiopians do in big pits, and made little round *gojos*, with nice straight sticks up the center like poles to hold up the roofs. I lay long blades of grass, one right next to the other all the way around, thatching my *gojo*.

A shadow swept over me. A plane passed, all military gray, only a few hundred feet high. Small gray rocket shapes nestled under its wings. Then it broke the sound barrier for the first time over Ethiopia. The concussion was a shock, but what I remember is the ghostly silence of that jet appearing so suddenly, so low overhead, with bombs ominously held under its wings.

Jeanie stared at the space where the plane had passed. "Aunt Esther said to come in if we hear shooting."

"That doesn't count," I said. I had no conception of lives and deaths, of flesh and blood at stake. Those bombs, dropped somewhere else, didn't scare me. What scared me was the bags in the house, under our beds. I would hoist mine over my shoulder, Ethiopian-Airlines-yellow with its green lion logo rearing up, reaching out to tear flesh. I would follow Aunt Esther and Jeanie over sparkling tarmac that smelled of hot tar. Onto a plane. And at that, my imagination ran dry. Evacuation alone was a cavern so deep, I couldn't see the bottom.

Downtown, army tanks burst through the palace gate where the Neway brothers were holding their nineteen hostages. The Imperial Guard, defending the palace, realized their own commander was the one who had deposed the Emperor. They faltered. Ethiopian Air Force Saber jets swooped in, breaking the sound barrier, to bomb the Imperial Guard headquarters.

Germame realized their cause was lost. He threw open the doors of the Green Salon and sprayed the hostages with machine gun fire. Most of them died immediately. One of the co-conspirators was killed in cross fire, another committed suicide. The brothers, Mengistu and Germame, fled.

I didn't know this was happening. The sun dropped below waving eucalyptus trees. Jeanie and I finished thatching our *gojos*. The light turned blue around us. Blue from dusk, and blue from the perfumed smoke of supper fires all over the city. Tragedy strikes, and whether we're directly affected or not, the living go on living. Playing, eating, sleeping. Reaching out for love.

Aunt Esther stepped out on the porch and rang the supper bell.

I stood slowly, stiff from squatting. "See, nothing bad happened to us." I said it like a mantra, like something I knew to the depths of my being was true. It was a conviction I'd inherited from Dad, though I'm not sure he ever said the words aloud.

We ran to the house, its window squares gleaming like gold in the dusk.

When news came over the radio that His Majesty's army was fully back in control, Aunt Esther invited us big kids to go shopping with her. "I had to scrape the bottom of the can for milk this morning," she said cheerfully from the front seat of the van. Her curls bounced with every pot hole.

Jeanie and I looked at each other. Yeah. The powdered milk on our oatmeal had been so thin it was transparent.

In the *piassa*, Demissie stayed in the car. We crowded up the four worn stone stairs and through the door of Up the Steps, the small grocery with imported food. Side by side, leaning on the counter, the six of us filled the store. Behind the counter, dry goods and cans lined walls eight feet high.

Aunt Esther squinted through her sequin glasses and pointed to what she wanted. The old Italian who owned the store, thin and bent over, veins showing blue under the shiny pink of his bald head, fussed at his Ethiopian workers in a mix of Amharic and Italian. Light came in dimly from one tall window, the green shutters pushed open.

One of the men coaxed cans and boxes off the high shelves with a pole. The other caught them as they fell, and passed them to the old Italian, who packed them into cardboard boxes with the tops torn off: powdered milk, canned tomatoes, tuna fish, and oatmeal in red cans with the smiling Quaker man on the front.

Aunt Esther stepped to the door and waved to Demissie. Jeanie and I scooted one box to the edge of the counter. JR and Demissie pulled another.

"Two hands. Hold the bottoms," Aunt Esther said.

Jeanie and I eased down the steps sideways, watching each other's faces, our feet feeling the rounded stones. Halfway across the sidewalk, us dancing a side-step and laughing, shots barked from the left. My ears burned. Cans tumbled to the sidewalk. The corrugated floor of the van came at me as I dived. Cold metal pressed one shoulder. Jeanie's shoulder touched warm against the other.

Demissie was lying beside his box on the sidewalk. His brown hands over his textured black hair. JR lay beside him. Up and down the sidewalk, other Ethiopians lay flat on the gray cement. No one moved.

Then Demissie raised his head slowly. *Tollo, tollo,* John. *Tollo, tollo.* He went on, like a chorus as they got up, tossed cans into the boxes: *tollo, tollo,* quickly. Demissie dived across the front seat and the engine roared. Aunt Esther and the other girls, like colorful, furtive birds, ran out of the store and jumped into the van. The green doors of Up the Steps banged shut. Demissie lurched out into the street and the van's sliding door rolled closed.

More shots exploded into the air. Shivers started deep inside my stomach and moved out in waves. I pressed my teeth together hard, but they chattered.

Once we got out of the *piassa,* Demissie slowed down a little. As we rolled through the mission gate, the *zebenya* holding it open with one hand and clutching his *dula* with the other, Demiessie ran his hands through his hair. He parked, and pulled on the emergency brake. He laughed, and suddenly we were all rolling against each other, laughing our fear.

Street news said that several people had been shot in the *piassa* that morning. It said that the round-up of rebels would go on for a while. It said that the Neway brothers might be hiding out in the forest behind Pasteur Institute, across the street from us. It said there would be a search that night. Maybe a shootout.

# CHAPTER 15

Late in the afternoon, the Mennonite kids evacuated their hostel behind the forest and arrived with overnight duffels and sleeping bags. I was resigned and only secretly bitter whenever Jewel was around. I hovered close to Jeanie and Jewel all evening.

The electricity went out as we were finishing supper. We had devotions together in the thin light of dusk: about twenty children, cross-legged in a ragged circle on the woven jute rug in the living room. Aunt Esther played the five-octave pump organ and led us with her warbly soprano voice. Jeanie, Jewel and I harmonized. Aunt Esther read that psalm of comfort, harkening back to the Children of Israel crossing the Red Sea and then the Jordan River on dry land: "When you pass through the waters I will be with you...For I am the Lord your God."

Light dimmed. Aunt Esther put the little kids to bed in their room and in sleeping bags on the hallway floor. She came into the living room, where we big kids were still sprawled on the couches and rug. She closed the door softly behind her. She pushed up her sequined glasses. "Candles are in the sideboard. If you promise to stay quiet and let the little ones get to sleep, I'll make taffy."

The boys sat on one side of the table and horsed around in the flickering light. We girls sat on the other side, heads bent over the wavering reflections of candle flames, laughing at the boys, pretending to ignore them. Pans clanked in the kitchen. Stretching my arm across the dark wood, I pinched the soft, warm wax at the top of a candle. If I lay my head on my arm, I could see Jewel, so beautiful in her white prayer cap and braids, just past the edge of Jeanie's cheek.

Aunt Esther pushed backwards through the swinging door with two pans held above her shoulders. "Hey, you've been great. John, get me trivets?" She set a pan down with a clunk, stainless steel on cast iron. "Green. And red. Christmas is coming! Butter your hands. Grab a partner. Pinch off a handful. Don't burn yourselves."

Benny shyly asked me to be his partner. I blushed, hot all over. But who else was there? He and I pulled seriously, silently. JR threatened

79

to put taffy in the seventh-grade boy's hair.

We pulled the glossy clumps into ropes. Beneath the peppermint flavoring, the ropes of candy smelled faintly of Blue Band margarine and gray Ethiopian sugar. The ropes turned opaque, and then hardened. We broke them into pieces and tossed them into a bowl: clink, clink, Christmas taffy, God-with-us, candlelight in the dark. We sucked and chewed, and stuck out red and green tongues at each other. The candles burned down into milky puddles. It was better than a slumber party.

There was no shootout that night in the forest around Pasteur Institute. Was there even a search? News like that didn't make BBC, and no one bothered to tell us kids. No news is good news.

The other good news was that we were so close to Christmas, Mr. Anderson closed school. Maybe he thought we needed a little extra time that year to be with our families. Though no one asked us about our fears. Maybe they thought we would be less traumatized if they ignored our emotions. And I certainly wasn't a girl who would bring up what the adults wanted to keep hidden.

I didn't know how the Neway brothers got away until I was old enough to read Ethiopian history. They had circled west and fled Addis Ababa to the southeast on foot. On Christmas Eve, the army found and surrounded them on the slopes of Mount Woochale. There are moments in history that are debated, but will be forever hidden in mystery. Germame seems to have committed suicide rather than be taken. But who shot and only wounded Mengistu? He was captured and taken to Addis Ababa to recover and stand trial.

Jeanie and I were put on Ethiopian Airlines to go down the Jimma-Mizan-Maji line and home. Two hours later, I sat in the shadow of the airplane wing in Mizan. I felt woozy from airsickness. I tucked my skirt under me so the crabgrass on the airstrip wouldn't prickle. Jeanie's mom held her in a tight hug and rocked her back and forth as though she'd thought she would never see her daughter again.

Off to the side, the agent had pulled Jeanie's father over. He came to me now, squatted down, and told me softly that Ethiopian Airlines wouldn't be going on to Maji. The police radio was broken, and the Maji police might not know the coup was over. They might think their patriotic duty was to arrest the pilot or impound the plane.

I sat, blank for a moment, until what he was really saying unfurled in my mind: I wasn't going home. Would I go back to Addis, or stay in Mizan for the week? I don't remember if the decision was given to me or made for me. I don't know whose responsibility I was at that moment. I don't know who would have picked me up at the airport in Addis, or how EAL would have contacted them: *We have a little girl here*...It was another moment when I channeled Dad's determined optimism that everything would work out just fine. I look back and feel retroactively protective of this girl, who tucked away her real feelings and trotted obediently along the path the grown-ups laid out, assuming they knew what was best for her.

Jeanie chattered with her parents as the Mizan Jeep labored up the road to the mission station. Dry season dust swirled around us from deep ruts. A dinged up black winch sat on the front bumper to haul the Jeep out of those ruts in the rains. Beyond the dust-encrusted windshield, a deep green forest jostled past, hung with vines, dark and still. I was three months into life away from home, experienced at being big and brave. I arranged my face to look acceptably pleasant, and told myself, in effect, that the Red Sea could not be expected to part just so I could get home.

Christmas week with Jeanie's family went fine. Even now it feels ungracious to imply that I was not merry. Jeanie and I played pick-up-sticks by the hour on the plank floor of her living room. I read Black Stallion books. We ate papaya at breakfast, something that didn't grow in chilly mountainous Maji. Jeanie called the BBC call-music *the banana song*, because when it came on the radio, her father was invariably just cutting a banana onto his hot cereal.

Dad had waited for me at Washa Wooha, then drove home empty. The next week, he made the trip down the mountain again. Hoping. Jane has told me about hovering anxiously at Mom's elbow as she made a cheese sandwich to send for my lunch. "Don't put tomatoes on it! Caroline doesn't like tomatoes!" She wanted me to feel all the welcoming love she held in her adoring second-daughter's heart.

But Mom didn't have room for the whims and preferences of her children, even one who had been away for three months. She put a big slab of tomato on the cheese and spread homemade mayonnaise over it. "She'll eat it if she's hungry. Won't she."

That evening, seven-month-old Chris hid his head in Mom's shoulder when I climbed out of the Jeep and reached out to take him—a dagger to the heart of the girl who had fancied herself his second mother after he was born. In Mom's letter on onionskin to our grandparents, she said: *Of course Chris had forgotten her, but they've had lots of fun*

*getting reacquainted.*

Another dagger—they had Christmas without me. *We had to make like God again and create our own Christmas tree,* Mom had written in her letter. Dad's face would have looked stern, as he supervised the strand-by-strand application of tinsel "rain." I could hear him, *Don't throw!* Here and there, Jane had flung clumps of tinsel when he turned his back. The cedar branch tree in a large bucket stood stiff and crispy now. Under it, my gifts sat in a sad little pile. The family gathered around as I opened them. It didn't feel like Christmas. The smell of orange spirals baking didn't waft out from the oven. Christmas carols weren't singing from the record player, powered by a truck battery. Dad didn't read the first Christmas story from the gospel of Luke, Mom the Christmas chapter from *Little House on the Prairie.*

"Why does *she* get presents?" Joy said. She was seven and a half. She'd gotten her presents on Christmas, when I wasn't there. Had she even missed me? I sucked resentment like a Desta, an Ethiopian hard candy, sweet but cloying in the throat. I picked the tape off carefully, to use the paper again.

Three books. A teal canvas jacket lined with flannel. A package of new panties. This was basically what we got every year, but this year I couldn't find the delight I should have felt.

My stocking in Mizan had held an orange and a turquoise leather manicure case with scissors, tweezers, and a cuticle tool, something I'd had to ask about, since we were a fingernail clipper type family. Under the tree, a packet of stationary had been wrapped and labeled with my name. Mom wrote, about my week with Jeanie, *They went on hikes, swimming, had picnics and a festive Christmas celebration and somewhere or other found things to fill an extra girl's stocking so she really wasn't as conscious of anything wrong as we were.*

Mom! How could I possibly be that oblivious? I later said to her, in a forgiving mood brought on by becoming a mother myself, "I get it why you didn't nurture us. Your generation thought if you kept us fed and clothed and clean, you'd done your job."

"Oh no," she said. "I was going to be a warm and nurturing mother."

And when we moved her out of her house into a care facility, we found a sensitivity-group exercise paper she had written at about age fifty, saying that she wished she'd been a better mother and wife. That turned me tender again: she did her best, but it wasn't what she had dreamed of. Have I done any differently? Maybe in saying they were conscious of something wrong, she was getting as close as she could to saying that she'd missed me. That she'd been worried.

And I—why didn't I snuggle up for comfort? I had already forgotten how to ask. I didn't understand why my Christmas presents that year felt so empty. I thought if I were a better girl, I would be happier to be home. I'd be more excited about my extra little Christmas. I'd be more grateful for the gifts.

*She is being so good to the others,* Mom went on in her letter. *But she also seems to want so much to be with Harold and me and is lots more serious and grown up acting than before.*

Ah. She did see the free-floating anxiety I'd carried home, as real as the rearing lion on my EAL bag. Maybe she couldn't bear to ask how I was, to hold me and tell me that she loved me, and how much she had missed me, because she knew I would cry, and if I cried, she would as well.

The fact is, I was born to a line of tough women who all buried their tender sides. Mom's grandmother had died six weeks after her mother was born, and her grandfather had split up the three children, left them with friends and relations, and married three more times before dying in Portland, Oregon. A rootless man who rolled West.

Or, as Grandma once said to Jane, "My father was a no-good-nik and I married a no-good-nik."

That second no-good-nik was Mom's dad. He had come home from WWI, body and mind broken. Mom had grown up drifting with him from one Iowa farm to another, part of the rural destitute during the depression. Later, Grandma committed Grandpa to a mental hospital after he chased her around the kitchen with a butcher knife. It's easy to see that Mom's childhood fears and sorrows were not treated with tenderness.

"If I start crying, I'll never stop," she used to say. *Better never to start* went unsaid.

At breakfast one day, Mom and Dad both frowned at the oatmeal. Another argument about a book. Mom told Dad he was ignoring the very same problems the book was about. "You can never admit when there's a problem. 'There was a good spirit!'" Her voice was sarcastic. That was their joke, which didn't sound much like a joke that morning. It's what Dad said about meetings, no matter how awful or boring they were. *There was a good spirit.*

Out at a corner of the *korkoro megazen,* the banging and clanging began, Dad's foreman hitting the iron pipe against that tire rim gong. The workmen would be gathering, waiting for him. Dad took his last bite of oatmeal and pushed back his chair.

Twenty minutes later, he was back. "Where's the pipe wrench?" He dug under a pile of papers and little kid clothes on the sideboard.

Mom wasn't done. Something about people not changing their superstitions, just because Dad preaches a sermon.

The mission headquarters had started sending books out for discussions in mission station meetings. The first was *The Crumbling Walls*. I had stared at the cover, the white block letters on a dark blue field. So ominous sounding. It had sat on the side table in the living room, face down, while Dad made his slow way through it. Now, in its place, *Things Fall Apart*. Spine bulging. On top of Mom's latest *Ladies' Home Journal*.

Dad answered, his voice muffled, his head down, searching for his tool.

Mom said Dad jumped to conclusions before he got the whole picture.

Dad found the pipe wrench and banged back out to the *megazen* to finish fixing whatever it was he was fixing. Mom turned back into the kitchen.

# CHAPTER 16

I picked up the *Ladies' Home Journal*, which looked a little beat up after its transatlantic crossing, its journey up the hot and humid Red Sea, its trip in the C-47 and then in the cardboard mailbox from Addis. I stretched out on the floor of the living room to read, smelling cement dust and feet, ink and shiny paper, onions sautéing and the remaining tang of coffee smoke from the day before. The loops of the green rug dug into my elbows.

Can This Marriage be Saved?

The woman says, *Here's what's wrong.* So surprising, every time—the man says it's something else. And then the counselor says what's really going on. The word divorce slipped between the lines, all the way through.

Mom opened the kitchen door and, with a cloud of steam and onion, swished into the dining room in her full skirt. "Clean off the table and set it for lunch," she said.

"It's Joy's turn," I said.

Mom got that tight look on her face. "Caroline. Do what I ask." She whirled back into the kitchen. I'd known it was a hopeless objection. I'd made it a dozen times before. If I stayed inside to read or sew, that's what happened. Jane or Joy would make an inconvenient fuss if she called them in from play. I was convenient and compliant.

I made the only fuss I could. Silently. Well, almost silently. I banged the plates onto the table just a little harder than necessary. My sisters, when we got older, said, "You must be adopted. You don't have freckles, you're blond, and you're *good.*" But I knew how resentment can hide under goodness. I took seriously what Jesus said about sins of the heart. They're the worst. I just didn't know what to do about them.

Before lunch that day, we sang another Maji hymn as the blessing, *For the beauty of the earth.* I peeked out at the Sleeping Giant hills and the big gray *gojos. For the glory of the skies.* I didn't mind that the *gojos* interrupted the view. They made the valley beyond a hidden treasure.

As soon as we sang amen, I said, "Daddy, I think I have a bojelee." This was the word we used, our mispronunciation of the Amharic *mujelie*, for an Ethiopian burrowing insect.

He said the mules were coming, but he'd take a quick look.

"Mule shots!" Joy said, and started eating faster.

A lowland tsetse fly sting itself felt like a shot, but the version of sleeping sickness they carried only infected animals. Without treatment, the mules that carried goods and people all over the Maji mountains got sleeping sickness when they dipped into the lowlands. I don't know what the muleteers did to protect their pack trains before Dad got there. It was one of the things he'd taken on, a role he could play: giver of mule shots.

The other girls finished and asked to be excused. "Don't go across the road," Mom said.

Dad sat down in the platform rocker. It creaked under his weight. He lit a match and, precise and methodical, ran a needle through the flame. Its tip turned iridescent blue and red in the heat. "Let's see what you've got."

I lay down on our loopy green rug, my chin on my hands and my foot up between Dad's knees. Cement dust tickled my nose. I loved the peculiar itch of a bojelee, deep and intense. It made me want to grind my teeth.

The point of the needle poked a spot in the corner between my flesh and my big toenail. I loved that gentle poking of the needle. I loved Dad's hand on my foot. His life was packed with important work. As his oldest, I had to have a big vision too, and accept that Dad had other things to think about besides my bumps and bruises. Or my feelings. I tried not to make him feel guilty by asking for something he couldn't give. But splinters and bojelees were Dad's jobs, and fair game for his attention.

"Yep," he said.

His thumb held firm on my arch. His fingers curved around my foot. He squeezed my toe. "Big egg sack."

The needle tip hit a raw nerve. I jumped.

"Hold still." He squeezed harder. "Whoops, I broke it. Hold on." He stepped over me on his way to get the alcohol.

I rolled over and looked. A little cavity had been eroded near my toenail, eaten away, I supposed. It held clear fluid with white specks swimming around in it. No blood flowed when a bojelee infection was opened. But if Dad left some of those eggs in my toe they'd hatch, and another bojelee would dig a cavern beside the first. Sometimes Ethiopians came to the clinic from out in the countryside where there were no needles, with their feet infected and swollen with bojelee colonies, one behind another.

Dad came back. The alcohol burned. I closed my eyes tight and pressed them against the backs of my hands. When Dad was done swabbing bojelee eggs, he wrapped a Band Aid tight against the burning.

I slipped into my flip flops and ran out to join my sisters. As I appeared, Ato Kulkai called to me, *Tell Mr. Kur-tis the mules are ready.* I would carry messages from Amharic to English, but not back. Uproarious laughter had put an end to any attempts to speak Amharic—I thought I was making mistakes, and I so hated making mistakes. People still burst out laughing when I speak to them in Amharic, but now I know it's the delight of hearing their language in the mouth of a white woman that makes them laugh. I wish I'd known that, then. I wish I had been bolder as a girl.

I ran back into the house. "They're ready, Daddy." He rushed past without looking at me.

As Dad disappeared through the tattered *korkoro* door of the *megazen*, a man led a white mule in, holding the mule by his halter, tight under his bottom lip, through the crowd of clinic patients by the gate. Another man carried a coiled strip of leather. The gathering of men and boys by the gate gathered close, black and mostly naked, chattering in their lowland languages.

The muleteers circled, watching the mule's hoofs. They were Dizis, stockier than the slender northern Ethiopians, and darker skinned, but not as tall, not as black as the lowlanders. One man threw the leather strap at the mule's back leg, but he flicked his hoof and the leather fell to the ground. The man gathered up the strap and flung it again—I leaned, as though to help—and it wrapped around the mule's hocks. The man circled the mule so the strap wrapped his front legs as well. The men counted in Dizi—*koi, tagen, kadu*—and yanked. The mule fell with a thud that I felt, twenty feet across the road. Joy cheered and clapped her hands. The clinic crowd shouted. The smell of men sweating and of grassy mule breath wafted to us in the tropical sunshine.

Before the mule could get back up, the men pulled the leather tight. One threw himself on the mule's bunched hoofs. The other grabbed his head and pinned it to the ground. Dad came out of the *megazen* with a huge syringe, held straight up.

"Eeeyoo, I can't watch this part," Joy said.

Dad swabbed the mule's neck and jabbed the needle in.

"It gives me the shivers," Jane said, lifting onto her toes. We'd stood in lines, our sleeves rolled up, our arms held tightly and our faces turned away for yellow fever and cholera shots, typhoid and tetanus boosters, polio. When we got the first set, Jane had been two. She ran away and hid behind the door of the clinic.

"The shots will keep you from getting sick," Dad said as he dragged her out.

"I want to get sick!" she wailed.

The men unwrapped the leather strap from the mule's legs and he scrambled to his feet. Ato Kulkai daubed a pink saddle sore on the mule's shoulder with bright purple gentian violet, a topical antiseptic. The mule lurched and swung around, almost lifting the lead man off his feet. Ato Kulkai jumped back. The men laughed, and across the road, we laughed with them. Purple rivulets ran through the mule's white hair.

That night, my toe was red and hot. Dad's hand felt so cool, holding my foot. After he checked it, he poured hot water from the huge water kettle into Mom's big bread-rising bowl. I rocked, and read, and dipped my foot into the scalding water.

Every night after supper for a few more days, Dad checked on my toe. I was sad when the flesh in the corner by the nail filled in and healed over pink and new.


I looked up from my book one afternoon as Mom came in from her afternoon women's Bible study. She had the double wrinkle between her eyes.

At the supper table, she sawed away at the meat, cutting it into bites for four-year-old Cathy. She usually told the same joke when we had meat—*This cow lived a long and useful life before it got to our table!*

"Admasu took his baby to the Orthodox church to be baptized," she said in a low voice to Dad. His fork paused on the way to his mouth. He stared at his plate. He chewed slowly. Admasu was one of the teachers, one of the church leaders.

Mom had frowned, in another *We don't do that moment*, when Jane once said she wanted one of those darling leather packets children wore around their necks. "Those are from the priests," Mom said. "It's a Bible verse to protect the baby."

Calling on a new mother with a baby was what everyone did, and Mom had taken Jane, Joy, and me when she went to call on Admasu's wife. The baby, with its still-light, creamy skin, slept with his eyes squeezed closed and his hair shiny with ghee. He was bundled in a flannel blanket I recognized, that Mom must have given. And he was almost lost among the blankets tucked around his mother. The room smelled of ghee and clothes and blankets. It smelled of the fresh smoke from the center fire, banked for the day, and of old smoke that coated the undersides of the eucalyptus rafter poles and the top of the walls. Now the baby had probably had his hair cut into a tuft on top, so the angels could snatch him up to heaven without a hitch if he died.

I ate as silently, thinking. Dad must have wanted to baptize Admasu's baby in our church. What was the theology? Couldn't he do both? Apparently not.

As soon as I had finished reading the new books that had waited for me in the lonely pile under the cedar branch Christmas tree, I passed them to Jane and started in on hers. Then I began my regular read-through of old favorites: the original *Bambi*; the sequel, *Bambi's Children*, where a misunderstanding between the deer families leads to tragedy; and *Caddie Woodlawn*. Caddie's real name was Caroline, and I adored her for being the free spirit I was not. I addressed my journal, *Dear Caddie*.

Perched on the knoll between childhood and adulthood, I did a lot of thinking that break. Mostly at night.

I was always the nurse when we played—clearly, the Ethiopian people needed nurses. But it didn't seem right *to serve the people of Ethiopia* while living like an American. The house Dad and Grandpa had built us, with corners, a *korkoro* roof, a cement floor and windows, was luxurious compared to the dim *gojos* of Ethiopians on the hillsides around. We had both a Franklin stove and a cast iron cook stove. Mom had a set of good dishes she brought out only on special occasions. We children slept in our angle iron bunk beds with cotton-stuffed mattresses, not wrapped in *gabis* on the floor. Our short Ethiopian sheets, gritty with DDT powder to keep down the fleas, were still so much more than anyone else had.

And pre-teen integrity demanded that I live like an Ethiopian when I came back as a nurse. I never imagined a husband or children—no, I was going to make the world better in my own right. Like the aunties. Like Dad. In the middle of my *gojo*, I would have three rocks for cooking. I would eat on my three-legged stool, hand-carved from a section of log, holding a plate. I would sleep on a hand-hewn bed with rawhide strapping under the straw-stuffed mattress.

I saw myself becoming more, not less Ethiopian, even as I was being sent to boarding school for an education designed to make me more American. Night after night, I lay and divested myself of American luxuries. It soothed me. I counted things I didn't need instead of counting sheep.

With my three-legged stool, I didn't need couches. No rocking chairs. No green rug, not with a cooking fire in the middle of the house. But in our living room, bookcases lined the walls. The one behind the platform rocker held our books. The other three overflowed with Mom's and Dad's. What about books?

Well, I could use a two-compartment wooden box the square kerosene cans came in. I could have a Bible. A few favorites.

But wait. Rainy season *gojos* were musty and damp. I could smell the mildew that would grow on the pages of my books.

Doubt crept in. If I lived like an Ethiopian woman, wouldn't I have to go down to the river to wash my clothes on a rock and drape them to dry on bushes? Wouldn't I grind my grain between stones? I'd gather twigs and branches for that fire in the middle of my floor. I'd carry cooking and washing water from the river. I'd have no time to read. I'd have no time to be a nurse.

If I could not live like an Ethiopian peasant, I had no business living in Ethiopia at all. Sadly, I rolled over and found a fresh, cool spot on my pillow.

# CHAPTER 17

It was Mom who taught me the comfort of reading. Her novels sat in piles on her bedside table. They lay on the coffee table and the sideboard. When the bookshelves got full, they were laid in on top of standing books. She read and napped for an hour after lunch, and in the evening, first by the light of the pressure lanterns, now by the electric light.

I read for hours that January, sitting sideways in the platform rocker. By tip-tipping my head, I could keep the chair rocking. In our chilly mountain house, with several inches between the tops of our walls and the *korkoro* roof, even if just ashes and coals were left from the morning fire, the round black side of the Franklin stove still radiated heat onto the soles of my bare feet.

Every morning Jane said, "Don't read." But she and Joy had made up new games since I'd left. I'd tried; they didn't work.

"Come play. It will be fun." Jane pulled on my hand.

"Don't. I'm reading."

"No! I beg of you," she said. We talked like our books.

"It won't be fun for me."

"It will be fun for me!" Jane grinned and cocked her head, clearly hoping for a winsome effect. But resentment tightened my chest: I knew it. No one really cared how I felt. What I wanted.

Jane's mouth turned downward as I glared. Her head drooped between her shoulders. Her flipflops shuffled to the door, sounding as sad as her face.

Duke-tebar, who worked all day for Mom, washing clothes in galvanized iron tubs, hanging the clothes and diapers on the line, and ironing with heavy sad irons heated on the kitchen stove, came into the living room to sweep. *"Dehena-nish, Kelen?"* Are you well?

*"Dehena,"* I said, and lifted my feet out of his way. Every day the cement floor had birthed new, gray dust bunnies. Every day we had tracked in orange dirt.

An hour later, footsteps ran along the veranda and Jane burst through the door. "Mommy's sorting boxes from the storeroom!" Jane's hands clenched at her sides. She often talked with exclamation points.

I stared, still out on the frontier with Caddie Woodlawn.

"They're houses! Houses for Teddy and Bunny!"

I ran with Jane to the bedroom and dug through the toy box. Teddy and Bunny were mine, pink and yellow and a snuggly eight inches high. Jane clamped her bear, dark brown and the same size, under her elbow. Tebby. That's how it was with Jane and me, her bear's name the same as mine except for a little dyslexic trick.

"Joy, come. I found your bear," I yelled. I held him up, draped backwards over my hand.

"Hurry," Jane said. "He's crying for you and we can't comfort him." That's also the way it was with us: Joy's bear was twice as big as ours, had lost half of his stuffing, and had no name. We kept Joy happy by making a big deal about his special features.

By the storeroom, cardboard boxes lay scattered on the grass. Jane and I snatched up the biggest. "It's called *dibsing*," I said, the streetwise boarding-school kid.

Cathy dragged her little box by the corner of a flap, bumping it against her heels, down to a sheltered spot between brushy shrubs and the false banana trees. Dad said yes, we could use bricks from the pile made so long ago by the Italians, but only broken ones. We gathered up brick couches, chairs, tables and beds. I picked castor bean leaf rugs, one for each of us, giant hands with seven shiny green fingers. Bits of grit packed under my fingernails when I pried up moss for velvet cushions. Calla lilies, unwrapped, would turn limp as thick satin sheets. Their stamens were corn on the cob. Grass-seed rice stuck to the creases in our palms.

People who came to the clinic were not allowed to wander the compound, otherwise dozens of patients every day of the week would have crowded around the windows of our house, staring in. And if we played on the side of the compound by the clinic, if we fell to fighting with each other, the crowd there would come to life like the audience at a circus.

Years later, in the States, I found I hated zoos. I thought it was because I had seen many of those animals in the wild. Then I realized the crowds of people pointing, laughing and talking about the animals were too much like the crowds that stared at me and talked about my every move as a child in Ethiopia. People thought my sisters' freckles were skin diseases. And I was the only person with blond hair that anyone in Maji had ever seen. My family acted as though my hair made me special. Ethiopians reached out to touch it, wondering what it was made of, straight, and streaked by the tropical sun. Kwashiorkor, a form of protein malnourishment, turns black hair a curious shade of yellow-orange. But why would the child of the richest people in town be malnourished? In the bell curve of my childhood, I was way out on the edge.

But now we braved our way through the clinic crowd. Chatter in all those languages followed us. A woman reached out and fingered my hair. I pulled my head away. A man brushed the peach-fuzz on my arm. At the clinic door, Joy, our extroverted spokesperson, knocked. People crowded behind us, surrounding us with the smell of cooking fire smoke and skin and hair. Northerners from town had dressed in their best clothes, the women with gauzy *netellas* wrapped around their shoulders, their hair modestly tied up in colorful nylon scarves. They stood back from what they would call "the blacks," who lived in the lowlands.

Lowland people had walked, sick, for miles up the mountain. Men had carried other adults in on stretchers. Some of the Surma women, whose bottom front teeth had been pulled at puberty and their bottom lips pierced, wore clay or wooden plates held by their stretched lips. Aunt Marge told stories, how women could put their pills on the lip plates and flip them into their mouths. When they took the lip plates out, their bottom lips dangled, black and wrinkled, below their chins.

Men from the lowlands stood on one foot, leaning against their walking sticks. Most of them wore only a string around their waists. Sometimes in the rainy season, they made capes from the same reeds they used to roof their houses. But their bodies didn't look all that naked to me, with none of that particular pink that made our bodies look so immodest.

While we waited for Aunt Marge, we gathered eucalyptus acorn caps under the huge trees that lined the fence by the clinic. Speckled shade shifted with bits of sunshine on the Jeep tracks. Birds nickered in the brush that crowded up to the *korch* fence. Fresh blue-green caps were still soft enough that we could pinch off the points and set them flat as cups and bowls for our bears. The dried pointy ones made nifty lids.

Aunt Marge came through the crowd with serum jars, one apiece, an inch tall. We tore off the aluminum bands, pulled out the rubber plugs that her needle had pierced, and turned them into teddy bear vases. For the next hour, we crawled across the yard behind our house, ignoring the chattering, watching crowd. We picked flowers hidden in the grass: white stars, purple dragon heads and pink baby fairy trumpets, flowers of the African grass which had no names—oral cultures can't remember by writing, so they save their words for what is important. Blades of grass dented my knees and pressed itchy grooves into my palms.

Mom called us for lunch; we left our bears eating lupine-seed soup.

Done, we ran back to the beautifully furnished boxes. I stood in the cool shade, looking around.

"Play." Jane sounded worried that I might go back to my books. I had enjoyed the home decoration stage of the game. But what would keep me there?

I answered soft and sad. The words came out of my mouth before I thought them. "Teddy and Bunny ran away from home."

Jane stared for just a second. "Oh no," she said, a mixture of tragedy and excitement on her face. "Tebby, too."

We ran through the sunshine with bears tucked under our shirts, down the hill, heels braced, to the bottom of the compound. Our bears disappeared into the leaves of the thorny, impenetrable fence.

"We have to forget where they are," Joy said.

*Now I sit in my house on a brick red couch, my elbow deep in moss green velvet cushions. I gaze at my wildflower bouquet in its crystal serum jar.*

"Tebby," Jane calls. "*Oh Tebby, where are you? I think he must be in the garden. I think maybe he's climbing the trees. I search. I listen. He's not answering me.*" She screams. "*Tebby's run away from home. I can't find him anywhere.*" She weeps.

I could count on Jane to make any idea dramatic.

Cathy jumped up and down. "Now me! My baby's gone, too!"

*We travel across oceans, in the depths of forests, through hunger and cold, searching for our children until our dying breaths should stop. But our searching is in vain. Our precious children are gone from us forever.*

*My elbows dig into the soil under the grass, my exhausted legs drag uselessly behind me along the top of the back hill, above the Maji Valley, across from the Gap. Soon I will die from a broken heart, and my agony will be over. Exhausted, collapsing, I lose my balance and fall over the edge, rolling, rolling, rolling down the hill.*

Jane, Joy and Cathy bumped behind me. Our grass stained bodies landed in a heap.

I raised my head weakly and peered into the fence. "I see a glimpse of yellow fur," I said. "Could it be Bunny?"

"No, not yet. We don't find them yet," Jane said. "We're still in utter despair."

I looked up to clouds tinged with the first wisps of sunset pink. "We have to. It's going to be supper."

"There, through the forest," Joy said, "what do I see...it can't be... it is! Oh Bear, come to Momma!" She snatched her no-name bear out of the fence, hugged his limp belly, and rocked him back and forth.

She threw Teddy and Bunny to me where I lay. They smelled of earth and leaves. An evening bird began its soft chatter. My chest hurt, I was so happy. I looked up again, into the sky that shaded to velvet navy above us, and without warning, tears poured in cool trails down my temples and along my ears and neck.

I could have stayed in that moment, crying for joy on the grass, under the Maji evening sky forever. All of us safe. All of us together.

The night before I left again for school, I wandered into the bedroom after devotions. The room felt cold. I drifted back out to the living room. Mom came in with a mound of diapers almost to her chin, the hand with her narrow gold wedding band on top. "Help me fold these."

The loops of the green rug dug in when I sat; the evening fire crackled and stung my back. Chris, who the Ethiopians called *Alga-werash*, Inheritor-of-the-Bed (not the crown), watched me from his blanket on the floor. The diapers smelled musky, of lye soap and bleach, and maybe mountain air and fog and cedars. The Maji wind had whipped them on the line, stretching out the corners. I shook one out. "Mommy?" I said.

"Okay, little guy," Mom said. Chris looked up at her and smiled as she pulled off his wet diaper. The smell of baby boy urine tickled my nose. I smoothed the pile of diapers, and pressed out the air trapped between all the folds. Sometimes, if we cried really hard, we used a diaper instead of a handkerchief to blow our noses.

I followed Mom to our bedroom, her full skirt swinging ahead of me in the dim hallway. I trailed my fingers along the mud plaster wall, over straw ridges under the yellow paint. When they'd left me with Jeanie Haspels and my roommates in Addis Ababa in September, after the Mission Association meeting, I'd been excited. Innocent. Determined. Now I knew the price boarding school extorted.

I'd had my hard times at home: a sprained ankle, my wrist sliced by a piece of *korkoro* I was fighting over with Jane, kittens that had died, days Mom made me set the table even though it was someone else's turn. I knew how to be brave, helpful and obedient at all times. But those well-practiced skills weren't helping me now.

"Into bed with you," Mom said. She lay Chris in his crib and covered him with the Little-Boy-Blue blanket that was hers when she was a baby. Careful not to gouge under my fingernail, I picked at the end of a straw in the wall. We weren't allowed to pull straws out of the mud plaster, it would chip the paint. But if I pulled carefully, straws slipped out like letters from an envelope.

Mom turned. "Caroline, why aren't you in your pajamas? Harold, is Cathy ready?" Mom had many gifts, but her empathy came and went.

"Almost." Dad's voice floated over the wall and bounced off the *korkoro* roof.

"Jane?" Mom said.

"Brushing my teeth," Jane called, her mouth full of spit.

Dad was in the living room, on the woven-jute love seat, snapping Cathy's footsie pajamas together. When he finished, Cathy laid her freckled cheek against his and he wrapped his arms around her until his fingertips almost touched his opposite shoulders. That was just what I needed.

"Run off to bed now." He leaned down to pick up the four-year-old clothes from the floor. He folded together the thin white anklets, still rounded from Cathy's feet, and laid them on top. He looked at me and raised his eyebrows. His forehead, always sunburnt, creased white and red.

"Harold, send Caroline in here," Mom called across the top of the wall.

Tears burst from my eyes. My breath caught. I wrapped my arms over the center of my body and rocked. Hot embers in the Franklin stove crackled, the pressure lamp hissed, and murmurs drifted over the wall from the bedroom. Where was my hug?

I peeked through silvery tears. Dad had slumped forward and hidden his face in his hands. Only his McLaughlin nose showed. His shoulders shook. He was crying.

Usually his crying made me cry. But this time, I took a deep breath. I hovered one of my hands over Dad's leg. Soft as fog, I settled it down onto the place where his thigh narrowed toward his knee. A log in the Franklin stove fell apart. Embers tumbled over each other with the tinkle of fine china.

# CHAPTER 18

Dad pulled out an engine-grease-smudged handkerchief. "You have to be a big girl about this." He blew his nose hard. "Mommy can't keep teaching you. You'll get behind." His voice still sounded tight.

I knew that. Joy was in second grade. She wasn't reading like Jane and I had. And Mom never had been one to sit down and patiently teach us. Besides, I loved school. Mostly.

Dad's voice evened out. "This is what it means, living in Maji. You don't want us to live in Addis, do you? Or go back to the States?"

I just wanted a hug.

"Maybe Maji was a mistake," he said softly. He hung his head down and shook it.

I sucked my tears back so hard they stung high in my nose. "It's okay, Daddy. I don't mind." Maji would never be a mistake.

"That's a good girl."

I didn't move anything but my hand, patting his khaki knee.

Early the next morning, Dad shook my shoulder. Dark windows in the dining room reflected my wavering reflection back to me instead of the Maji view. Dad loaded my footlocker and EAL bag into the Jeep. He came back into the house and nodded to Mom. I hugged her waist so I didn't have to look at her. She patted the spot between my shoulders, then unlocked my hands and rushed to the kitchen. I wiped my eyes.

"Load up, girls," Dad said. Jane was coming along to Washa Wooha.

The air felt wet with *goom*, and the Jeep headlights created a gray tunnel running ahead of us. At the side of the road near Maji town, a ferret-like *shele-metmat* blinked, its shining eyes disappearing into a furry face, and then slipped through someone's *korch* fence. Roosters heard us coming and called. A dog barked, raising the cry, and the message was relayed through town. Jane, sitting in the middle, curled her legs up, laid her head on my shoulder and fell back to sleep. Her body sagged against me. The canvas door had torn off the Jeep long ago so I held tight to the panic bar over the glove compartment. As the sun rose, the fog glowed around us like a lampshade.

The road wound down and down, always with mountain on one side and cliff on the other. Always holding out against the encroaching forest, whose green understory reached in and swiped at the jeep. Always littered with fist-sized stones and carved with ruts. Always demanding all Dad's strength and attention.

After a couple of jarring hours, Dad braked in a spot of sunshine. He stepped out, shook his legs and poured coffee into the lid of his thermos. He passed a plastic container, greasy from the brown lye soap the school boys bought on market day. Mom had spread bran muffins with jam for us. Dad pointed to places where he'd trekked on the ridges of navy-blue mountains—Gurfarda, Mule-Ears; Temenj yaz, Grab-Your-Gun; Jemu. Jane and I tried to sound interested, as though he hadn't told us dozens of times. Our feet made dark footprints on the grass, still silver with dew.

Back on the road, Dad disappeared again into wrestling the steering wheel. Sometimes when he did that, I tried to talk to him, to keep him near. But his vague *mmm-hmms* made it obvious, even to a hopeful girl, that he wasn't really listening. The Jeep lurched steeply downward, over rocks laid into the road's deep ruts that otherwise turned into rivulets for the torrents that descended in rainy season afternoons.

Jane and I looked for wildflowers along the side of the road—the four-petaled orange creepers with black centers; the vine with fluorescent blue blossoms that I'd named Rocky-feller; the clusters of white florets with honey in each little stem. Jane thought we should name that flower Puff. I thought Puff sounded like a cat, not a flower.

In the damp shade of the Siski Chaka, Dad peered up through the buggy windshield and pointed. A branch high above us trembled. A family of *guereza* monkeys, making their deep hoo-hoo sounds, leapt across impossible spaces, long black and white hair floating behind like cloaks.

"Daddy, is *guereza* English or Amharic?" I asked.

"English, of course," Jane said, her voice full of confident scorn.

"No," Dad said. "I don't know the English. America doesn't have *guereza*."

I thought about that for a long moment.

We got to the lowlands around midday. Heat radiated through the Jeep's gray canvas, and sweat prickled my scalp. My legs stuck to each other under my skirt—even in remote Maji, we dressed up for the plane. A tsetse fly buzzed into the Jeep and circled our heads. Jane smacked it with her sock monkey when it landed on my shoulder, but tsetse flies are tough as rubber, and it revived and stung the back of my knee. I screamed. The ache raised the hair on my arms.

It seems that we saw the plane circle over when we were still some miles away. Mom wrote in her weekly letter, *Sure was hard to let Caroline go. Jane got to ride along to the airfield and when the plane came in before they got down there, the girls were so in hopes it wouldn't wait and would be gone before they arrived. As they went around the last bend and saw the plane waiting, both girls burst into tears. But Jane reported that Caroline said to her, 'What must be must be, and we must try not to cry.'*

Such grown-up sounding words for a ten-year-old.

The pilot that day was a short, dark-haired American. When I described him years later to Dad, he laughed. "That was Captain Brown. He had quite a temper. The Ethiopians called him Khrushchev."

Dad shook hands with Captain Khrushchev and the Ethiopian co-pilot. The three men in khaki, with shirtsleeves rolled up to their elbows and crescents of sweat under their arms, waited under the flat acacia thorn tree that served as the Washa Wooha terminal. In the blinding sunlight, sweating workers in torn shorts and bare feet finished loading the plane. Heat waves flickered over the dry plains. The airplane glittered. The Lion of the Tribe of Judah reared up, and green-yellow-red tail feathers stood out bright against the savannah of dun and golden grass. Jane's hair tickled my cheek and her t-shirt sleeve brushed my arm. Dad's hand lay warm and heavy on my shoulder. Oppressive as a wool blanket, heat pressed down on my head.

*Negadies* argued over their goods out in the sunlight—cases of soap, enamel trays, and swaths of fabric tied into bales. Fearing a disease Ethiopians called *bird*, which could cause anything from a stiff neck to pneumonia, they wore black wool greatcoats buttoned up in the heat. Their faces shone with sweat. Their mules kicked and whipped tails against the tsetse flies. A man braced his foot against a mule's stomach and cinched the packsaddle tighter. The mule grunted.

The agent waved his clipboard and his pink manifest fluttered. "*Mengedegnoch!*"

That was me. A person of the road.

Jane threw her arms around me and wept into my shoulder. Dad patted my back. I pulled away, not daring to look at either of them.

An aluminum ladder with three steps hung from slots in the floor of the plane, too high for me to reach. The agent put his hands under my arms and lifted. I scrabbled my fingers to find a hold on the ridges of the floor, and my toes, in brown and white oxfords, searched for the bottom step.

Along one side of the plane, the agent had lowered the green canvas stretched over aluminum, a bench that American GIs had sat on in Europe not that long ago. I leaned back against the fuselage. A young Ethiopian passenger dipped his head to greet me. The only other passenger stared ahead over hands propped on a cane, his wrinkled face framed in a thick white *gabi*.

The rest of the plane was filled with quintal sacks of raw coffee lashed to rings in the floor with thick brown ropes. A pile of untanned cowhides buzzed with flies. Gasoline fumes leaked out of the empty barrel Dad was sending to Addis in exchange for the full one that had come in that day for the Jeep. I took shallow breaths of the rancid air. A sheep in a burlap bag, the opening cinched around its neck with twine, struggled to get purchase on the slippery metal floor. It lurched and bleated, then finally laid its head down in passive resignation.

The men who'd flown in to unload and load the plane climbed back in. The smell of their sweat burned in my nose and masked all the other smells. I twisted in my seatbelt and looked out the small greasy window. Dad was looking down. His arms were wrapped around Jane. Her face was buried in his shirt. My eyes prickled. I watched them until Jane looked up and waved a limp hand. I waved back solemnly.

As we took off, the plane bucked in heat currents rising off the lowlands. The agent came out of the cockpit and gestured to me with his clipboard. I followed him up the vibrating metal aisle, knees bent and legs braced.

"Your dad told me to take care of you," Captain Khrushchev said, turning his head, but not far enough to really look at me.

I pressed the back of my hand against my mouth. Maybe Dad did know.

"Why are you going to Addis by yourself, eh?"

I sniffed and took a deep breath. "I'm going to boarding school."

The co-pilot picked up the snakehead radio transmitter and pressed the button. His thin black mustache brushed the grille. "Ji-ma, Ji-ma, Ji-ma. Come in Ji-ma."

"A school girl, eh? How do you spell 'cat'?" Captain Khrushchev said.

I might be small, but I was *not* in first grade. The radio crackled and buzzed. I looked past the black hair on the pilot's white neck, out the smudged window, through the propeller's transparent gray shadow, at the tan earth in patchwork below.

"C-A-T," I said.

He nodded, reached over and turned a dial.

I leaned against the co-pilot's seat. He spoke into the mic, rolling his r's in the familiar Amharic accent, and substituting z for th. "This is Echo three-seven-niner calling Jima. In the air over Maji at thirteen hours, do you read, over."

A voice spoke out of the static. "Copied. Over and out."

The co-pilot switched the radio off and looked over his shoulder at me. His eyes shone black, ringed with reddish brown. They looked as though they might be saying, "*Izosh*, be comforted. *Berchee*, be brave."

The plane shimmied sideways and my hipbone bumped the metal frame of his seat, where military green paint had chipped, and ragged aluminum continents shone through. I picked at the paint, and a sliver ran under my fingernail. Sucking it, I watched red and green instrument dials jiggle. The artificial horizon dipped and swung in its liquid sky. It wasn't until my own daughter turned ten that I realized just how young I was.

Two months later, as we drove home from school one day, Demissie braked suddenly. I looked up from my book. Jeanie pulled herself forward. Demissie shifted into reverse, turned in his seat, and waved her to sit down. He looked over his shoulder with his mouth open slightly and his eyebrows low. But cars had come up behind us. Haystacks bobbed by the window, donkeys loaded high with fine teff straw. It was the *mercato* road in the middle of the afternoon. We were hemmed in.

The square in front of Teklehaimanot Church was full of people, as it always was. But the people should have been squatting on their woven reed mats, with piles of potatoes, onions, spices or coffee beans for sale. I should have heard the sound of voices rushing like the sound of the ocean. Instead, the square was silent.

"Oh." Jeanie's voice breathed in my ear. She grabbed my arm hard. One of the little girls screamed. Her big sister pulled her head against her shoulder.

# CHAPTER 19

Across the square, a man's body hung from a tall structure. A brown cloth bunched at his neck, over his face. His hands were pulled behind his back. He was dressed in khaki, and his feet pointed downward in black shoes. His body twisted in Addis's mountain breeze. My stomach lurched, as though the van had hit an air pocket. A nerve whirred in my ear.

I turned away. People huddled on the sidewalk against the spiky wrought iron of the church fence. A beggar looked at me. He stretched his hand out and bobbed it up and down, begging. His knee was a big knob against his chest. His shoulders were thick from hoisting himself on a thick piece of rawhide along the streets on his hands. His clothes might have once been white, but they had turned earth brown. A blind woman sat next to him. Something like half-cooked egg whites covered her eyeballs. She raised her hand and her brown sleeve fell away from her fragile skin.

A woman in her white traditional dress—a rich woman with a wide red border on her shawl and dress—bowed and dropped coins into the man's hand and the woman's cup. Maybe the rich woman was going to the church to light a candle and pray for a relative who had died.

The beggars' mouths moved. They would be saying, *"Yibarkiwot."* That's why people gave to beggars in front of churches. To be blessed.

The gears of the van ground, and we lurched and started to move again. I kept my head turned, to the beggars in front of the church, and the wrought iron fence around it, and its brown stone walls and the cross on top, and the dome that was once white but was now rust streaked. Jeanie sat back. The little sister whimpered.

No one said anything the rest of the way home. I left my finger in place in my book and held it tight. Out the window, dingy shops and coffee houses floated by. Someone pushed aside strips of plastic hanging in a doorway to keep out flies. They twisted around each other, untwisted and shuddered back into place.

We passed bulging fences that forced pedestrians over onto the edge of the street. Past the cream-white statue of Abuna Petros chained to the Italian machine gun. Closer to home, Demissie sped up. The towering trees around Pasteur Institute loomed over us. They cooled the air. We pulled up to the metal compound gate, painted green. Demissie honked and the *zebenya* yanked the bent iron dead-bolt out of the hole.

Here's what I learned when I researched the coup: when Mengistu Neway and his brother were run to ground on Christmas Eve, after he was wounded and captured, he was allowed to recover in prison in Addis Ababa. His friends urged him to grovel before His Majesty as he came to trial—HIM might give Mengistu imperial mercy.

He said, at his trial, that he had left his life of privilege for the sake of his people. He was not sorry. "I did not kill His Majesty's friends. I wiped the dirt from his eyes."

He was found guilty of treason and condemned.

Because none of the adults ever spoke of the hanging, my memory sat like an undigested lump until, years later, I wondered if I'd made it up. "Oh, no," a friend said at a school reunion in the mountains of Colorado, an appropriate place for children from the mountains of Ethiopia to renew their connections. "No, I came the next year, and the boys all talked about it. I was mad that I'd missed the excitement." And yes, we could be awfully cavalier as children, about the real lives of people in the country that was hosting us.

The afternoon Mengistu Neway was hanged, I practiced my piano lesson, a simple two-handed tune. Both hands stayed just as I placed them, slightly rounded, thumbs hovering above Middle C. Only my fingers moved. After supper, I lay on my bed on my stomach and did my arithmetic. If I didn't concentrate, I saw him again, Mengistu twisting there, brown cloth over his face, and shiny black shoes that pointed down.

This is how mish kids calendar their childhood memories—was it before or after we moved to Maji? Before or after the furlough in Boise, Idaho, or the one in Pasadena? Was it before or after I started at Good Shepherd, before or after my one year of boarding school in Egypt?

As soon as mish kids start boarding school, they drift between two homes, settling into one only until time to go to the other. Dad still fixed things, tramped down to the mill and the ram, and drove to Washa Wooha. My sisters made up new games. Mom managed without my help. I felt dispensable, a vague soul who came and went.

At Good Shepherd School, our friends came and went, too. We carried on—with them when they were there, without them when they were gone. Some of us responded to all this uncertainty by hanging onto the names of everyone they'd ever known. As adults, those folks' address books are rag-eared, scribbled, corrected and re-corrected, spilling a litter of torn return-address corners from friends all over the world.

Others of us learned how not to miss anyone.

Jane joined me at Good Shepherd the next year. We hugged Dad good-bye at Washa Wooha, crying as we clambered up onto the sun-hot aluminum floor of the C-47. We sat together under the wing in Jimma, in the eye-watering-jet-A-1 fumes of refueling. We landed on the cool rainy season tarmac in Addis, and someone met us, as they always did, even though Mom and Dad had no way to confirm that we would be on the plane, and we'd have had no way to call if we'd been forgotten.

I crossed my fingers all the way to school: *Just let me be a big kid.* Mr. Anderson rattled us through town, down the hill past the wine factory and across a rickety bridge with eucalyptus railings that wouldn't keep a child, much less a van, from falling into the river. Up the hill and onto the new road, no longer granite gray but striped with muddy tire tracks. And there stood Baldy, Crew Cut, the low silver and stone school building.

Over the summer, the dorm had been finished, across a wide gravel driveway from the school. Fingers still crossed, I followed Mr. Anderson and one of the many workers who built, cooked, washed clothes, cut grass and cleaned our classrooms. He carried my footlocker on his shoulder with his head crimped away, the edge cutting into his neck. Another man carried Jane's. She huddled close as we walked through a dim entryway.

The dorm opened up to a large courtyard, an open rectangle with rooms encircling a wrap-around veranda. A sidewalk criss-crossed the courtyard, cement still wet between blocks of granite. Deltas between the sidewalks lay muddy and empty.

The right side of the dorm was for girls. Jane was shown her new room, with three girls her age. I left her there, shyly looking over her new roommates and being looked over.

Next door, I stood in the doorway of my new dorm room, smelling fresh paint and new fabric, feeling bleak. Last year, sixth-graders had been big kids. Now I was in sixth grade, and the prize had moved out of reach. The four seventh and eighth grade girls were in the end room together and I was stuck in with three fifth grade girls. One of them was mean as a mule, another moody, always wearing a turned-down mouth. Two angle-iron bunk beds, painted emerald green and clad in gray Ethiopian wool blankets, lined one wall; on the other side two dressers—two drawers per person. At the other end of the room, a window framed Baldy Hill.

The others had already claimed the top drawers. I stooped to unpack into bottom drawers, and hung my dresses on the iron rod that stretched across the closet alcove.

Jane knocked on my door that evening. She gave me that smile, the one that was supposed to win my heart. She didn't yet know how I treasured my sisterless status at school. I frowned, already not in a good mood. I was not seduced by her smile.

"Caroline, I forgot my toothbrush. Would you be averse to my using yours?"

I was not seduced by her precocious vocabulary, either. "Yes. I would be averse."

Worry lines formed around her eyes. If I noticed, I didn't soften. "Go ask Mrs. Anderson." I firmly shut my door.

To be fair to the big sister in this situation, I didn't yet know how anxious it made Jane to ask people, strangers especially, for help. When we traveled together for a college visit back home to Ethiopia, we had a shouting argument in the Rome airport because the Ethiopian Airlines desk was closed and she wouldn't let me ask the Alitalia agent about our boarding time the next morning. Not even when I told her to hide behind a pillar.

Jane's bigger problem, she didn't even mention. She still wet her bed. Did Mom and Dad think she'd magically stop? How did they think she was going to manage? Did they even let Mrs. Anderson know? For several years, Jane wet her bed at school. When I brought that up in my adult circle of sisters, Cathy said, "Why not send her to boarding school? Mom wasn't helping her at home."

It's true. Mom had spanked. Then she'd tried cold baths. Then there was a period when Jane huddled, naked and crying on a stool in the bedroom, as Mom swept in and out, shouting at her. Joy, Cathy and I hovered, watching in pain, not knowing how to protect our sister. Maybe our loving witness softened the blows.

And maybe Jane was better off at school. We got clean sheets and showers once a week. I remember that she often smelled faintly of urine. Jane just remembers that her cotton mattress got pretty stinky by the end of the year. She says she and the roommate who had warts on the backs of her hands were definitely at the bottom of the cool-listers. But she says no one tormented them. I remember that about Good Shepherd. Everyone was a little fragile. We were mostly—there were some exceptions—protective of each other. Jane coped until she grew out of wetting her bed.

She also says she probably had what she calls a helpful margin of illusion—*It's not that bad.*

The flurry of moving-in energy lasted for days, as kids and their footlockers arrived from down-country mission stations at Haile Selassie I Airport on various plane days. Screaming, giggling reunions. Boys shouting. I caught bursts of high laughter from my friends next door through the cement block walls. *Pull up your socks,* Dad would have said. *You're fine.*

Jane, like me, was a socks-puller-upper—at school she had to live in her little kid world, I in my big kid world. Our table assignments in the dining room randomly moved each week, so from time to time we ended up together. When that happened, our friends were surprised. They didn't know either of us had a sister—we didn't look related, she dark and freckled, me blond.

I didn't want to be in charge of my own sisters at school, but that year I was assigned a first grade Mennonite "little sister," whose long, never-to-be-cut hair I braided for her every morning. And the boys in the dorm were like brothers, the brothers I hadn't had. The boys' dorm rooms stretched along the other side of the courtyard. Little boys ran across, touched a post on the forbidden girls' side, and dashed back to safety. Little girls screamed at the incursion and other little boys cheered.

In the early evening, a bell rang and we poured out of our rooms, with teeth brushed and faces scrubbed in cold water. We trooped along the veranda in pajamas, bathrobes, and flip flops to devotions in the dining room. Mrs. Anderson played the piano and we sang the harmonies we heard in her chords and lovely arpeggios.

Benny was still my only classmate. We were plugged in between the bigger classes on either side of us. Boys tried to tease me: "Benny likes you!" I just made a face and ran off to play with Jeanie Haspels. Benny was so not my type. I wasn't even tease-able when it came to Benny Gamber.

The next year, in seventh grade, Benny went on furlough. I sat in a row of one, behind the sixth graders, across the aisle from Jeanie Haspels and the eighth graders.

Joy joined Jane and me at Good Shepherd that year. She still wasn't much of a student. Unlike Jane and me, she was actively miserable at school. She began to say that she had a sore throat several times a month, and stayed in bed all day. When Mrs. Anderson came around to do room check—*beds made? floors swept? clothes put away or hung up?*—she would ask Joy how she was feeling. That moment of attention was like a drug. Joy eventually got her tonsils taken out, the adults thinking that would take care of her sore throats.

Joy and Jane shared a dorm room with two other girls. That was a bad idea—they fought fiercely. Joy tried calling me in to help them only once. I should have known better: I had forfeited any rights to be the big sister at school. Besides, you couldn't argue with Jane, and Joy was that much more stubborn. They turned on me together. I lost purchase on my wise persona, screamed at both of them, and stormed back to my room. But by the time we went home for vacation, we were so united in our happiness to be back in Maji, it didn't matter how mad we'd been at each other at school.

Jeanie Haspels, now in eighth grade, was still horse-crazy. I did my best to hide my fear when we rode the school horses, skinny Sparky and rotund Musfin. My happiness to do anything just to be Jeanie's friend also overrode the ambivalence I felt about being a horse. We were Black Stallion and his mare one evening, galloping down below the dorm in the blue dusk, in the tall grass that clicked with insects settling for the night and scattered little pollen rods on our pedal pushers as we ran through. Suddenly Jeanie stopped. She pointed to the trenches workers had dug for a new dorm. First one boy's head and then another peeked up and ducked back down.

"Ignore them," she said. We tossed our manes and cantered further down. Below us, a boy in a blue and white plaid shirt ran hunch-backed through the tall grass. We veered toward the school building. Someone was there, too. My heart started to pound.

# CHAPTER 20

Black Stallion galloped for all he was worth, his mare close behind. I pointed. "I think we can get through there." I looked back once. Sixth grade boys and Benny had jumped out of their hiding places and were running to catch us. They were gaining on us, but not by much. We'd make it to the dorm, easy.

But Tim Johnson, aka Skins (I don't know why) came through the entryway just then. Silver blond, a Baptist kid from Minnesota, he leaned a shoulder against the wall, arms crossed, pretending not to notice us. We turned and ran to Jeanie's window. She banged on the glass. One of her roommates opened it.

"Quick," we shouted together. Jeanie boosted me up first. Then we pulled her in. Climbing in the windows was highly forbidden, but this was a case of emergency.

That Christmas, Dad surprised us with an envelope hidden on branches of the created Christmas tree—the picture of a bike cut out of a Sears catalog. In Addis for a committee meeting later, Dad bought the bike and brought it out to us. Mustard yellow. A full-sized bike, so we could ride it no matter how much we grew. A man's bike; Dad proudly patted the bar. "This makes it much stronger."

It was too big for any of us, even when Dad cranked the seat all the way down. It was especially high for Joy. But she demanded her turns. Her friends held the bike while she climbed up. She tilted it and hopped on one foot as she came to a stop.

One day Joy's friend, panting, banged on the door of my room. I ran with her to meet Joy, weeping, limping through the entry and along the veranda. Friends were holding her on either side, and leaning in to her. Blood seeped through her pedal pushers, down her inner thigh. Joy wailed when she saw me, and buried her face in my blouse. She'd fallen on the bike. It had cut her. *Down there.*

In town, at a clinic, I stood by Joy's shoulder at the operating table. The smell of rubbing alcohol tingled. The doctor didn't talk to us. He ran a needle and black thread through Joy's tender flesh. Joy winced.

Whimpered. Held my hand tight. The doctor leaned over the delicate dance; tying, snipping. Tying, snipping. I could hardly breathe.

Two weeks later, Joy got her stitches out. In the waiting room, piles of *Reader's Digest* magazines lay scattered on the table. I didn't understand most of the jokes; I loved the vocabulary quiz; I could always lose myself in a story. I read while Joy sat beside me, looking around the room, jiggling her feet. When the nurse called her name, I read on, pretending to be absorbed. Feeling awful. But not awful enough to watch again what was happening to Joy. She came out, wiping a tear away.

"Oh dear," I said. "Did they call you?" Not that I would outright lie. "Are you Ok?"

She nodded.

"Did it hurt?" I was so hoping she'd say no.

"Not as much," she said, and wiped her nose with the back of her hand.

When I later asked Joy what she remembered about this, she didn't remember that I left her to her stitches without support. "You were kind to me that year," she said. "You let me hang out in your room sometimes, and you sat on my legs in the middle of the night when I had chicken pox so bad I couldn't stop twitching." It brought tears to my eyes, that Joy would remember my being kind to her.

After Jeanie Haspels and I galloped by the dorm one day on Musfin and Sparky, Mrs. Anderson took Jeanie aside. She needed to start wearing the bras her mother had sent with her to school. She needed deodorant.

"What's deodorant?" I asked. And even though I was only one year younger than Jeanie, I had no sign of what Mom would call a bosom or Mrs. Anderson would tell me I had to corral in a bra. I still had the shape of a slim boy. A tiny slim boy. What was wrong? I struggled with my problem inside my own head, as I did with all my problems. And, as it always did, my own head yielded up a plan.

There was that girl a year younger who was chubby. She had breasts. I could get chubby, get breasts. Get skinny, keep the breasts. Perfect! I began my breast development project by going on a diet to lose weight. To make sure that I could.

I passed the blue melamine bowl of boiled potatoes in their skins straight on to my neighbor at the table. I sniffed the steam that she released when she pierced her potato. The aroma of margarine slathered on the mealy crumbs, the salt and pepper—delicious. I picked at my slice of roast beef. At my cooked green beans.

As for dessert, I was crossing my fingers the dining room staff would serve "saliva," a lemon pudding that had been whipped, and sat in a foamy glob in the blue dessert bowl. Or spice cake with disgustingly swollen cooked raisins. But what if dessert was chocolate pudding? Or yellow cake with butter frosting?

It only took a couple of days before I abandoned the plan. I may have decided to bravely face the tragedy of never having breasts. Or maybe I decided breasts were over-rated. That part of the memory has faded away.

Back in Maji over break, Mom said, "You're growing up. In Ethiopia, women wear dresses." She avoided my eyes and left my room, full skirt whirling. My face burned. What was shameful about pants? And with no breasts, how was I suddenly a woman?

I went out to the musty storeroom. Dust and fine teff straw lay in drifts on the floor. When I wrenched open the lever that sealed the supply barrel, the smell of mildew and fabric starch sighed up into my face. Dim light filtered in above my head, between the mud plaster wall and the *korkoro* roof, and through a hand-planed set of wooden shutters that didn't meet in the middle. The *korkoro* pinged as it expanded under the afternoon sun.

The storeroom was my special place, because I was the seamstress of the family. I had spent hours alone in there, sorting through the fabric barrel, planning dresses I would make. Measuring by holding the fabric to my nose and stretching out my arm, as Mom had showed me. "It's a yard," she said.

"For everyone?" I asked, amazed, trying to reason out how that could be true. "What if someone's nose is longer?"

Mom threw back her hair-sprayed curls and laughed. Mom was like that. Like a flashlight, often turned off to conserve batteries. But oh, when I found the button and the beam of delight shone on me, what joy.

That day, I dug into the clothes-to-grow-into barrel. There were things Mom couldn't wear any more. I laid them aside. Dresses for the little kids. Baby clothes. I was looking for an everyday dress.

And then I found it, a shift with a white Peter Pan collar and French knots scattered over vertical variegations of brown. I marched into the house, into my bedroom, and changed out of my Sunday dress, with its wide wasteband and and a gathered bodice that suggested some bit of swelling in the breasts. The shift was more like a tent. A nun's habit. It had absolutely no shape. It hung below my knees. Perfect. I came out of the bedroom and glared at Jane and Joy, dashing by in their elastic waist jeans and pedal pushers.

A few days later, Jane sat on the couch reading, knees up and heels braced on the front bar of the jute-strung couch. She was ten now, almost as tall as I was, and more ready to burst into womanhood. But Mom hadn't noticed that.

"Jane! Feet on the floor!" Mom said, on her way to the kitchen, where bread needed to be baked, where chopped onions were ready to be sautéed for spaghetti sauce, where turnips and carrots from Dad's garden needed to be scrubbed, peeled and sliced for supper. When Mom came back through, Jane's heels had crept back up. Mom said, "If you don't sit modestly, I'll make you wear a skirt."

A skirt was punishment for immodesty? My cheeks stung. Jane didn't care if anyone saw her panties, anyway. How could Mom not know that Jane would sit with her knees in the air in a skirt.

It only took a week for Joy to comment. "Are you wearing that dress *again*?" she said, hands akimbo. "I am so tired of looking at that boring old dress. When you throw it in the wash, I'm going to cut it up with scissors."

"You wouldn't dare." I took *Little Women* and stormed out the door to read it for the zillionth time. I sat in a wheelbarrow by the *megazen*, where the workmen would greet me and then leave me alone. Where I could pretend, once again, that I was Jo. But I knew I was only Meg. Boring, good, womanly Meg.

That summer, when I was twelve, hanging between childhood and womanhood, a marriage was arranged and announced—the groom was Wondemu, who helped Aunt Marge in the clinic. He was handsome and the marriageable age for a man—maybe in his early thirties. The bride was Negatwa.

For a short while when I was younger, Negatwa had been my friend. Her name means *The Dawn*—or does it mean *The Morrow?* The difference between those two words is only a momentary rest on the *g*. With her beautiful, rose tinged brown skin, Negatwa was the daughter of a policeman, a transplant into Maji from somewhere further north. She and her sisters were the only two girls in the Maji mission school.

She had come to play sometimes after school, wearing her hair tied in a nylon net scarf so that it pillowed above her forehead, a soft pink or purple aura. She was close to my age, but Ethiopians then had only a vague notion of when they and their children were born. She always wore a long skirt.

She tucked it modestly, with the deftness of practice, when she squatted to make petunia ladies with me in the soft dirt of Mom's garden. Amharic filled my world and I knew words, but I couldn't put them into sentences. Negatwa and I played our fantasies in parallel, each speaking her own language. The petunia ladies danced and twirled. We smiled at each other.

We had been children together for a short time. Then I went off to boarding school and Negatwa went home after school to work beside her mother, learning how to make *injera* on a hot clay griddle, *injera* with "eyes" even and regular all over on one side. She learned how to pound coffee and spices. How to pick carefully through the lentils for stones and dirt. How to brew beer and mead.

A week before her wedding, Negatwa's wedding drums began. The drums went on late into the night, muffled and deep, less heard than felt. Their vibrations came to me over the hill between the mission and town, down past the swale and the school, up through the gate and through my glass window.

# CHAPTER 21

Mom and the aunties and I went one afternoon to congratulate Negatwa's family. She was nowhere to be seen. In the corner of the room, a boy beat a cowhide and hollow log drum between his knees. The boy, his face shining with sweat, looked in a trance. The hair had worn off the cowhide drumhead where his fingers struck. The aunties and Mom sipped hot, fresh coffee in tulip shaped *sinis* from China, and visited with Negatwa's mother. I nibbled roasted barley. I drifted on that lovely sea of Amharic, understanding the sounds but not their meaning. The drum vibrated my heart.

Negatwa and Wondimu were married in the school hall church. She wore a new, blindingly white traditional dress with a wide woven border of red and blue. She stood with her face down, never looking at us or at him, never smiling. I watched her closely, but as though from a long way off.

Our family and the aunties walked up the hill that evening for the *digiss*. Tables and benches had been packed into her family's front room and wobbled on the pounded earth floor. Old sheets of newspaper, the *fidel* like lacey designs, plastered the mud walls. The mountain chill came in through wooden shutters, closed for the night over glass-less windows. Negatwa and Wondimu were being feted in some back room. The feast was not for them, but for the family and the community, celebrating together.

As we ate, a troubadour squeezed between benches, standing now by this guest, now by that, singing to the whiney sound of his *mesinko*, a single-string lute. Its diamond shaped sound box was covered with hide. The bow looked as though it might have been made of any old knotty branch, stripped of bark and arced to hold the horsehairs. Every song held "wax and gold," that literary form—the wax its obvious meaning, the gold a pun, a simile, a hidden meaning (usually salacious.) The troubadour stood by Dad. He smiled gamely. The crowd hooted and shouted.

"What? What?" I said at Mom's shoulder, but she laughed along and shook her head to say that she was maybe not even catching the wax, and for sure, the gold was completely obscure. Dig as they may, there are very few foreigners who ever find the gold beneath the wax.

Jane nudged me. I rolled my eyes and hitched my shoulders. We both went back to eating—members of the clean plate club. This is terrible training for a child at a wedding *digiss*. I knew that only leaving the plate piled high would prove I had satisfied myself. The servants ate the left-overs in the kitchen later, so they had added incentive: more *wat*, another roll of *injera*, only one more drumstick, *What's wrong don't you like the food?* A meatball, another dollop of *ibe*, the cooling homemade farmer's cheese. Jane, Joy, and I ate like troopers. We shouted to each other above the noise and the music. How could I stop eating—no butter spared. Spices. Onions. Finally, my stomach grew tight as the drum. I couldn't swallow any more, even the *birz*, mead that hadn't yet been fermented, sweet and waxy, hinting of meadows and flowers.

Suddenly a shout. Men danced out from a back room carrying aloft a white cloth. A sheet, it looked like, with an irregular scarlet spot of blood. Mom stiffened. The room erupted with clapping, shouting, and the joy cry, "*Li-li-li-li*," shrill and high. Mom stared at her food. Her hands gripped each other in her lap. Jane leaned across me.

"It's just something they do," Mom said.

Jane looked at me and frowned. I had no idea. I felt the shame pouring off Mom. I shook my head and Jane sat back.

My world and Negatwa's, which had crossed for a short time in the dust by the petunias and roses, had now diverged. She was no longer a virgin, and I didn't know what a virgin was. I was headed off to eighth grade, where my ongoing crush on JR would be thwarted by his going to ninth grade at the boarding school in Egypt.

I had finally begun to grow. Mom later told me I looked like someone took me by the hair and toes and pulled me like taffy. And one day late that summer, Mom came into the bedroom where I lay reading on my top bunk. She laid a packet of something soft, wrapped in Ethiopian brown paper, on my pillow. I looked up at her face, even with mine, and before I could say, *What?* Mom laid a pamphlet on top of the packet: *Growing Up and Liking It*, by Modess. "This will explain." She spun back out of the bedroom.

On the pamphlet cover, a girl stood looking in a full-length mirror. Jeans rolled-up, Keds, a flannel shirt only half tucked in, her hair in a bouncy blond ponytail. Looking back at her from the mirror was a girl with a shoulder length flip. A frilly pink dress and pointy flats. She smiled like Cinderella did when her prince rode up on the white steed.

I flipped over. The bed creaked. I bunched the pillow double under the back of my head. Inside the pamphlet, I studied the line drawings of a woman's torso. No head, no legs. Seahorse organs. Organs I didn't know I had. Reading about those organs, my body went hot, then cold. My stomach clenched. My eyes burned.

Another torso. A baby curled upside down in there. And how it got there...Surely nobody...all these nice aunties and uncles...I buried my head under the pillow and panted my own used up air. I made a tunnel for fresh air and fell asleep until Chris shook the bunk bed to wake me for supper.

Mom's plan must have been that I would pass the pamphlet along. But the next day, I hid it under the cardboard bottom of my dark yellow EAL bag with the rearing lion. To save Jane from the shock and shame. She got the news from roommates, and kindly told Joy. Mom never did talk to any of the others about menstruation—or even about deodorant or leg shaving.

Back at school one day, sweet little Sarah Wenger, Jewel's sister, slipped me a note in a laborious fourth grade cursive. *Chester likes you. Do you like him?*

My heart went pitty-pat. Chester Wenger's complexion absorbed the mountain sunshine and turned to bronze. He had hazel eyes and hair some color between hazel and gold. He was fun and funny, and he was the fastest runner in the school. Bar none. When we played pom-pom-pull-away, which we did every evening between supper and study hall, Chester was always the last one running. Even when the other thirty of us had only Chester left to tag, he dodged like a dancer from one base to the other. Everyone liked Chester.

But Chester was a year younger. And a girl who had a boyfriend a year younger seemed desperate. Like she couldn't attract someone her own age.

But there wasn't anybody my age. Only Benny Gamber.

*Yes*, I told Sarah. *Tell him yes.*

Sarah slipped a note into my hand the next evening, and smiled up at me as though I had just become family. *I want to kiss you*, the note said. *Meet me in the water heater room. Chester.*

I popped open the door with a clang. Sweat tingled my forehead. Was everyone watching? No, kids were running and shouting in the grass. No one was paying any attention to me, sneaking into the water heater room, where Ethiopian workers built wood fires to heat water for our Saturday showers. I perched uncomfortably on a split piece of eucalyptus log. The room smelled of fresh wood and old smoke.

I hadn't latched the door behind me. It squeaked open and my heart felt as though it would burst apart. Chester peeked his head in. He grinned.

Our knees touched when he sat on another log in the tiny room. A slash of sunlight fell bright across Chester's face. He still smiled, watching me as he leaned forward. His hazel eyes shone. So close.

At the last possible second, I turned my face away. His soft, dry lips pressed against my cheek. I didn't open my eyes. The door squeaked. The light behind my eyelids brightened and then darkened.

I also lost my next boyfriend over a kiss—Slinger, with wild curly hair and ruddy cheeks. Early in GSS history, when we read about Samuel anointing the young shepherd boy, David, Benny Gamber had asked Miss Wilkins, "What's *ruddy* mean?"

"Ruddy is like Jim Sperry," she said. And ever after that, Jim was Slinger. Even the teachers called him Slinger.

The dorm went all atwitter about Slinger and me—*It's high time Core has a boyfriend!* And to prove it, we had to kiss. Slinger took my hand in the cool, dim entryway of the dorm. My heart lurched. I didn't know a boy's touch on my hand would do that to me. He led me out behind the dorm, back where Musfin and Sparky were stabled. We sat down on a huge log. The smell of horsey sweat and digested grass wrapped richly around me. Slinger's chest along my arm, through his red plaid flannel shirt, felt warm. He leaned over me and said, "I know you don't want to do this. We can just pretend."

No real kiss? I felt dizzy with the shock, the shame that I'd wanted it, and the gratitude that Slinger would protect me. Dozens of eyes watched from behind the cinderblock corners of the dorm. Someone tittered. The horses behind us nickered. Slinger leaned in closer. I closed my eyes. I could feel his breath on my face.

"There," he said. "Now they'll leave you alone."

That Friday, Jane banged on my door, breathless from dashing across campus. "Come! Slinger is on the swings! Setting a record!"

I ran with her, leaped the granite steps of the school building two at a time and stopped, panting, in the entryway.

Slinger was swinging with the girl who always pumped so high in a dress. The girl was in fifth grade now, and Slinger in ninth. They stood face to face on the swing, pumping in rhythm, until the chains slacked at the zenith. A kiss at each end of the arc. A glimpse of her panties on each descent. The whole boys' dorm, gathered below them on the ground, cheered.

I pressed my lips tight. Jane studied my face. "Thank heavens," I said. She knew what I meant—thank my heavenly stars that I had been saved from that bad boy.

"You're such a goody-goody," Timmy, Slinger's younger brother, said to me a few weeks later. We were playing pick-up basketball on the packed earth and cinder gravel court above the swings. "What you need is a kiss." I wanted to say, you wouldn't dare, like I had to Joy and her scissors, but I thought my glare would say it all.

And of all the sixth grade boys, Timmy would dare. Suddenly he jumped on my back as I ran down court. Arms around my neck as I stumbled for balance, he craned around and planted a big smooch on my cheek. The other boys laughed.

I jabbed as hard as I could with my elbow.

He jumped down, and ran past me laughing, holding his ribs.

A couple of weeks later, I was playing with Jeanie Haspels around the back of the school. Before we saw them coming, we were surrounded by eighth-grade boys, the ones who had gotten some growth and some muscle. The biggest boy tackled Jeanie. As she fell, she shouted at me to run. But one of the others had already gotten his hand on my arm. I fell on the pile of sand by the hand-crank cement mixer. He pinned me down, his body crosswise over mine. I could barely squirm under him. I could barely breathe. Skins leaned down, one hand on each of my shoulders. His blond eyelashes were invisible on the edges of his eyelids. I screamed. He kissed me hard, his mouth on mine.

Before I could even open my eyes again, the boys were pelting back to the dorm. Jeanie sat up. She shook sand out of her hair. "I'm sorry," she said. "He was bigger than me."

I didn't answer. I stumbled to my feet. I wobbled as I ran. I popped open the metal door to the girls' bathroom. I threw myself headlong on the black and red tile, sobbing. The floor cooled my burning cheeks.

When I was empty, and my tears had dried, I splashed them off my face. I marched to the principal's office, and told Mr. Anderson, my voice hot with outrage.

At supper the boys grinned, the girls watched me when they thought I wasn't looking. The news was already all over the dorm: *Skins kissed Core!* I held my head high, with wounded dignity.

A few days later, my sister Jane banged on my dorm room door. "We saw Skins going into Mr. Anderson's office!" I held my breath. "When he came out, he was smirking."

That's not the way the story was supposed to end. Rage and shame rushed in again. I burst into tears. Jane and her roommate hovered over me, patting my shoulder.

Would it have mattered to the boys to know that I wasn't trying to be superior by being good? They didn't know I was driven by my own reasons, like Dad, to be perfect; driven like a sailboat, all the sails let out, running before private winds of doubt and self-reproach. Or maybe all the drama about kissing Core was just the beginnings of a sexual power dance, and the talk about *too good* was a cover.

For Christmas that year, one of Mom and Dad's gifts to me was a small hardback book, *A Diary of Private Prayer*. The Very Reverend John Baillie, theologian and professor at Edinburgh University, had composed morning and evening prayers, one for each day of a thirty-one-day month. The prayers sat on the right as I opened the book. To the left, a page had been left blank so I could write my own prayers or prayer requests.

I started that evening, the twenty-fifth day: *I grieve and lament before Thee that I am still so prone to sin and so little inclined to obedience.* There followed a long list of the specifics. Some didn't apply to me (*fond of idleness, indisposed for labour*). Others smote my conscience (*eager to find fault, resentful at being found fault with; brisk in the service of self, slack in the service of others*). It ended: *Hear my sorrowful tale and in Thy great mercy blot it out from the book of Thy remembrance.*

I could have thought, *Oh good grief, I'm just a kid!* But I didn't. I was too prone to taking up any call to perfection, too averse to being my own best friend.

I lay on my top bunk every evening, under the itchy wool blanket, the comfortable scent of my own skin and hair on the pillow, the gritty DDT dust down by my feet, and wrote prayer requests in my immature handwriting. Patience with my sisters. Dry weather so Dad could get down the Washa Wooha road and back. Our missionary aunties. I had nothing specific in mind that they needed from God. I was just trying to pray like John Baillie would.

At our evening devotions, the night after we took down that year's cedar-branch Christmas tree, Dad taught us a new hymn. He did this by reading a line at a time for us to repeat until we knew it: *Now on land and sea descending...jubilate, jubilate, amen.* Then he asked us the usual questions: for Cathy, not yet in school, "Who was the first man and the first woman?" For Joy, "Who led the Hebrew people out of Egypt?" Jane and I grinned at each other and waited. We knew who

Abraham, Isaac, and Jacob had married. We knew who killed Abel. We knew plagues, who called down fire on the sacrifices of the priests of Baal, and whose blood the dogs licked up on the streets of Samaria. That night we had a question for Dad: *Who was Ruth's sister in law?* Sure enough, Dad couldn't remember Orpha, even though Mom laughed and said, "Don't you remember? Lila Stites's sister."

Then Dad pulled out his torn envelope bookmark and read the evening's story from *Hurlbut's Story of the Bible.* It's incredible that we could read from that thick, mustard colored retelling of Bible stories night after night, and never get to the New Testament, but that's what I remember.

And after the Bible story it was time for prayer requests. Mom and Dad didn't talk about their struggles, or invite us to pray about real fears or problems. We offered banalities—prayers for our grandparents and a few vaguely remembered friends in the US. The weather.

We knelt, elbows on the chairs and couches, and prayed our boring prayers. Chris toddled around and climbed on Joy's back, which made her giggle. I peeked at Mom, who pulled Chris down and frowned at Joy. I struggled to keep my eyes shut. I hung my head between my shoulders. I wondered if anyone else noticed that the cushions smelled of dust and faintly of farts. I shifted around as the loops of the rug dug into my knees, and tried to find a John Bailie-like reverence. Dad prayed last and led us in reciting the love chapter from I Corinthians: *Faith, hope, love abide, but the greatest of these is love. Amen.*

But Maji station prayer meeting night—that was a different story. The aunties came to our house for dessert and a shortened devotion before we were sent off to bed. I made sure the hall door was left open a crack. As my sister and brother quieted on their pillows, as their breath deepened, I lay still under the wool blanket. There were no boring prayer requests at Maji station prayer meetings. Any rustling of my sheets and I might miss a tidbit.

# CHapTer 22

In prayer meeting, the adults talked about things Mom would have shut her mouth into a tight line about if I'd asked. They knew intimate things about the lives of our workers—it was from a prayer request that I first learned about Negatwa's marriage.

Now Dad told the women about a school boy, who had started school as a teenager. He got as far as fourth grade, then came to Dad and said, "My brain is full." The grownups laughed softly together. The young man wanted to go back to his village and start a school with what he'd learned. Dad asked prayers for wisdom.

There was trouble between mission families in Dembi Dollo again. How did Dad know these things? Prayer request time lasted for over an hour. Even adults can be confused, can get discouraged, can behave badly. Prayer enfolded my life: thanks and a blessing on every meal, in church, and at the end of every day in devotions, prayer meetings and in the dorm. Out in the living room, they genuinely wanted the best for everyone. But the line wandered, gray, between gossip and prayer.

And when it came to prayer, Mennonites took things a step further. The girls, like Chester Wenger's sisters, wore prayer caps, an elegant solution for two of St. Paul's admonitions: pray without ceasing and women, cover your hair. But if prayer caps were the solution, why didn't Presbyterians wear them? Maybe it had to be the whole Mennonite package or nothing at all: the uncut hair in long braids, the slightly longer plainer skirts, the dark complexions and the history of persecution from both Catholics and other Protestants.

It hadn't taken me long to figure out denominational differences. Some of the Lutheran fathers smoked. And they used wine for communion. *Wine.* Presbyterians were next worst: women like Mom wore lipstick. Mennonites were strict, but they didn't expect anyone else to let their hair grow or wear prayer caps. They didn't foist their beliefs on the rest of us. Baptists, on the other hand—they thought they were absolutely right about everything. Like I would go to hell because I had been baptized as a baby. Also, the Baptists were the naughtiest kids in the school. It was pretty clear, the stricter the parents, the naughtier the kids. Skins, for example. Slinger.

*The Diary of Private Prayer* was my Presbyterian alternative to prayer caps. It quoted Wordsworth: *The world is too much with us, late and soon. Getting and spending, we lay waste our powers.* I was stirred. Exalted. Convicted. My powers would not be laid waste.

I read my evening prayer every day. My cross-stitched linen book-mark, a gift from a missionary auntie, I tucked in next to the binding. Whether I was at home on my tufted cotton-filled mattress, or at Good Shepherd between rough-woven sheets, I laid my head at night on the pillow over John Bailie's prayers. I turned my mind to God and fell asleep, on a good night, praying.

On the blank pages I listed my besetting sins. I didn't ask to move mountains. I pleaded for patience, believing it would be a small prayer for God to answer. During those middle school years, before breakfast had even ended, one of my sisters inevitably said something stupid, or refused to cooperate, or knocked over her glass of milk. Jane, who loves me dearly, says to me now, "You sure don't suffer fools." It would have been easier for God to move a mountain than to change my oh, so human heart.

On summer break in Maji, I sat in the platform rocker, like a nest by the Franklin stove. I had grown out of the games outside. I wanted to read and be left alone by the rest of my chaotic family. But from there, I was easily summoned to change a diaper, set a table, or sew on the hundreds of name tags it took to send three girls to boarding school.

"Caroline, help me pick up," Mom said to me one morning. The living room floor was scattered with little kid toys. Duke-tebar would be there soon to sweep. When the living room was cleared, I flounced back to the rocker. "And if you don't take that scowl off your face, you're going to your room."

Joy beamed her dimples, as if to say *Don't worry, I've got this.* "Caroline's not scowling, Mommy," she said. "That's just the way she naturally looks."

My cheeks burned. Had my resentment etched permanent lines in my face?

Mom had bought three colors of flannel for night gowns. I was planning to cut them out, cozy in the dining room as rain pinged the *korkoro* roof and rivulets ran down channels of corrugated iron and splashed into the gravel below. My own nightgown factory assembly line. I wandered into Mom's bedroom first, looking for the always-missing hairbrush.

As I came around the corner, I startled Mom. She turned quickly from where she'd stood in front of our only mirror, that spanned the double set of drawers in her cherry wood dresser. But I had seen her face. Crumpled and wet with tears.

"Ato Jimma killed himself," she said in a low voice, when I asked.

I felt a cold shock. I'd never known anyone who died. Ato Jimma often preached in the school hall church.

Mom just shook her head when I asked *why? how?*

"We don't need to talk about it." She wiped her face with a strip of TP, and blew her nose. I imagined Ato Jimma in a casket. Mom ran the hairbrush I'd been after through her hair, shook her head once and studied how the curls fell. Then she sprayed a cloud of Hairnet over it. I stepped back, still looking at her red face, tiny drops of spray landing sticky on my face and hands, its perfume tingling my nose.

There weren't very many people who came to our Maji church. After devotions one evening, I asked Dad if God would send the rest to hell. Dad only talked about hell as a joke when we had guests: *You'll be banished to a place where there is weeping and wailing and gnashing of teeth!* That or Siberia.

While I was waiting for Dad to answer, in the back half of the house, Mom was bustling from bathroom to bedroom, keeping the other girls on track for bedtime—pajamas, tooth brushes, and the potty: *Just try.*

Dad said God is so pure and holy he can't abide sins. Dad went over the plan of salvation, Jesus taking on our sins for us. Dad said God wanted everyone to hear about his plan for forgiveness. That's why we had come to Maji.

A piece of firewood broke. Sparks, all shades of red and yellow, billowed up in the Franklin stove. "I know, Dad," I said, I'd heard all that in dozens of sermons. It was the small print I was concerned about. "What about the people who died before we got here?" Dad got up to put another piece of wood on.

One of the little kids had put bits of crayon on the lip of the stove, even though we were not allowed to. A shiny puddle of purple bled into green and red. There were spankable transgressions, and there was naughtiness. And there was getting caught. Colors on the stove were too beautiful for my sisters to resist, and if they didn't get caught, there was eye-rolling but no follow up.

When Dad didn't answer right away, I said, "How is that fair?"

He didn't have any small print explanation. I argued with him until I was weeping. If God was love, why would he be so careless, so sloppy as to leave some people out through no fault of their own?

Dad finally said, "Caroline, God is wiser than we are. I'm sure he has a plan."

Not reassured, I stormed off to bed. "How could he?"

Mom wasn't responsible for our souls. Her job was to teach us character. She unveiled a wonderful plan she'd seen in the six months delayed *Ladies Home Journal. TaTa!* on poster paper: *Model Child Chart!* She brought out a box of gold stars, as enticing and precious as real gold. She promised a star for every task—bed made, teeth brushed, chores done cheerfully. At the end of the week, a prize to the star-winner. Cathy was excused, she was too young, but Jane, Joy and I needed character stars.

Mom didn't consider whether her premise was actually true. I brushed my teeth without being reminded. I brushed my hair, no matter how long it took to excavate a hairbrush. I liked my bed made, my clothes hung up. Soon my row of stars marched serenely across the Model Child Chart. Jane's and Joy's rows looked ragged and gappy. It didn't take long for them to yield the high ground. What was the use? I was born a Model Child.

Pretty soon, Jane and Joy mocked the Model Child Chart. Mom's prizes got more perfunctory—*Oh, you again?* I was mortified. No one knew how to get the Model Child Chart stopped. It might have worked, redrawn just for Joy and Jane, but Mom noticed our personality differences only in the broadest possible outline: Caroline the Responsible One; Jane my Dennis the Menace; Joy my Social Butterfly.

We have agreed since that we both benefitted and suffered from her benign neglect. She modeled a woman living her own life. She didn't communicate anxiety or fear for our safety. And—and it was hard that we had to fend for ourselves emotionally.

Back at school, Mrs. Anderson announced her own new plan—individual devotion times. I sat alone with my dorm mother in her living room in the awkwardness of intimacy without safety. When the fifteen-minute devotion and prayer was over, she gave me a slip of foolscap, the paper we used for homework, shiny smooth on one side, pulpy on the other. Mrs. Anderson had chosen a Bible verse specially for me. The words flowed in her even, slanted cursive: *Be ye therefore perfect, even as your Father in Heaven is perfect. Matthew 5:48.*

# CHAPTER 23

Walking along the granite veranda, I was blind to the riotous orange canna lilies that now grew in the courtyard. This Bible verse confirmed my worst fears. I folded the narrow strip in half. In half again. Again. Until it was a tight roll of paper that could easily get lost or misplaced.

Jesus was supposed to be helping me be good. I hadn't realized just how good. Surely God knew how hard I was trying, but I knew I wasn't a Gentle Jesus Meek and Mild kind of disciple. There was nothing mild about me. Being responsible was how I compensated. The only solution I had found for my failures in the perfection department, until God answered my prayers, was to hide them as best I could.

The summer before I started high school I realized that no, bras were not part of *growing up and liking it*. I was about to be sent off to a *boarding* high school, with a name-tagged supply of undershirts with tiny pink bows where there would someday, hopefully, be cleavage.

Before I threw myself down the Bat Cave waterfall to a tragic death on the valley floor—but a doom preferable to high school in undershirts—I snuck the key to the storeroom, unlocked the padlock, slipped in and closed the door tightly. The fifty-gallon drums stood lined against the side wall in the dim light. I'd seen no bras as I dug through them before. When Mom had shopped for that five years-worth of clothes in Boise, I'd been a tiny ten-year old. Now I was going on fifteen. I guess Mom didn't do the math. It was a hopeless quest. But one I had to make. Praying for a miracle.

On top of one barrel sat a battered cardboard box. I leaned close and peered through the gloom—Mom's name, smudged by mud from the mule trip up from Washa Wooha. In the corner, Aunt Lois Haspels's name. I opened the flap, holding my breath. Lying on top, straps.

I held up the bra and studied it in a ray of sunlight spotted with dust motes, a ray that pierced down through a nail hole in the *korkoro* roof. The bra was gray. It was really just two triangles of soft fabric attached to a stretched out elastic band with one hook and eye. I didn't need any more than triangles of soft fabric. I didn't mind gray from boarding school wash tubs. My eyes teared up. It was a miracle, as unimagined as crossing the Red Sea on dry land. No lacy lingerie has ever made me happier than worn out bras from Jeanie Haspels.

That evening, I followed Mom from the cluttered supper table to the kitchen. I followed her down the dim hall to our bedroom, where she gathered up Cathy's pajamas. I followed her up the hall again, past rhomboid shapes shining through the doors. Finally, I caught her alone in her bedroom for a moment. I grew damp under the bangs. My mouth got dry. But I ratcheted up my courage. "Mom, I found some bras from Jeanie. Can I have them?"

"Sure," she said, on her way out to the next bedtime chore.

The next day, I carefully hand stitched my name tag over Jeanie's. I locked myself in the bathroom. I reached awkwardly behind my back and fumbled with the worn hook and eye. I felt...sexy, I would have said, if I had known the word. Covered there, and bare everywhere else. When my straight brown dress brushed my midriff, tingles sprinkled through my groin.

The day I threw my shift into the wash, I put on a skirt and white blouse. Now my triangles showed up like those under all the *ferenji* women's blouses. When I walked through the kitchen, Sagu made a comment. I didn't understand one word he said, but I knew he was talking about me. My ridiculous white triangles. The other boy cracked up.

I fled to the safety of the living room. But I wasn't sorry. Wearing dresses, my periods, they were no fun. I wasn't going to let anything ruin the one glory of growing up: a bra.

The Schulz American School of Alexandria, Egypt, in a poor neighborhood whose streets smelled of stale gray water, was where Presbyterian kids went for high school from all over Africa.

Once again, off I went into worlds unknown without my parents or sisters. Seniors, who had done the trip before, took charge of the rest of us. But they didn't tell me not to leave my customs declaration on the plane. Holding up the whole gang, I filled it out again, shamed and sweating, under the frowning eye of a large Egyptian man.

After a long, sweltering bus ride through the desert from Cairo, I followed the other girls into our dorm. "You're there,"

I took a deep breath. A big square room. Two platform beds with drawers. A bunk. Dressers. A desk. A door on one side, open to the adjoining room where two girls were hugging and dancing in a circle. A door on the opposite side, open into the bathroom, tiled white from floor to ceiling.

Eight ninth grade girls shared this suite: Chloe, Alice, Eloise and Barbara in one room, Ruthie, Marilyn, Carolyn and Caroline in the other. Maybe the dorm mother chuckled as she assigned us. Thankfully, it wasn't long before my nickname from Good Shepherd caught up with me to relieve the congestion—I became Core.

I kept a diary that year. What interested me as a fourteen-year-old was not Alexandria, but mostly my hair, my grades, and whether my period was starting. Letters home, on tissue-thin paper with the school logo in English and Arabic, are cheerful and brave, since I had learned from Dad to show a good face. In contrast, my memories are shaded with loneliness. My roommates already had friends or were too moody to be friends.

We walked every week to church along the *corniche*, smelling the salt water of the Mediterranean. I didn't want the *corniche*, I wanted a friend. We took school outings to swim in the sea at Sidi Bishr. I wanted a friend. I went on a camel ride into the desert over spring break, but where was a friend to laugh with as we joggled side to side on those wobbly humps?

I walked down the hall one afternoon, past the laundry station. The girls whose job it was that week to read name tags and stuff clean clothes into cubbies were horsing around. As I passed, one shouted. "Look't this!" She summersaulted a thin gray thing through the air. I would have known it anywhere.

"Oh my gosh!" the other girl said. "Who..."

At that instant I passed them. At that instant they went silent. I stared straight ahead. I hoped my footsteps sounded just as jaunty as they had been seconds before. Small schools have no bell curve.

For months that year, I mooned over JR, my perennially unavailable crush, sure that only his attention would brighten my gray world. Adolescence had turned the boy I loved even more moody-broody, but I didn't care. On Sadie Hawkins weekend I invited him to the movie, *Ring of Fire*. I bought us a bag of popcorn. The delicious, buttery smell, the huge splurge it represented—my heart squeezed tight with hope. JR and I awkwardly passed the oil-stained brown paper bag back and forth. We munched silently as the movie lights flickered over our faces.

The credits rolled. The fluorescent lights went on. I squinted painfully. JR and I joined the flood of kids in the aisle of the assembly room turned cinema. In the granite entryway, JR mumbled, *Thanks*, and ran down the stairs toward the boys' dorm.

I fled up to the dorm's flat roof. The evening air was Mediterranean-warm. The waist-high wall cast a shadow from city lights. I leaned against it. Ceramic tiles radiated heat on the soles of my feet. A cat who lived up there came by, and I stroked her tragically. But she didn't want to be my solace. She squirmed out of my arms. I threw myself onto the dusty tiles, and sobbed.

A boy named Paul had been watching me as I watched JR. Back on October twenty-fourth, I'd called him by his last name and noted in my journal, with prim disapproval, that I could smell he'd been smoking. In November, one of my friends told me he liked me. In February I noticed that for myself. In March I got a nice note from him. But it wasn't until April that I raised my gaze from my broken heart to really look.

His dad was the Charge d'Affairs in Yemen, so he took it on himself to inform me that we could never marry because I wouldn't know what fork to use at a banquet.

*Boy howdy,* as my people would say. My dad was from Eastern Oregon, where a juniper fence post could wear out five post holes. My Great Uncle Lee had been run out of town as a cattle rustler. I was from Maji, remote and beautiful Maji. I wouldn't know what fork to use, and proud of it.

"Listen to this," I said one day, and read Paul a passage from *Mill on the Floss.* He was not transported by George Eliot's gorgeous prose. I tutored him in algebra. *He finally got it,* I wrote home. *He just wasn't trying.* Paul wasn't trying to be a good student. He wasn't reading the classics. He was too busy having a good time. Paul was funny. He teased me. We wrestled and chased each other around.

"You two have the healthiest relationship of any couple on campus," our Bible teacher's wife told me.

In the back of the school van, on the way home from a year-end field day in Cairo, Paul tightened his arm around my shoulder and drew me closer. He leaned down slowly, and pressed his lips against mine. He pulled back, and we looked at each other, inches away. So this was the kissing that was so sinful, that the GSS boys thought would bring me down to earth from my heights of goodness? It was nice. But kind of innocuous. He kissed me again. The tip of his tongue moistened my lips. I opened them.

When we pulled away, my heart wasn't pounding as much as reverberating.

"Where did you learn to French kiss?" he whispered.

"I didn't," I said. I hid my face in his shoulder. I could have said,

*I guess I was just finally ready.*

Paul's parents came from Yemen for his sister's graduation, and invited me to her graduation party at the embassy compound in Alex. I sat beside Paul, afraid to look at him. I shyly answered his father's questions across the dining table, which glittered with silverware—yes, multiple forks—and crystal glasses that the grownups filled with deep red liquid that must be wine.

It got late, and his mother said, in her British accent, *Poo-poo, we're not driving you all the way across town at this hour.* She gave me a white cotton nightie with lace, and put me in a bedroom with its own private bathroom. I waltzed around on the cool tile floor in virginal white, shutters open to a Mediterranean garden with dark Bird of Paradise flowers and palm trees.

Paul and his family flew out that weekend for furlough in Ohio. The next day, I lumbered in the Presbyterian bus across the desert to Cairo. I had a day in Addis, so I rode the van out to Good Shepherd. A boy named Mark had heard that Jane's sister from Schutz was coming. He watched me step off the bus. He watched me hug Jane. He watched Joy run over and throw her arms around me—we hadn't seen each other for nine months.

I didn't notice him, and didn't know he would be waiting for me when I got back from furlough.

# CHapTer 24

In Maji, our furniture would stay in place while we were gone for a year—other than Mom's cherry bedroom set and the rocking chairs, we had basic furniture, with mission inventory numbers written on the bottoms in pencil. Mom emptied cupboards and dressers. I cleaned the dresser in the bathroom. The top drawer was full of medicine—was it expired? Would it be expired by the time we got back? Globs from lidless tubes of A&D ointment had attracted stray pills, lint and dust. Baby powder had spilled from bottles not twisted shut. I wiped and tossed and sorted in a miasma of powder and chemicals. Chris and Janice played outside, as we had when we were their age.

I had reached a mellow fifteen and cheerfully helped Mom now. I was grateful to be saying au revoir to Maji before leaving. The hills, nubby with brush or cropped close by cattle. Sunset. A see-you-later lift of my face to the waterfall's spray. The evening *goom* spilling into the valley and tumbling over itself as it came up our side before dark fell.

My relations with the kitchen crew were more civilized, too, as though they saw that I really was a woman now. Sagu was tall and handsome. I felt shy around him. We smiled at each other when I passed through the kitchen, but we didn't talk.

When the day came, and the idling Jeep rattled outside on the dirt track, Mom, Dad and the aunties and I stood by the front door in an awkward cluster, the little Maji *ferenj* team. Dad gave final instructions. They wished us traveling mercies. We shuffled and waited for some intangible signal that it was time to be off.

Sagu stood in the door between the kitchen and dining room watching, waiting, maybe, for a turn to say, *May we meet again in peace.* No one else noticed. What were the conventions for a young man and a young woman so different—our status, our nationalities, our races? The grown-ups would all turn and watch if I walked over and shook his hand. I felt hot at the thought, and took my sweater off. I gave Sagu a quick, embarrassed smile, and turned away.

Later that summer, I decided: when we went back, I would finish high school at Good Shepherd, not Schutz. I'd spent the summer suffering the agony of no letter from Paul, followed by the lurch of my heart when I saw his handwriting on an envelope. He had terrible handwriting. I could see he wasn't going to be much of a letter-writer. And I didn't know how to miss someone or how to tell them so. I wrote Paul a prim little letter: *We'll never see each other again.* I told myself I was being noble, setting that cute, funny, sophisticated boy free for some other girl. Paul didn't answer, and I never saw Alexandria again.

Nothing had prepared me for Pasadena, California. Based on the mission rental allowance, a local church had found a three-bedroom house in Watts for our family of eight. I scrubbed ancient linoleum in the bathroom on hands and knees. Its rust colored pattern had worn through to the tar layer between the sink and a scratched claw foot tub. I thought we could make do—I thought we *should* make do, it was much more airtight than our house in Maji—but Mom made a vague comment about this not being a good neighborhood for us. I only understood later, when I read about that summer's race riots.

Mom and Dad moved us into a house on the dividing street of the school district and I rode the school bus across town to John Muir, Pasadena's racially-mixed high school. Black and white students glared at each other in the halls. The parking lot was crowded with mobile classrooms for us—three thousand teenaged Boomers.

I'd been in classes of two. I'd eaten breakfast, lunch, and supper and hung out with my friends through languorous, sun-soaked weekends full of cricket song, grass seed and dust on the Good Shepherd acres. Or, at Schutz, I'd played volleyball in the blistering tile courtyard, ping pong on the cool cement veranda, or dodgeball in sweaty Egyptian heat. Now, at John Muir, I found my way from classroom to classroom, through packed hallways. I saw thirty different faces in every class. I walked home from the bus stop in smog that burned my eyes and made them weep.

Dad was in a master's degree program. He traveled on weekends, speaking in churches, passionately promoting the "Fifty Million Dollar Fund" that would support innovative work in Ethiopia, Egypt, and India.

Always wanting to encourage his most spiritual—even ascetic—daughter, Dad gave me a booklet, *The Practice of the Presence of God.* Brother Lawrence, a Carmelite monk in the 1600s, had manned the monastery kitchen. He dedicated himself to do all things for love of God, and to cultivate the awareness of God's presence, whether scrubbing scorched pot-bottoms or peeling potatoes. In interviews and letters, he said this practice gave him great comfort and joy.

This is what I'd been longing for. John Bailie admonished me in confession and nightly rededication to faith, but faith fell short in the chaos of the day. Brother Lawrence gave me hope. I read and reread his booklet, searching for clues for how to practice, but there wasn't much to go on. Desire was not enough to find the promised peace. Maybe peeling potatoes was boring enough that Brother Lawrence could concentrate. I was busy suffering in the miserable hallways of John Muir High School without a friend. I was desperate to get through the year and back home to Maji and Good Shepherd. God seemed more absent, not more present, after I read about Brother Lawrence and his luminous joy in the monastery kitchen.

We sang a song at Second Presbyterian Church that year. It expressed an ecstasy like Brother Lawrence's: *And he walks with me and he talks with me...And the joy we share as we tarry there/None other has ever known.* But God didn't walk with *me.* God didn't tell *me* I was his own. What was I doing wrong?

I should have known that if people were actually experiencing God in this tangible way, somebody would have been talking more about it. Instead, we were all longing to experience the spiritual in the middle of our disappointingly mundane lives. We were all groping for something more, and raising our voices from the same frail boat on the ocean.

One evening, I sat at the yellow formica and chrome table in the nook of our rented house, crying. "If I fell down dead in the hall, people would just step over my body and keep going." That got into the family book of quotes, but Mom's amusement at my dramatic despair did nothing to comfort me.

I did make one friend, Josie Pepito. She was an army brat, also raised in the crevice between her parents' and her host countries' cultures. With a mysterious homing sense, we found each other in the sea of three thousand. We ate together every day after English, and talked about *The Good Earth*, and Guam, and Ethiopia.

I didn't know to ask Josie where she lived. I was shocked to learn, late in the year, that she had a brother. Did I mention that I had sisters? We appeared in English class, ate lunch together, and disappeared again. If she didn't show up, I ate alone.

Josie and I walked through the gray painted, gray tiled hall that smelled of dust and sweat and books one noon. A lanky black boy grabbed my arm as we passed. He rotated me to face him. The girls behind him snickered. I looked up into his face. His lips twisted to the side. His black eyes, surrounded by short black eyelashes, ran from my hair to my shoes, but skipped my eyes. The hall expanded, gray and empty around me. People in Ethiopia stared at me, but they were just curious. They pulled my hair, but only to see if it was real. There were thousands of them, and only our family.

"What a dud!" the boy said. Another boy punched his arm. He danced in a circle, clapping his knee.

I hugged my books against my chest. Josie bumped the crash bar with her hip. It clattered. She faced straight ahead as she held the door with her body. I slipped by. She followed me to our table. We unwrapped our bologna sandwiches.

Maybe it was my hair, the perky morning flip that had drooped by noon, in spite of my prickly curlers. Or maybe it was the stupid pea-green shift that Mom had gotten on sale and that I wore in its turn, even though it made me look and feel as gray as I got when I was airsick on the C-47s.

Or maybe. Maybe it was my shoes. They were black velvet oxfords Mom and Dad had bought in Boise. The shoes had spent five years in the supply barrels, waiting for me to grow into them. A mouse had nibbled on the leather in one spot, but you could hardly notice. Otherwise they were in perfect shape. They would never wear out. A girl in Ethiopia would have been delighted to have those shoes. I wore them with thin white anklets. The other girls at John Muir wore stockings and kitten heels, or bare legs and sandals, like Josie. But I would never throw away perfectly good shoes just to be fashionable.

After school that day, I walked down Hill Avenue. Behind me, the rocky bluff had disappeared in smog. Cars purred by. Pasadena on the left. Altadena on the right. I squeezed my eyes shut, and they watered enough to relieve the burning. In the front door, I went straight to the baby grand piano in our furnished rental. It gleamed like a black mirror in a nook off the living room. I lost myself for an hour in a lachrymose Venetian Boat Song and the sad and easy parts of the Moonlight Sonata. My piano playing still exhibited more passion than talent, but it filled the hole of my shame with something beautiful I could create.

I opened the front door on another afternoon that spring, and this time stopped on the threshold to stare at a tape deck and a box of Kleenex sitting in the middle of the living room floor. Around them ringed the sectional couch and several easy chairs. "Mom? Dad?"

Mom's voice came muffled from upstairs. "Are Jane and Joy home?"

Seconds later, they banged in, off their middle school bus. They stopped short to stare, as I had. We sat on the couches and waited, fidgeting, not looking at each other. Cathy, home from fourth grade, came downstairs. Chris and Janice were six and four. Mom called them in from play, and they curled on the couches between us.

Dad came down the carpeted stairway. I studied him, to see from his face how I should feel. His face looked sober, but shone with a muted excitement. That was a confusing mixture, unreadable even for one who'd spent her life reading Dad's face. Mom tried too hard to be serious. A smile kept softening the corners of her mouth.

Dad cleared his throat, intoned some words about *something we all need to hear*, and leaned down to turn on the reel-to-reel tape deck. The tail of brown plastic rubbed in pattern as the reel slowly spun. The tape hissed a little, then our missionary Uncle Mal's voice greeted us. He was speaking after the Association meeting the month before, and the tape had made its way from the mission compound to the post office at the bottom of the *piassa* in Addis Ababa and onto EAL, to arrive at our house.

The mission aunties and uncles wanted Dad to pass on to them what he was learning at Fuller Seminary. Could he help them figure out how Jesus was good news to indigenous mountain and forest peoples of Ethiopia? Instead of being a strange, foreign religion? Could he help them start oral-only churches where local languages weren't written? Could people write church music of their own, instead of singing hymns translated from English and German? The Association had voted Dad to be Country Representative, to advocate and advise in the gap between New York and the field.

Tears flowed down my cheeks. I mopped and wiped. They kept coming.

"I knew it," Jane sobbed. "I knew someday we'd lose Maji."

"No," I wailed. No, because who would dare move the Kurtzes from where they belonged? No, because a treasure shouldn't ever be ripped away, even for the noblest of reasons. I opened my mouth to ask what Dad was going to tell them. But I saw the answer in his face. I sobbed, my sixteen-year-old dignity gone entirely. Jane buried her head on my shoulder. Maji had been a talisman. The basis of our identity. What anchored us when we were at school.

I hadn't known that all year my future had been hanging in a balance. Demoralized by his failures in Maji, Dad had written to his bosses to say he was a failure at mission church planting, he thought he should go back to Portland where he had been successful.

Uncle Fred had assumed, after he spent eight years in Maji, that the church didn't grow because he was only an agriculturalist, no matter how devout. What Maji needed was a pastor. Dad had kept the mission station running for ten years. He gave people a mill, he soldered a few dozen aluminum pots for the women, he fixed alarm clocks and watches for the men. Took our nurse auntie out on mule-back mobile clinics. Started satellite schools. But he hadn't been able to grow the church.

There was Admasu and others who took their children to the Orthodox Church to be secretly baptized. Except there are no secrets in an African community.

There were the people in a village across the ridge, who'd asked for someone to come and teach them about Jesus. Dad had thought it was his breakthrough. But the Orthodox priest heard of it.

A deacon, in white jodhpurs and *shemma*, led the priest's mule. The bit jingled. The wooden saddle, padded with a thick *gabi* and an embroidered saddle blanket, creaked under the priest's weight, in his long black robes, his hair bound up in a turban. He carried his ornately carved ceremonial cross. He swished the flies away with his horse-tail fly swatter. He was a big man. An emissary from God. Protecting the true church from heresy.

When he got to the village, he called the elders together. They sat under a tree, sipping scalding coffee in white *sinis* made in China. Coffee with butter and salt. When the needful hospitality had been enjoyed, the priest warned the elders they would not be allowed civilized burial if they were baptized by the missionary.

The priest went back once more, to sprinkle holy water in the direction of the gathered villagers. He assured them the church graveyard and heaven would now be theirs.

Dad had been crushed. But he hadn't talked about these things with his daughters at the time. He had kept his brave face on.

And then Ato Jimma. Dad's hope for a local church leader had hanged himself.

When Dad had written in despair, on that tissue-thin airmail paper, his bosses hadn't been ready to let him go. They convinced him to do a master's degree. A wise old missionary from India was starting a department at Fuller Seminary—anthropology and mission theory, a new field called Missiology. All I'd known at the time was that Dad wanted to take some courses and it had to be in Pasadena. And that's where Uncle Mal's voice on the scratchy brown plastic tape found us.

Mom whispered to Dad and went to make a phone call.

# CHAPTER 25

When she came back into the living room on the day our Maji lives ended, Mom announced in a bright voice that we were going swimming at a friend's house. They'd invited us over. *Any time.* We'd never accepted that invitation. No one objected to this bizarre plan for the rest of the afternoon.

Peering through puffy eyes, I gathered my yellow swim suit with its white piping and boy-shorts legs, and my white swim cap. The eight of us piled into the station wagon, four girls on the wide middle seat, little kids in the back.

Janice and Chris must have been mystified at the air of tragedy filling the car. Mom passed Kleenex back to us, with the print and scent of her blotted lipstick.

*No more boarding school.* We would be day students, those lonely souls who missed the heart of what Good Shepherd had been to us. Joy sat silent and relieved beside me. Only Jane understood how my world had imploded.

In the pool-blue water, I swam back and forth. The salt of tears and the burn of chlorine mixed in my mouth. I bent my arms awkwardly back to hang onto the cement over-flow trough beside Mom, who was more of a side-clinger than a lap swimmer.

Mom said, "Now that we'll be in Addis, we can have a piano!"

I launched out for the other side without answering. A fresh up-welling of tears left warm tracks on my cheeks in the cool water.

At the end of the year, I took an unspoken vow: I was not going to risk being bra-less ever again. On a shopping trip with Mom to Macy's, supplying the family for the next five years, I firmly, breezily said, "I'll be up shopping for panties," and ran to the elevator. Five years. Who knew what could happen in five years? I grabbed a cart. The happy, blue-printed women on the fronts of bra boxes hanging from display stands all looked the same. I turned a box over, hoping for words.

Hmm. Numbers. Letters. I remembered the formula for buying

shoes in Boise: a size up every six months. I pulled boxes off their hooks and dropped them into the shopping cart: 34. 36. 38. I was counting years and sizes with complete concentration when Mom found me. She looked at the pile in the cart. She picked up a box. "44D!" She gasped. "I only wear 36!"

I stared at her chest. She looked marvelously well endowed. I pulled the bra from the box. Its huge cup unfolded slowly, stiff with circular stitching. The four hooks and eyes in back could have fastened a suit of armor. I gave a soft scream. And suddenly, there in the lingerie department, Mom and I were giggling. Mom's dark, curled hair shook in spite of the hair spray.

I sagged against the cart. "I'm going to wet my pants."

Mom laughed harder. She finally wiped her eyes. She chose a few 32A and 34A bras for me. She threw in a 34B or two just for good measure, marched to the cashier, completely unembarrassed, to pay. Amazing. I fled to the bathroom.

I waited at the elevator for Mom, who laughed again when she joined me. "Size 44D," she said, and shook her dark curls. I laughed with her, and reached for the red and white striped Macy's bag with my haul.

The sunshine of that moment had driven away any thoughts of Jane, who needed little white triangles more than I had at her age, but who had endured eighth grade in Pasadena in undershirts. Jane would now go into high school in those undershirts, until I outgrew some of the bras in the little blue boxes that I had been so determined that day to buy.

In view of our grief over losing Maji, in view of our having to suffer as day students, Mom and Dad gave Jane and me one last year in boarding. I wasn't all that grateful. It seemed like the least they could do. We were to go home on weekends, something we quickly promised, and then wrangled out of as often as we could.

Moving into the dorm, back in one of my lands flowing with milk and honey, I sat on Jeanie Haspels's bed, leaning against the green cement block wall, watching her rifle through the detritus in the bottom of her footlocker. The homey smells of local wool blankets, fresh paint, and cement filled my head. Out on the granite veranda girls' footsteps dashed back and forth, high voices screamed, laughter burst and bubbled. "Hey. Let's go see what's happening," I said.

Now that Jeanie had grown out of some of her horse mania, there was no more galloping. No more flicking our ponytails. She had a sixties flip and I'd had Dad give me what I called a Julie Andrews cut, after we saw *Sound of Music* in Pasadena. We found Bob Sandbagger and Mark Rasmussen on the basketball court playing Around the World.

"Do you let girls in?" I asked.

"Sure we do, don't we, Moosie?" Bob said.

Donkeys clip-clopped by the barbed wire fence along the dirt road past the basketball court. The Ethiopian boys driving the donkeys shouted, as they always did, to get our attention: *"Ferenj ferenj!"* And we ignored them as we always did. In September, at the end of the big rains, storm clouds still gathered by noon most days, but that day our mountain afternoon was sunny, the air cleared of dust by the daily scrubbing. Flies whined, buzzards drifted overhead.

The four of us lined up under the basket on the right side. Bob put his shot in and went on. Jeanie laid hers in. Mark hitched one thin leg and arched his arm over his head in perfect hook-lay-up form, but the ball hit the backstop too hard and ricocheted out. Mark's next try bounced off the rim. So did the next.

"Concentrate, Moosie!" Bob said.

We laughed at Mark as we moved around the key and he tried again and again under the basket. His straight dark hair flopped across his forehead and into his eyes. His cupid's bow lips were as dark as if he wore tint. He blushed and laughed with us. I knew I was the reason he never made even one basket that afternoon.

A month later, we ended up on the same team in a pick-up game of softball. I hit myself a single, and Chester Wenger, now a tan and muscled sophomore, followed me with a hit into right field. I took off from my lead, a yard from first base. As I approached second, Mark shouted from the third baseline, "Keep going!" I rounded the base wide, and flew to third as fast as my Keds would take me. "That's my girl!" Mark yelled.

We exchanged a shocked look as I pounced onto the base. The stunned silence around us on the diamond erupted into hooting and whistles. I drooped, my hands on my knees, panting, breathing the dust I'd raised, and the smell of tropical sunshine on my hair and face, my lungs burning. I kept my eyes down, on the third base, a square of gunny sack with red dirt in every fiber.

In the dining hall line that evening, Mark's brother said, "Forget Moosie. He would rather take an engine apart than go with a girl."

I was ambivalent about Mark, anyway. It hadn't challenged my genius to see how shy he was. And he hollered at teammates who missed a pop-up or fluffed a lay-in. But he watched me. He smiled at me, his green eyes warm behind tortoiseshell rimmed glasses. After my lost year in Pasadena, that attention felt delicious.

Still, it was my last year in boarding school, and there was no hurry to solve the boyfriend question. I was busy gobbling up every moment of what, this time, I knew I would lose.

Before breakfast, I ran across the gravel road and dew-sparkled crab grass to the practice room, where I pounded out Liszt and Rachmaninoff, Chopin and folk songs. I played basketball every afternoon with Mark and the other boys. I played Emily in the junior class production of *Our Town*. I took up the cello. I aced Algebra 2 and Trig, and no one could beat me out in Honors English.

Benny Gamber warned Mark in study hall one night, "Don't you know walking encyclopedias are reference material and can't be taken out?"

That note made its way into my hands. I unfolded it, chalk dust making my fingers rough against the foolscap paper. I looked up and smiled at Mark, at Benny. Reference material? You bet!

Off the bus for an at-home weekend one Friday, a huge crate greeted me as I opened our front door. When he heard Jane, Joy, and me slam into the house, Dad dashed down the hall, calling the troops together. I crossed my arms—this must be the piano that was supposed to make losing Maji all better. It had taken most of a year en route by freighter—through the Panama Canal from Oregon, around the cape and up the east coast of Africa to Djibouti.

Dad had a pry bar ready at hand. He pulled out nails he had loosened earlier. With a grand flourish, he peeled off a board. Out tumbled ivory pieces, chips of wood, bits of dowel, green felt hammer heads. A gust of dry air smelling of sawdust and old glue. It appeared that longshoremen had moved the piano down the gang plank end over end.

Dad's excited expression froze. I saw the soft, vulnerable fear of failure there at the edges of the big smile he was trying to manage. It softened my heart just a little.

By that time, I had achieved near resignation over the move into Addis—I'd had seventeen years of practice at tamping down my desires, submitting to the family's greater good. And I was an old hand at putting on a good face for Dad. But as I went back to my room that afternoon, I felt a secret thrill of satisfaction that Mom's piano bribe had failed. It wasn't going to make everything all better.

Dad wasn't that easily thwarted. He recruited Cathy, home recovering from hepatitis. Over the next three weeks, she and Dad poured over the broken piano bits as though they were pieces from a giant 3-D puzzle. They got the hammers glued back together and the keys working. Only two notes at the very top, and three at the bottom, had to be cannibalized, and sat, forever depressed and mute.

When that school year ended, Mark wrote in my yearbook, *See you next year*. I knew exactly what he meant. I spent the summer thinking about it. Yes, he was moody. He was insecure. He was shy. But wouldn't my love give him more confidence?

I was Mom and Dad's responsible one, committed to the premise that doing what other people wanted earned me love. Though it had never quite worked out that way, I still hoped earned love came packaged with happiness. I was also practical. None of the other boys in our class of sixteen seemed like boyfriend material.

It took Mark most of the first semester to work up the courage to ask me out. But when he did, when we talked together, just the two of us, his shyness fell away. I was delighted. Jane was not. "He's always touching you," she complained.

One Sunday after we were officially going together, I asked Mom if I could invite Mark for lunch after church. He walked into the house, past the infamous piano, and straight to the kitchen. "Can I do anything to help?" he asked.

Mom told me that evening, "Mark can come over any time."

After another Sunday dinner, Mark and I planned to write an essay together about *Catcher in the Rye*. Dad got excited about our project, and waxed passionate about Holden Caulfield's scorn for preachers' Holy Joe voices. *As if Dad didn't have one of his own*, I thought. But I sat quietly and let him have all Mark's attention. Our time ran out, and it got too late for Mark to hitchhike back to school.

"Spend the night here," Dad said. "Take the school van with the girls tomorrow morning."

Mom brought sheets, and Mark and I stood on opposite sides of the hide-a-bed couch, shaking out the top sheet between us. Suddenly I saw us lying together in that bed. I wasn't ready to think about passion. Sex. What I saw was tenderness. Our bodies safely spooned and resting.

At the end of the year, when we were about to leave Ethiopia for college—he to Ohio and me to Illinois—I was left in charge at home, and was finishing up a typing job. Mark and I lay on Mom and Dad's bed, propped against their pillows, proofreading the old flimsy duplicating paper, delicate as ancient silk. The job took all afternoon, because Mark kept interrupting to snuggle and kiss. Chris and Janice peeked in the open bedroom door and ran away giggling.

When I got up to make supper, Mark hugged me in the doorway of the room. Before we met, he had planned to be a forester, living high in a fire look-out tower, safe and alone. Now he sang me the Monkees' song: *Then I saw her face, now I'm a believer.* And he couldn't let me go, even to the kitchen.

The day after we graduated, Mark left with his family for the States. Two months later, my parents put me on Swissair. In New York City I bought a Greyhound ticket to Mark's new home in Carthage, New York, up by the Canadian border.

The conditioned air in the bus smelled of dirty upholstery and feet. I watched trees passing by along the side of the highway: maples and birches, so different from *korch* and *zigeba* and giant ferns in the viny forests of Ethiopia. I'd been traveling alone for a week; silence was beginning to feel like my new native language.

After supper that night, I offered to dry the dishes his mother was washing. She stood just five feet tall, and her yellow rubber gloves came to her elbows. Mark had followed me into the kitchen, and now he picked up a second dishtowel. His mother laughed. "That's a first."

When we were done with dishes, I followed Mark out to the front porch. He didn't reach for me. His shyness was back, with his family watching. I felt awkward. He sat down on one side of the front steps and I turned to the other and sat stiff and upright against a column. Porch and pillar both radiated summer heat. In the unfamiliar humidity, my clothes clung to my skin. Summer cicadas made a shrill racket.

"How does it feel?" he asked. The words sounded innocent. But he twisted his Cupid's bow lips into an ironic curve. That was the first time I considered that his feelings for me might ever change.

# CHAPTER 26

On the porch that night, Mark sang a Tom Rush song: *No regrets No tears goodbye. Don't want you back.*

The cicadas' incessant buzzing invaded my temples.

*We'll only cry again, say goodbye again.* Mark's bass voice was sweet.

I hid my shock until I could say good night and stumble to the guest room. On top of the white eyelet bedspread, fully clothed, I lay down in a fetal position. The embroidery pressed rough against my cheek. The world heaved and spun around me. I opened my eyes to steady myself. The room stilled. I closed my eyes and the whirlpool pulled me down again. My chest hurt.

In Zurich, rowdy German boys had accosted me on the street. A Sudanese man had rescued me, then pressed me to have a beer with him. In Geneva, a boy had tried to pick me up on a park bench, where I'd carried my journal to sit in the sun. On the Greyhound bus to Carthage, I'd fallen asleep and the sailor who'd climbed on at a later stop and sat beside me reached over and cupped his hand on my breast. I froze. I pretended I was still asleep. I'd thought Mark would be my protector in this frightening world of men.

Staring into the dark in Carthage, I didn't think of my other losses: Maji, Good Shepherd School, my sisters, beautiful Ethiopia. Everything I loved lay nine time zones away. Sometimes one final blow carries the weight of all the others.

I had felt like a misfit at first at Good Shepherd. For most of the year at Schutz. All year in Pasadena. The reprieve, back at Good Shepherd for my last two years of high school, popular and smart, had given me hope that I had left my misfitting ways behind in my journey to the Promised Land of happy adulthood. Leaving my family and Ethiopia, and losing Mark on the way to college, drove me back into the wilderness.

I didn't know the names of rock stars or movie stars. I had never been to homecoming or a prom. Who was Howdy Doody? I'd never seen the Micky Mouse show. I sat, feeling lost, as my roommates laughed about their shared experiences.

"I don't know why you're so homesick all the time," one of my roommates said. "I went to summer camp every year and I never once cried." I gave up trying to explain how a small country in Africa could feel like home to me, and how far away from home I really was. I began to tell people I was from Des Moines, Iowa, where Grandma lived.

"It's time for my show," Grandma said the day after I got there on my Christmas break. She looked excited and a little shy, nestled down in a big, brown tufted swivel rocking chair. Her house was so small, a person had to slip sideways past the stove, between the chair and TV, between the bed and the dressing table, past the toilet into the shower. It was stuffy and warm, and smelled old, like the musty paper that lined the steamer trunks where our aunties stored linens in Maji.

I curled my feet up under me on the end of the couch near Grandma. I smiled reassuringly at her. Maybe I would catch up on TV, and have something to share with my roommates. The music started. *As the World Turns.* No, I was sure this was not what my roommates were watching. I still put my book away, and watched with Grandma every day.

Grandma fussed over me. *This isn't much of a life for an eighteen -year-old.*

Her pastor and his wife had hosted an exchange student from a Middle Eastern country. *Two lonely teenagers!* They came to pick me up, and in the basement family room, he put on a record. "Dance?" he said.

"I don't know how."

"I'll teach you." He laid the grasshopper arm of the turntable carefully down with the tiniest of scratching sounds. *Wise men say...the* voice crooned. The boy took me by the waist and shoulder. I tried to follow where he was going to move his feet next, and sway with him. He pulled me close. I smelled wool, sweat, and Aqua Velva. He pressed his groin into mine, hard against my pelvic bone. Beads of sweat lined my hairline. I held myself rigid and pulled away, my back against his hard arm muscles.

"It's okay, Grandma, I'd rather just be with you," I said when the pastor's wife called again.

Sunday brought the highlight of her week: *The Lawrence Welk Show.* I knew *The Lawrence Welk Show* from the year we lived in Boise. Jane, Joy, and I had pretended to be the Lemon Sisters, wearing our fluffiest slips under full skirts, and swishing them back and forth as we sang.

I embroidered a handkerchief for Grandma for Christmas. I read half the nights because I couldn't sleep. Then I slept restless and hot until late in the morning. When I thanked Grandma for supper, she said, "Such as it is." That was about all I could say about my life.

Back at college, second semester started. It turned out that I, who had never heard the words sorority, fraternity, or kegger, had chosen a party college, populated by a mixture of Chicago city kids and Illinois farm kids. I eddied into backwaters, as currents carried the rest of my classmates effortlessly along together. I didn't look foreign. I didn't sound foreign. But I couldn't find a way out of my lonely tunnel to where the others sat together in the sunlight.

I had never dated a boy I didn't already know, his hair askew at breakfast in the dining hall, cleaned up and sharp in the classroom, mesmerized, as I was, by the African insect chorus in the delicious, drifting, semi-boredom of weekend afternoons. I'd been popular. Jane and her roommates had told me I was pretty. Now, on Friday and Saturday nights, the dorm emptied out. I wandered the halls, looking for someone, anyone, to talk to.

One boy did finally ask me for a date that year. Michael Somebody. I thought maybe, maybe my losing streak was over. My heart flushed with hope when he asked me out again. Maybe...He took me back to his frat house after a movie, and we sat on a love seat in front of a crackling fire. *Maybe* he'd seen something in me to like. Maybe I could safely tell him who I really was.

"So...I grew up in Ethiopia," I said, smiling.

Michael stared at me. "Where?"

"Ethiopia. You know. Africa?"

"What in the world were you doing there?"

The crackling of the fire began to sound harsh, the heat oppressive. I was so, so sorry I'd brought it up. "My dad was a missionary." Why hadn't I stuck with Des Moines?

"What was he doing messing with other people's religion?" he asked.

Now the firelight on my face was unbearably hot. There was no way to explain about the Washa Wooha road, the mule shots, the evil eye, the *goom*. I'd been a fool.

Michael stretched and gave a fake yawn. "Well, it's getting late. I'd better get you back to your dorm."

I put on a dress as a matter of course on my first Sunday in

Monmouth and walked to Second Presbyterian Church at nine-thirty, the Sunday School hour. The man at the door greeted me with a look of panic. In a college town, I was apparently the only college student who had showed up at the church in quite a while. My *Diary of Private Prayer* sat, worn and full of childish prayer requests, in the dark at the bottom of my footlocker. I'd given up on figuring out Brother Lawrence's secrets. But I continued to creep quietly into church services. I clung to my hope that church would somehow, yet, give me the way to still myself and know that God was God.

By that time, the church that had sent my folks into the world as missionaries had begun the slide that no one has been able to explain or halt. In Germany and France, empty cathedrals are sold to museums, breweries and restaurants. Protestant churches in the US stumble on, struggling to keep up buildings that were meant to serve congregations four or five times their size. Friends in their seventies tell me they are the youth of their church; the death rate of church populations in 2015 was four times that of the general population. Sunday School classrooms that bulged with kids when we visited them on our furlough years now store stacks of child-sized furniture and old flannel story boards—Moses in the bulrushes, Jesus feeding the five thousand.

European post-modern philosophers suggest the credibility of the church was destroyed by the horror of the "Christian" nations of Europe slaughtering each other in two World Wars, the churches in Germany and Italy supporting brutal nationalism.

Of course, the Crusades, the greed and violence of the papacy in Rome, church-sponsored violence against "pagans" and "witches," against women, against reformers and Bible translators, against Jews, against the citizens of what they called the "dark continent," had already cast plenty of doubt on church credibility for anyone who wanted to think about it. But American Christians in the fifties and sixties, like my parents and teachers, hadn't wanted to think about it. They didn't see the murky marriage between power and spirituality that had given birth to our churches.

Life is so tenuous. Sooner or later we're all brought to our knees by sorrow or tragedy. Is it any wonder that we need to believe in something larger than ourselves to keep hope alive? Spiritual leaders make promises that can't be kept: *Faith in Jesus will protect you from illness and death; science will solve all your problems; learn not to desire and you will not suffer.* My son-in-law says, "At heart, we're all animists." By that he means we all look for something we can do to appease evil spirits roaming abroad.

The next year, Jane joined me at Monmouth. We both dressed up as we'd been trained to, and she joined me at Second Pres. Until one Communion Sunday, we missed each other and I slipped into the pew alone. I looked around at the middle-aged congregation. The women wore dresses in pale colors. The men wore suits. Sounds were muted. No one greeted or even looked at me. The organ began a prelude.

I stood and put my bulletin down on the pew cushion. I sidestepped out to the center aisle. Not looking to either side, not making a sound on the deep carpet, I walked out. I'd had it with taking communion alone.

Jane arrived at church after I left. She suffered through communion alone, and neither of us went back. I never said I left the church—I figured the church left me.

As the draft began that winter, and birth dates were read, I lay long into the night, listening. A future brother-in-law listened in Chicago to his birth date pulled out ninth. Paul from Schutz was thirty-sixth. Mark, in Ohio, number two hundred and forty-seventh. The church was making a loud noise about our long hair, short skirts, and sexual sins, but had nothing to say to us about our boys being randomly sucked off to Vietnam.

And in the US South, the church was justifying the unjustifiable. Hadn't we WASPS and WASCS learned anything about justice and mercy? The church was obsessed with private pietism (good behavior), and the Old Testament was out of style. No one was reading those prophets who ranted about justice. And no one was taking seriously that rabble-rouser Jesus, who had challenged the pietistic rituals of his day.

With Mary Travers and Cher, I stopped putting my hair in curlers every night. My hair grew long and my bangs grew out.

By my junior year, the college men were noticing me. It was worse than being invisible. I drifted, unmoored from all the tense teachings of my parents and teachers, into unhappy sexual relationships. I watched from the sidelines as the Vietnam War chaos unfolded. I wandered from one unsatisfying class to another, living with roommates who may have thought we were close. But how could we be close, if I never spoke of Ethiopia? Eventually, Jane and I roomed together. When I'm in a mood to wallow in regret, college is what I think about.

Dad had glowed when he hugged me after my valedictorian speeches in both eighth and twelfth grades. I knew he was proud that I was smart. But my smarts didn't produce a vision for my future—in me, in Dad, or in anyone else at Good Shepherd. Was the conservative religion at fault? Maybe it was just a sign of the times.

"Get a teaching certificate. A woman never knows," Dad had told me, as he brought me the big gray suitcase where I would pack all the worldly goods I would take with me for college. That was the only career advice I ever got.

I escaped Illinois to a five-month archeology program in Costa Rica. I thrived there. I learned Spanish on the hoof, and dug through fish bones, pottery shards, and shell fragments. Next, I signed up for a Washington DC program for art and political science majors—they needed warm bodies. I didn't know that Mark, now a poly sci major, was also on his way to DC to be an intern with an Ohio Representative.

# CHAPTER 27

The coincidence of Mark and me independently signing up for programs in DC seemed so unlikely that Mark believed God was giving him another chance. He wasn't going to blow it this time. First, he sent me flowers. Then he called.

I sat on the rough stones of our brownstone program residence. The weather was spring warm, the asphalt dappled by sun shining through chartreuse leaves. Mark came up the sidewalk in an army-surplus jacket and boots, his Cupid's bow lip now hidden under a mustache. His face looked pale and tight. He could hardly smile. My heart went out to the shy boy I'd known so well.

He rented a boat that day, and rowed me down the Potomac River. The peak of cherry-blossom season had passed, and pale pink petals lapped against the boat. The river smelled faintly of mud and of fish. I talked enough to put us both at ease.

The next weekend, I sat in the little glass phone booth in the living room of the brownstone room talking and laughing with Mark, who had called from a pay phone in his dorm at American University. After an hour, one of the boys in my program banged on the glass and scowled at me. "I'm expecting a call!" he shouted. I smiled and turned my back. There was no end of what Mark and I wanted to say to each other again. What we didn't need to say was even the word, *Ethiopia*.

When I got back to campus from DC, I was a senior. I was several credits short of a math major and no longer interested. I was short of a psych major. I'd been excited about anthropology until the anthropology professor Monmouth hired was a bore. My mish-mash of credits didn't add up to anything. Sinking back into my on-campus depression, I thought I should just drop out. I've forgotten why Dean Beherens called me to his office: *Let's see if we can't get you your degree.* He suggested a *topical major*, something Monmouth had designed to be with-it, relevant.

I was cynical about the dean's intervention with me—he just didn't want a good student dropping out and blotting Monmouth's statistics,

I told myself. That's all anybody ever wanted from me. Being a good girl. Now I have a more nuanced sense of what he did for me. Now I remember him with gratitude. A college degree has served me well.

The dean and I pored over my transcript, looking for any threads we could follow. Disillusioned with my own education, I was reading the thick *Crisis in the Classroom*. I signed up to spend the second half of my senior year in Chicago as an intern in Wonder, an alternative school within a Catholic girls' high school. With that I had a topic for my major: *Psychology and Educational Change*.

The program staff in Chicago welcomed me—they'd been missing a math teacher. Mark hitch hiked out from Ohio to see me every few weekends. Spring is the Windy City's best season. The dark clouds over my head broke up and my life felt *partly sunny* again.

Mark and I married at the end of July. Mom sent me a dress she made from Ethiopian fabric, green and white and silver, and I made a tunic for Mark to wear with his best moss-green cords. I arranged daisies and tiger lilies into a bouquet for myself that morning, while my sisters cleaned the house and baked a strawberry shortcake.

A dozen friends—the women in long loose shifts, the men in bell-bottoms—gathered around us under a weeping willow tree in the back yard. Summer insects hummed in the background. Jane, braless, with her long hair wound up on her head, sat on a stool with her guitar and sang. No sentimental song about the rapture of love for me, but St. Francis: *Make me an instrument of thy peace.* My years at Monmouth had only deepened the earnestness I inherited from Dad.

Jane had bought crab with the very last of our money, and served it on crackers. We laughed at the Matterhorn of shortcake, layered and covered with whipped cream. Joy and one of our professors opened a bottle of champagne. Jane's boyfriend passed a joint.

Mark got a part time job and I signed up to work for one hundred dollars a month in the Wonder program. Vatican II had opened up the Catholic Church, and I was among the first Protestants working in Catholic high schools. Mark and I covered housing by becoming dorm supervisors for the next crop of urban student teachers from small midwestern colleges like Monmouth. The program was housed in a former convent where the walls had been painted with layers and layers of glossy, dove-gray paint. The speckled linoleum floor had been waxed and re-waxed until the tiles along the edges had turned yellow. Down the hall, we cooked our meals in a kitchen full of big old commercial stoves and sinks. Gold flecks embedded the white counter tops edged with aluminum strips. The bedrooms smelled like dust of the ages.

Mark wired two single beds together for us, and I hung my clothes in what had been a nun's closet. There wasn't room for a bedside table, and I reverted to keeping my bedtime reading materials under my pillow. I loved this ascetic situation. No selling out to middle class respectability! The misery of college was behind me. I was an adult now. A wife. I had work that I believed would help tilt the world back toward justice.

The Wonder program occupied the back corner of the third floor. Our girls didn't wear the plaid skirts and navy sweaters of the girls downstairs. Wonder staff didn't wear dresses or suit coats. We all wore the t-shirt and jeans uniform. We talked about freedom. Relevance. Empowerment. We talked about what was wrong with mainstream values. With the powers.

On my way upstairs one day, I joined three of my students in the hall. A nun stuck her head out a classroom door. "Girls! Get upstairs before I give you demerits." We laughed and ran together to the safety of Wonder. I didn't look any older than my students. I'd finally found my people.

A Wonder colleague I'll call Jen taught history and philosophy. She had the girls reading *Siddhartha*. Their discussions overflowed class time and into the lounge—Jen sat on one of the donated brown couches, its legs unscrewed. The students sat cross-legged or lay flat on their backs, staring at the ceiling. They waxed passionate—*if a tree falls in the forest but no one is there to hear it, does it make a sound?*

My answer to that, as I half-listened, prepping Algebra I and Geometry lesson plans, was, *Who cares?* A tree falls, a tree falls. Between her classes, Jen played her guitar and sang Cat Stevens songs with the girls: *I'm being followed by a moon-shadow.* I wished I was popular like she was. But I was more reserved, more businesslike. There was nothing to sing about in Algebra I.

Halfway through the first semester, Jen disappeared.

At the end of that week, Wonder staff gathered, sitting on the legless tufted couches or cross-legged on the floor: Timothy; a science student teacher; a part time English teacher from downstairs; a retired nun who acted as our director and was as radical as the rest of us; and me.

Timothy pulled on his dark brown mustache and said, "Are all the girls gone?" He got up and closed the door. He sat down again. He sighed. "Jen had a nervous breakdown. I visited her in the hospital yesterday. She doesn't want the girls to know."

I had envied Jen. The guitar. Cat Stevens. The cluster of adoring students.

Any psychologist would tell you: whatever happened with confident, beloved Jen, don't disappear her from her students with no explanation. Don't hire someone more reserved and more business-like in her place. But we were so young. Self-help books hadn't been invented. Wonder immediately hired me.

The girls took all that talk about empowerment and made it their own. We had been the generation who said, *Don't trust anyone over thirty!* We, who had seemed so radical and cool to the girls just the week before—we, who were only in our twenties—were now the ones who couldn't be trusted. And in particular, I was the snake in Eden. By the end of the month, at the top of students' list of demands, was that Wonder fire me. I left that Forum meeting trembling.

Night after night, in the corner room Mark and I used as a sitting room, I told him every mean thing the girls said to me. I trailed behind him down the wide hall to the chrome and Formica kitchen where he pulled the tuna noodle or mac and cheese casseroles he'd cooked out of the oven. Oblivious to the smells—cheese, fish, the student teachers' toasted sandwiches or bologna—or the other conversations around us, I went on and on. What I said back. What I wished I'd said.

I trailed behind Mark again, back to our corner room, through the dim hallway. Ignoring the sweet smelling smoke that crept out from under a student's bedroom door. Into the evening, Mark stood at our buffet, his back to me, building a turntable and amplifier from kits. He said, *Hmmm*, every so often so I would know he was still doing his best to listen.

When I finished, I started over. To this day, I can't listen to Cat Stevens.

We planned a Wonder staff retreat in a cabin on Lake Michigan for a snowy weekend, to figure out what to do. Call meetings with parents? Put girls on probation? Kick some of them off the program? Disband Wonder? We were ready to consider just about anything. Of course, telling them Jen's secret was not on the table. I also remember it this way: what to do about the girls' irrationality was how we framed it; rallying around me and helping me cope never came up. Did no one notice how I was struggling? Did I hold myself at a distance and cut them off before they could even reach out? I must have put on a good face. I'd always tried to be right. To be above reproach. To earn approval and assume it was love. I knew nothing about getting help.

Friday came, and I breathed a prayer of thanks for getting through one more week. Twenty-five feet from the front entrance of the school, Jen's number one defender came through. A plain girl, she wore a black and white knit cap over sandy hair that managed to look the same color as her face. She twisted her mouth into a sneer when she saw me. "Hypocrite," she said. "Power-hungry hypocrite."

I started screaming at her. Right there in front of the principal's office. In front of everyone on their way out the door for the weekend. My rational brain shut down completely. I didn't care who heard me or what they thought. I had no idea ten seconds later what I had said.

Telling Mark about it, over the rattle of our bug on the way to the cabin in Michigan, I started to cry. I cried so often during those years after I left Ethiopia. I'd failed to thrive in college. Now I was failing adulthood. Mark had nothing to say. Eyes on the road, he drove us through grimy, run-down Gary, Indiana. I progressed from crying to sobbing.

Mark carried a bag in each hand into the cabin, and hustled me up the stairs to our room. I fell face down onto the bed. My tears wet the colorful quilt, with its puckers and stitches. Timothy and the others had gathered around a potluck supper in the dining room. Their voices trailed up the stairs with the scent of warmed up casseroles.

"Do you want to eat?" Mark asked.

I stumbled to the bathroom and splashed freezing water on my face. But then I pictured walking into the dining room, everyone looking at my swollen, red eyes, wondering. Or worse, politely not looking at me. Hands trembling, I undressed and turned on the shower. Hot water pelted my face. I could hardly breathe. I slumped against the shower stall. My head knocked against the tiles. Something solid. Bump. Bump.

"What are you doing?" Mark asked.

Bump. Bump. Bump.

# CHAPTER 28

Mark turned off the water and pulled me out of the shower. I hid my face in my hands. Tears dripped between my fingers. He wrapped a towel around my shoulders, and another around my long hair. He patted me dry like a child.

"Climb in," he said, and held my jeans for me.

Mark crept me down the stairs. The fake fur around my hood hid my face as we went by the dining room door. He led me by the arm down to the dark, hissing lake. I kept stumbling. I couldn't see.

Mark didn't say anything. He walked me through the snow.

Maybe it was the cold that finally stopped my crying. Mark didn't turn us around until I was calm. Heading back, the snow sparkled blue-white ahead of us in the moonlight. Both of us shivered. We stepped back into our own footprints. The lake lapped up and turned the edge between water and snow to crystal. Mark held my arm firmly, through the silvery snow, through the gloom, along the lake's gurgling edge.

After that weekend in Michigan, Mark said, "How about I move us next year?" He had always wanted to work on a farm. The school year whimpered to a close, and we moved to Hills, Minnesota: last town west before South Dakota; last town south before Iowa; population 463.

Our brief sojourn in Hills, on the Jacobson Place, spanned a summer in which the herbicide failed and Mark worked sun up to sundown chopping pigweed out of the soybeans by hand. I spent my days in the hundred-year-old, two-story farmhouse with tall front windows, surrounded by giant trees to keep it cool in the sweltering summer. The kitchen sat on a slab, added later, with lowering ceilings and insufficient light. We got permission to buy new floor tile. I covered the pitted linoleum counter tops with orange contact paper. I spent all day every day alone and dull with depression.

Moses struck a blow for his people and killed an Egyptian slave driver. It didn't set his people free, it got him exiled. Years later, he was still herding his father-in-law's sheep like a teenage boy. I had failed just as badly at setting the world right. Now, having Mark's dinner on the table on time was all the world asked of me.

Mark came in from the fields at noon, exhausted and grimy. He splashed in the bathroom for several minutes, and when he came out, the dust coating the hair on his arms was gone from his elbows down.

Our dim kitchen, tilting as though it wanted to fall off the back of the house, smelled fragrant with my meatloaf. Green Jell-o with cottage cheese and pineapple jiggled on our plates when he bumped the table leg.

I let my hair curtain my face. Tears ran secretly down my cheeks. Mark was working so hard. There wasn't anything he could do for me anyway. He ate as fast as he could. "Thanks," he said, and pushed back. In the living room, he lay down on the cool floor. He slept for a few minutes. When he trudged back out to the fields, I went back to bed.

Just before Christmas, the Jacobson Place burned down. In Chicago for Jane's wedding, Mark and I were left with the clothes in our overnight bags. We looked at each other and tried to think of anything we would miss—our couch? His turntable and amp? Our dishes? We reverted to missionary asceticism, to gratitude—*the Lord giveth, the Lord taketh away, blessed be the name of the Lord.* All our things could be replaced.

We drove our bug back to Hills in a snowstorm that overwhelmed the tiny windshield wipers. Mark sat forward, gripping the steering wheel and peering out the small, clear delta.

In below zero weather, we wandered around the site, laughing and stamping to keep our toes from turning numb. In the bitter cold, there was no smell on the ash pit that had been our home and belongings. Trees stood, winter-bare and scorched on the side toward the house, in a circle around us. The fire had burned so hot, there weren't even cinders. The only thing we recognized were the gears of Mark's bike and the hide-a-bed mechanism that had fallen through the floor into the basement. Something aluminum had melted itself around two square iron nails like a sculpture. We saved that as a memento, and said good-bye to the farmers who had hired him, worked him to the bone, and had hinted that they wouldn't keep him on through the winter. I said a delighted good-bye to my second career attempt: hired hand's wife—lower in status than the hired hand. And much lonelier.

We accepted my teacher friend Timothy's invitation to move

into the narrow, four-bedroom apartment he and his wife Ellen were renting in an old Chicago duplex. We bought a bed. I got a part time teaching job. Mark enrolled in electronics school.

Mom still wrote her weekly family letters from Ethiopia. I snatched them off the hall table as soon as I saw the familiar blue air form rimmed with red hatch marks. I slit them open carefully, because Mom filled every centimeter of available space. I scanned through her breezy social and political commentary on life in Ethiopia. Struggled to read the fuzzy carbon. Stared, unsatisfied, at the *Love, Mom* she scribbled into the margin. I was nothing more than part of her American public.

It was 1973. When Emperor Haile Selassie became emperor in 1930, he had been a visionary and a modernizer. Only slightly over five feet tall, he was a man of dignity. He had involved himself in all the daily details of leadership. He had promoted African self-rule decades before colonial rule unraveled in the rest of the continent. He had started the Organization for African Unity, in whose hall shone a full-wall stained glass window—the peoples of Africa marching, led by Ethiopians dressed in the ceremonial white dress of the Ethiopian people, colored borders gleaming, holding a huge torch of liberation. The first major stained glass art installation by an African.

But now, Haile Selassie was in his eighties. He completely misunderstood the winds that were stirring. His medieval autocracy had been untouched by the Neway brothers' socialist reproaches during the coup. His version of land reform after the coup had been to officially annex Eritrea and give land grants to loyal military and police officials.

As 1974 dawned, and Mark and I settled back into life in Chicago, the non-commissioned army officers' water pump broke at a camp in a small, dry corner of Ethiopia. The officers wouldn't share theirs. Soldiers mutinied. The functionary sent to settle the problem was made to drink from the soldiers' contaminated water supply. When he got sick, the officers were forced to share their pump.

And word got out that the soldiers had not been punished. Within the month, the Air Force (now an efficient body of pilots trained in the US) mutinied. Then the soldiers in Asmara. Then at the headquarters in Addis Ababa. The issues were all economic: living conditions, pay, food, and clean water. Snowballing mutinies began to give the army a sense of its muscle.

His Majesty shuffled cabinet ministers around. He appointed a new Prime Minister, who promptly squandered good will by announcing a fifty percent increase in the price of fuel. Taxi drivers, who carry people to and from the corners of Addis Ababa like a swarm of ants, raised a collective howl of despair. OPEC had raised oil prices—eighty percent in one quarter—but HIM backed off the increase to twenty-five percent.

The new Prime Minister doubled down with his tin ear for the people. And why wouldn't he? In Imperial Ethiopia, no one had ever worried about being popular. He announced that teachers would work forty-eight weeks per year. Schools would run morning and afternoon shifts. Class size would jump to sixty-seven.

The Ethiopian Teachers' Union called a strike. University students took to the streets, as though the past fourteen years had been prac-tice for that moment. Taxi drivers jumped in, and together they shut down Addis Ababa.

Eastern European countries crowed that the Ethiopian people's "creeping coup" had begun. In her letters, Mom took a patronizing tone about Ethiopian Socialism. The US couldn't possibly lose the Cold War in Ethiopia. Stalin was gone, Mao was gone. How grim could socialism possibly get in backwater Ethiopia?

And truly, in rural areas, peasants farmed with oxen, as they still do forty years later. They harvested with scythes and threw their grain into the air so the wind would carry the chaff away. They ate what they grew. Only a few dollars passed through their hands, only enough to buy soap and salt, and in a good year, pencils and notebooks for their children. In their world, God had ordained His Majesty to rule.

In Ethiopia, the brightest students from every corner of the country rose through the education system. Sagu from Maji, for example, was now in Addis Ababa University. These children of peasants who passed the School Leaving Exam went to university, their education paid for by the government. When they graduated, they would be guaranteed bureaucratic jobs for life, part of Ethiopia's army of well-educated civil servants. These elite young people didn't watch cattle, they watched TV. They drank Coke. They listened to BBC. They studied economics.

They discussed Marx.

The year 1974 saw another year of failed rains in Northern Ethiopia. I heard more about that in Chicago than Mom and Dad heard in Ethiopia, because His Majesty's advisors shielded him from news of the drought, averted their own eyes, and censored news from foreign journalists. When I was a kid, the starving children of Bangladesh were invoked to make us clean our plates. Now the people of my beautiful Ethiopia stared, gaunt and big eyed, from the pages of *Time* magazine.

Eventually, when His Majesty visited the North, where a sea of devastated farmers were on the move in search of food, he had nothing to say to them. He met with local officials and only gave them the bizarre advice to get their arrears taxes up to date.

This botched response to the drought is what finally brought the two worlds of Ethiopia together. E-TV aired a British documentary of the famine intercut with shots of lavish feasts in the palace, liveried servants feeding slabs of meat off silver trays to His Majesty's favorite dogs and pet lions.

A shadowy group of low-ranking officers called the Derg had been operating behind the scenes for some years. Now they called in their bet. On September 12th, Derg member Number Eleven was chosen to read the edict deposing Emperor Haile Selassie. The papers rattled in his shaking hands. Soldiers in the room wept so violently they had to leave the room.

His Majesty listened with dignity. Then he said it's the responsibility of an emperor to stand by his people through good times and bad. If this decree was for the greater good of the Ethiopian people, he would comply.

He was escorted to the door. As he came to Number Eleven, he paused. "Why are you holding your gun like that?"

Number Eleven stammered. "It is easier to hold like this."

"I think it is easier to shoot like that," His Majesty said, and swept on.

The emperor had ridden triumphantly into Addis Ababa after WWII in the back of an Alpha Romeo. Now a non-commissioned officer drove him to house arrest in a baby blue VW bug. A gaggle of young men followed, shouting, "Thief Tafari!" Were they common people of Addis Ababa who had read the newspapers accusing him of hiding Ethiopia's wealth in Swiss bank accounts? Or were they soldiers, commanded to appear in civilian clothes and manufacture a ground-swell?

Eastern European leaders hailed the next step in Ethiopia's "blood-less revolution." Ethiopia's Marxism was a textbook case.

In the summer of 1975, Wonder staff invited me back to teach. The program was moving out of the Catholic school and into a storefront on Wilson Avenue. Some of the girls who had been so angry at me had graduated; others seemed to have forgotten that I was the source of all their pain. I felt wisps of hope for myself again.

Mark, Timothy, Ellen, and I found a food co-op, and a store in our neighborhood that sold whole grains and legumes out of bins. Then

Timothy discovered Movement for a New Society (MNS), a cluster of communes in Philadelphia. We ordered their course called Macro Analysis: economic injustice, power inequities, racism, sexism—everything was interrelated, they said. It made sense.

Mine had been the generation of the Civil Rights Movement. We were the kids Chicago police beat and arrested at the Democratic Convention in 1968. Ours were the boys drafted for a war that seemed more and more pointless. We were the kids shot at Jackson and Kent State Universities. *Silent Spring* had been published, the first cry against pollution, and Lake Erie had been pronounced dead. Now we were wading through the morass of the Nixon years. The cultural disenchantment made a convenient narrative for me. I didn't have to explain why I was unhappy. I could let politics cover my unhappiness living in the US ever since—well, really, ever since that lonely year in Pasadena. In MNS, I was going to be a modern-day prophet, like those who railed at Israel for oppressing the orphan and widow.

We started talking with another couple I'll call Avril and Roxanne—maybe we could buy a triplex together. Finding friends had been so long in coming. I was giddy at the thought of having a community.

MNS came out of the Quaker Action Group that had organized Vietnam War protests. So we had *clearness* meetings with Avril and Roxanne. Meetings to *discern*. We told our life stories. We got excited about pooling our appliances and furniture, moving into a struggling neighborhood, making our lives count. Timothy and I waxed passionate about our storefront school. Even our collaborative structure was revolutionary. Next we would start an alternative college.

Avril and Roxanne were psychiatric social workers. They had two boys. In the months we talked about living together, they got pregnant, lost the baby, and adopted a three-month-old from Guatemala. Roxanne was going to change the US policies toward Guatemala as soon as baby Anna got old enough.

No one knew Avril's dreams. He missed most of our clearness sessions. When he did attend, he rocked silently in a wooden rocking chair, stroking his strawberry blond beard and the mustache that hid his mouth.

"What about you, Avril?" I asked one evening.

Half his answer went into his beard. "Social change, mumble, mumble. Reaction formation." He chuckled and rocked. I looked at the others, to see if they'd understood. Timothy picked lint off his flannel shirt. Roxanne's straight hair curtained over the baby's head as she tipped the bottle higher. We wouldn't have recognized a discernment if we'd had one.

The day after Thanksgiving, the six of us stood outside a house on Malden Street, a house with square pillars holding up a wide, low-browed porch. Stained glass lights flanked a gigantic oak door. I took my shivers, in the wet winter wind off the lake, for shivers of excitement. *Georgian Mansion*, the real estate printout said. Our faces were alight.

# CHapTer 29

The real estate agent arrived. We clustered behind him as he rang the doorbell. We trooped into the house, to the smell of over-cooked cabbage. The entryway stretched longer and wider than our apartment living rooms, and a staircase covered in red carpeting, frayed on the front edge of each step, soared to the second floor. A floor-to-ceiling stained glass window on the landing offset the cabbage. Colored glass sparkled with winter sunlight.

In a sitting room to the left of the front door, brass harp sconces shone on both sides of a huge mirror. In the dining room, mahogany beams. A chandelier with brass and green marbled glass dimly lit the room and reflected off the stained glass doors of a built-in china cabinet at one end. A butler's pantry led to the kitchen.

Roxanne tucked her straight dark hair behind her ear as she leaned toward Ellen and me. "This kitchen has a lot of features...missing," she whispered.

The house had been built by a doctor who'd kept his patients right there. Each bedroom on the second floor held an antique pedestal sink. A man named Drago owned it now. His grown son and family lived with him, and boarders rented three of the eight bedrooms. The third-floor rooms, with dormer ceilings and a steep back stairway off the kitchen, had obviously housed the servants. In a house like this, I thought, we really could change the world.

By the time we walked out of the house, we were clear. We had discerned. The six of us had fallen in love. With the house. With the selves we saw living in that house. With our first communal family joke about the kitchen. With belonging to each other, battling injustice, setting the world straight. Together.

Mark and Avril tore out the old linoleum in the kitchen with the features missing. When they were done sanding, the maple floor glowed. We didn't have money to replace the tin sink cabinet, but we didn't believe in spending money on things like cabinets, anyway. And who cared, with a floor like that.

The two families would take the second-floor bedrooms. Mark and

I helped them hang wall paper, paint trim, and scrub Ajax around every white octagonal tile in the huge bathroom.

Mark and I took one of the third-floor rooms, up the back stairs. A charming dormer ceiling met the carved headboard Mark found in an alley and restored. My spider plants arched in the window alcove and African violets bloomed shades of purple, pink, and lavender on the windowsill. We didn't need curtains.

We started our communal social change work with ourselves. Simple lives. Macro Analysis. House meetings on Mondays. Communal suppers. *Diet for a Small Planet. The More with Less Cookbook.* Vegetarian meals cooked from scratch in that honey-colored kitchen. Each couple would run the kitchen for a week.

Almost immediately, Avril stopped coming to house meetings.

"He thought he'd be the big Papa of everyone," Roxanne said. "If he can't, he won't have anything to do with us." No one said anything more about it. No one said anything when Avril started missing suppers. When it was their turn to cook, Roxanne struggled with three kids and supper for ten. Timothy pitched in. Roxanne left clean-up and Avril did it sometime late at night.

By that time, depression had swamped me again. I made it to the end of the school year and collapsed. All I knew to say to Mark was, "I'm not doing well." In my family, not doing well had never been allowed. But I didn't have to tell my family, they were halfway around the world. Every week I skimmed those fuzzy letters from Mom. I looked for some reminder of who I'd been, where I'd come from. Some explanation for the sad woman I had become. That place, those people, even Mom and Dad, seemed out of another lifetime. I no longer belonged in Ethiopia. But I didn't seem to belong in Chicago, either.

Mark framed an Ethiopian Tourist Organization poster, and hung it on the wall at the bottom of our bed. *Thirteen Months of Sunshine*; the green-yellow-red tail fan of Ethiopian Airlines; a girl in beads with a gourd on her head looking straight at the camera, calm and self-assured.

I discovered a row of Doris Lessing's books in the dusty stacks of our Chicago neighborhood library. She wrote that Africa is like a relapsing fever in the blood, one that has no cure, but flares up from time to time for the rest of a person's life. I read from one end of the row to the other. She was aspirin for me. She brought my fevers down.

Timothy, before he'd become a teacher, had been a pastor. He suggested we start a house church, to make our faith part of our radical lifestyle. We recruited two other couples and met every other Wednesday night in the Music Room with the brass sconces. There was no altar. No flowers. No organ. No singing. The only stained glass was Edwardian. Stripped of ritual of any kind, nothing about our meetings suggested worship. We discussed theology or a Bible passage. The conversations wandered, unfocused.

One week, sitting on the carpet, smelling feet and dust from the light green shag rug, I asked how redemption works. Sacrifice—the blood of the lamb—salvation through Jesus? This had been my sticking point since I had asked theological questions of Dad on the jute and foam rubber couch in Maji so many years before. Michael tried as Dad had to answer. I leaned forward. My anxiety increased with every answer he gave. I kept saying, "Yes, but *how*?"

Suddenly I stopped. I would never fully understand, unless God was no more complex than my own so often overwhelmed brain. I just needed to walk humbly with my God, as prophet Micah said. To embrace the unknown. My life was no longer steeped in hymns, but where they left off, the Beatles picked up: *Let it be.* Even if the darkness around me sometimes felt as thick as it had felt in the bat cave when Dad turned off the flashlight. At that moment, on the dusty green shag rug, I made room for mystery. I was no closer to answers, but I stopped thrashing.

Decades later, after Dad died, I took a sabbatical. My spiritual director gave me a book called *Centering Prayer and Inner Awakening*. I began to meditate. Finally, the spiritual discipline I had been searching for so many years before with John Baillie at Good Shepherd, Brother Lawrence in Pasadena, the house church in Malden.

Until then, I had prayed like an anxious child clutching at a mother's apron. Now for twenty minutes every day, I felt like the Psalmist: *I do not occupy myself with things too great and too marvelous for me. I have calmed and quieted my soul.* Every thought did not need to be thought. Every word did not need to be spoken. I began to recognize guidance. To feel reassurance. I learned to listen to something I could not hear.

But a thirty-year journey still lay between that moment of accepting the *cloud of unknowing* in the house church and my discovery of Centering Prayer. I was willing to let go of *knowing* in Malden, but I was still an anxious, uprooted soul.

I said I was going to organize demonstrations against US support of Pinochet, but I couldn't leave our third-floor bedroom. When the gritty heat of summer days woke me, I rolled over and sank back into groggy oblivion. Some days I lay and stared at the Ethiopian girl in the poster. Surely I could be more like her. If I tried harder.

Starting a kitchen duty week, I ricocheted around the kitchen, getting more and more tense. Cooking made me anxious—watching more than one pot at a time. And the kitchen was chaos. Pans were piled willy-nilly. Utensils were tossed in random places, never the same one day to the next, in our kitchen with so much storage missing.

As soon as we had all gathered around the big table and had blessed the rice and lentils, I said, "I have something I want to talk about at our house meeting."

"Avril's here for supper tonight," Timothy said. "Why don't you go ahead?"

Avril didn't look up from slapping rice on plates, one for each of the boys and a pile for himself. Words disappeared into his beard. We were used to disappearing words from Avril. No one even asked *What?*

"Here's the thing," I said. "We spend so much time looking for stuff in the kitchen. It gets crazy. Nothing's ever in the same place." The dark windows behind Mark and me let in a chill.

"Some of the Life Center houses put labels on their drawers and cabinets," Timothy said.

Avril, across the table said, "Control. That's what this is about."

I looked up.

The tines of his fork pointed smack between my eyebrows. He enunciated clearly. "There are terms for people like you." He didn't blink. Strawberry blond eyelashes fringed his eyes.

I couldn't look away. Blood fizzed across my shoulders and up the back of my neck.

Avril broke his stare, wadded up his cloth napkin and slammed it onto his plate of rice. He stood so suddenly, his chair tipped backward in slow motion. Timothy caught it halfway down. One of Avril's shoulders crashed into the door jam to the kitchen. His work boots slammed up the back stairs.

I looked at my plate. My knuckles ached from holding my hands so tightly together on my lap.

Ellen brought us out of our spell. "Why are you the one he attacks?"

I shook my head.

"You're so easy to get mad at," Roxanne said, balancing Anna on her knees. "I don't blame him. I feel the same way sometimes."

Mark was his silent self at the table. In bed, he pulled me close along his warm side. He patted my back. My tears puddled in the hollow between his neck and shoulder. I felt sick with shame. Why was

I so hard to live with? The despair I'd been feeling that summer swelled up like a tsunami. Mark's breathing evened and slowed. His arm fell away.

I lay in the darkness, alone. Something deep inside had fallen apart when I left Ethiopia. I thought my new home would be in the Malden community, but it wasn't. I could be cut out of the herd.

Mark and I wandered in our American wilderness, not for forty years, but for too long. We worked. We made money—but not much. Mark started remodeling apartment buildings with Avril. I clung to my dreams of bringing peace and justice in the world. I got curious forty years later, and googled MNS. We have a page in Wikipedia: *members were significantly influenced by a variety of anarchist titles published in the 1970s.* Yeah. That was us. I attended MNS leadership training based on those anarchist writings at the Life Center. But when it came to putting social change theory into practice, I floundered as though I really was walking through desert sand.

Then, unexpectedly, I got pregnant in 1976. My belief that I had to earn my space on earth, to pay with good works for the air I breathed, evaporated. I was participating in a miracle. I was doing something really radical—renewing the human race, betting on hope that the world would go on. The feel-good hormones flooded my system. Not a lasting solution, but what a relief.

Mark and I counted our savings and bought tickets for Ethiopia. *I want to be a daughter once more before I become a mother*, I wrote on a blue aerogram to Mom.

# CHAPTER 30

By the time Mark and I went back to Ethiopia together, His Majesty had died. The Derg announced he'd died of natural causes, being eighty-three. He was not laid out in state. He was not given a funeral. No one in Ethiopia dared to mourn. No one in Jamaica mourned either— the secrecy of his death, the fact that the public did not see his body, fed the Rasta mythology: their African messiah had risen straight to heaven.

It wasn't until later that a military underling confessed that he'd been commanded to suffocate His Imperial Majesty with a pillow and bury him by the back fence. His body was exhumed in 1992, from under a slab of concrete or under a latrine, depending on your sources. His body was held while the courts quibbled about the circumstances of his death. Finally, in 2000, the Ethiopian Orthodox Church got tired of waiting for the courts and held an imperial-worthy funeral for Haile Selassie's body. Bob Marley's wife Rita and other prominent Rastafarians attended, but most believers still maintain that the Lion of the Tribe of Judah lives on, an immortal deity.

But that was years away. From Chicago's gritty snow in December 1976, I emerged into dry season Ethiopia, to the kind of Christmas I'd grown up with: clear hot days, clear crisp nights and roses in bloom. Not even the drift toward socialism could change the sensory welcome of Addis Ababa: intense mountain sun warm on my skin at 8,000 feet; thin highland air, at first feeling so inadequate in my lungs; the farm smell of dust, donkeys and sheep on the streets; the incense of eucalyptus fires and coffee roasting; *berbere* spicing the air and tingling my nostrils; women's startlingly white national dress, with gauzy *netellas* resting lightly on their hair. I reveled in the music of Amharic—explosives popped in the back of the throat and on the tip of the tongue. The "r" rolled lavishly. The rhythm of unaccented words lilted. My senses said I was home.

Dad sat at the table with Mark and me to catch us up on Ethiopian politics as Mom cleared the dishes and stacked them for her kitchen worker to wash. The week Haile Selassie was deposed, university

164

students had voted with their bodies, the only votes Ethiopians had, in demonstrations calling for social security and minimum wages.

The Derg answered, Absolutely not: security forces fired on the demonstration and killed several students.

"What's *Derg* mean?" I asked.

"It's Ge'ez," Dad said. "It means committee." A secret committee of 180 non-commissioned officers. After that demonstration, the Derg declared a state of emergency and disappeared trade unionists, teachers and students. Ethiopian socialism might be just a mask for a totalitarian face.

Derg sloganeers shouted. "Land to the Tiller!" as they announced land reform; "Labor is Supreme!" to combat a deep-seated cultural obsession with status; "Ethiopia *Tikedem!*" Ethiopia First, ironically echoing Mussolini's *Sempre Avanti Italia*.

Ethiopians love political jokes: *President Brezhnev of Russia and President Carter come on a state visit to Ethiopia. A Derg official meets them at the airport, and the three limousines drive down Bole Road toward the palace. At Revolution Square, the Russian limo signals left and turns left. The American limo signals right and turns right.*

*The Ethiopian limo driver, in a panic, says, "Min yeshal-al? What shall I do?"*

*A calm voice comes from the back seat. "Signal left. Turn right."*

Propagandists borrowed more words from Ge'ez for Marx-speak. Dad's high cheekbones bunched as he translated for me: revolutionary from the old verb *to defy*. A reactionary as one-who-walks-backwards. Broad masses as *sefiw hizb*, wide peoples, running dogs of the capitalists as *capitalist buchilla*, puppy dogs, and an unpronounceable word for socialism: *hibretesebawinet*, the equality of mankind.

Ever a word lover, a culture lover, I couldn't get enough.

The Derg divided Addis Ababa into *kebelles*, neighborhood associations. Small business owners, teachers and students were banned from *kebelle* leadership—to keep bourgeois and reactionary elements from infiltrating, the Derg said. It placed its bet instead on young men who had flocked to the city looking for a better life. What Marx would have called the lumpen proletariat, what Ethiopians called *balegay*, or hicks, rose into leadership all over the city.

As Mom and I got out of the car in the *piassa*, boys with trays hanging by dirty twine from their necks ran up. They waved Kleenex packets and Chicklets in my face. I shook my head. "Yankee go home!" one of the boys said.

"Whoa," I said to Mom. "What happened to *fereni, fereni?*"

Mom chose one boy out of the crowd to guard the car. When we came back, he was rubbing it down with a filthy rag in hopes of a few more centimes in tip.

"*Tew, tew,* stop!" Mom said, but it was too late. She ran her fingers over fine new scratches cross-hatching the hood. The crowd of boys had waited for us, and now they all reached their hands out, shouting and shoving. She dropped coins in the hands of the boy with the rag. We dived into the car as a fist fight broke out.

"The next generation of *kebelle* leadership," Mom said, and her dimples punctuated the smile she flashed me as she backed out.

We drove to the grocery store, through what had been the Square of the Cross, where Orthodox Church festivals drew tens of thousands on holy days. Now it was Revolution Square. On the south side of the wide intersection, faces of Marx, Engels, and Lenin glared down at us from a huge billboard.

Mom's kitchen worker had chopped onions, left carrot sticks in a bowl, and water ready to boil. Mom bustled around getting supper ready, just as she had in Maji. Instead of wood smoke, the kitchen smelled slightly of propane gas exhaust. Out on the street, mega-phones blared.

"They're reminding the *kebelles* to send their quotas of demonstra-tors to Revolution Square tomorrow for a spontaneous demonstration," Mom said. "Some spontaneous demonstrations are more spontaneous than others." She gave an ironic twist to her scarlet lips.

A few weeks later, the *kebelle* at the mission station in Dembi Dollo announced that the wide-peoples of Ethiopia were going to take over the hospital where Mark's dad had been the doctor—one of two hospitals within several hundred miles. They took the only doctor hostage. Dad packed up quickly, sat all day in a gas line to fill the mission vehicle, and drove down.

When he got back and told us the stories over supper, he looked wan. He kept shaking his head. Every fifteen miles, militia lowered eucalyptus pole road blocks. They elbowed for their chance to frisk the *fereni.* The business end of Kalashnikov rifles waved wildly as they pawed through Dad's suitcase. Ethiopia *tikedem.*

Thousands of leaflets appeared in Addis Ababa one morning: the new government is fascist, the army out of line, signed, Ethiopian People's Revolutionary Party. No one knew who EPRP was. Security forces and police shot teenagers for shouting slogans. They lashed out at university students, who had sung, *Like Ho Chi Minh and Che Guevara, oh ye rebels, go to the jungle to lead the struggle.*

Dad got news every day from street news sources; every night from BBC and Voice of America.

A Derg member, Major Mengistu Haile Mariam, made a bid for power. The Derg sidelined Mengistu, reorganized, and elevated the popular General Tafari Bante. To widespread relief.

Then one morning, the sounds of vehicles; of soft city bird chatter; of people walking and visiting together through the neighborhoods; of donkeys clip-clopping by; of sheep running by to market, looking fearful as sheep do, with their droopy ears and tails—these familiar sounds were interrupted by the sounds of big guns at the palace. The city turned into one big surround-sound stereo system tuned to Radio Ethiopia.

*A coup. Mengistu Haile Mariam, shot. No. Yes.*

And then Mengistu's own voice rose in flowery high Amharic. He shouted victory over the reverse-walking *adharie*s who had threatened to turn back the people's *abiot*. Traitor Tafari Bante was dead. "Ethiopia *tikedem!*"

The real story came out much later. During a meeting of the Derg, Mengistu had nodded to his cronies. They rose and walked out. Security guards opened fire from the perimeter of the room. When the massacre was over, Mengistu had them go on shooting to make it appear that a fierce struggle was taking place. He sent conflicting announcements to Radio Ethiopia, then stepped grandly into his role as the conquering hero, reassuring his anxious subjects that their revolution was safe in his good hands.

Colonel Mengistu Haile Mariam. His name meant The Government by the Power of Mary. He had transformed the military junta into a dictatorship, just as the EPRP predicted.

Silence settled all over the city. The fatalism Ethiopians know so well says, *The sun that rises tomorrow will be our sun. The government that rules tomorrow will be our government.* It is not for common people to control the sun or the government; their place is to submit. But submission doesn't rule out satire.

*One Ethiopian says to the other, "Have you heard? During Russia's bloodless revolution, fifty million people were killed."*

*"Weygudie!" the other man laments. "Where will Ethiopia find the other twenty million?"*

But the revolution had not yet changed my experience of being an

American in Ethiopia. As a child, when I got irritated by people staring or shouting, Dad got irritated at me. "Ignore them if they bother you," he'd bark. I found that worked as well for socialist harassment as it had for curiosity.

Mark put himself to work on the mission compound where we'd been teenagers together. The ubiquitous fix-it problems were his specialty, and he thrived on the appreciation he earned. I joined Dad and his Ethiopian office staff for tea break every morning. They talked and laughed together. In the mellow second trimester of my pregnancy, I sipped sweet cinnamon-and-clove spiced tea and let their Amharic and English mixture wash over me. The children of Israel, when they crossed the Jordan River and found themselves in the land of their father Abraham, couldn't have felt more blessed than I did.

Rhetoric about evil aristocrats increased. A wealthy Ethiopian friend brought her jewelry over one night and asked Mom and Dad to hide it for her. They worried for her safety, but not their own. Maybe it was the legacy of His Majesty's policy of forgiveness toward the Italian settlers after World War II that made Ethiopia still feel so safe to us.

Or maybe Mom and Dad's comfort in the middle of revolution was the next iteration of the blithe optimism—or was it faith?—that had served them so well in Maji. Taking my cues from them, as I always had, I felt as relieved to be home as if I were back in my idealized childhood, even as Ethiopia marched into a violent identity crisis.

Or maybe our family was just intent on enjoying our adopted homeland for as long as we could. It was a fragile time. Everything was about to change. Dad was working hard on transferring all the mission land, buildings and bank accounts to Ethiopian church leaders. Soon the mission would be no more.

Near the end of our visit, Mom pulled Dad away from his worries, convinced him to use some of their precious, rationed fuel, and we drove about fifty miles to swim one last time in the bottomless volcanic cone of Lake Bishoftu. Ten years before on a choir tour, Mark and his roommate had conspired to throw me off the floating-barrel dock. Now Mark went out with a sailboat in a steady, sunny wind. Several thousand feet lower than Addis, hot sunlight bouncing off the lake tingled and burned my face. The water, full of bright green algae, smelled of growing things—of chlorophyll. I bobbed around, feeling tippy, as though the cool lake was trying to equalize with the water in my belly.

Back in Addis Ababa, Mark wasn't interested in food. Mark was always interested in food. He took to sitting on the couch all day. Mark never just sat around.

Mom leaned close to feel his forehead. She pulled down his bottom eyelids. She bit her bright scarlet lip. "I think you may have hepatitis," she said.

"Nah," Mark said. But every day that week he sat, and every day his body listed toward the cushions of the couch.

On the night before our flight back to Chicago, Mark lowered himself onto the edge of the bed in our musty basement bedroom. His face looked sallow, framed by his neat beard and dark hair aslant over his forehead. He lay down slowly. He lifted a thin arm over his eyes. The bare bulb in the low, stained ceiling glared down on him.

"You rest," I said. "I'll do the packing." He nodded and moved his feet out of the way. I lifted the suitcase onto the bed so I wouldn't have to lean down over my seven-months pregnant belly.

Before light the next morning, Mom shook my shoulder. I stumbled upstairs after her, the wooden steps creaking under my bare feet. Sandy-eyed, I rested my arms on the chilly dining room table. The house still smelled faintly of coffee-roasting from the day before. A hyena's faint whoop came from out in the dump at the edge of town.

Mom leaned toward me, as though her intensity could carry me with it. "I woke up in the middle of the night." She hadn't been able to sleep, worrying about Mark.

I pictured Mark's exhausted face the night before. "Yeah, he can hardly walk."

"You'll look pretty silly pushing him in a wheelchair." We giggled together—my heart full, as always, when my mother focused that beam of delight on me. "Imagine if he turns yellow during your layover in Paris. They'll quarantine you both."

My first thought: I'd be fluent in French by the time we got back!

"Stay at least until we make sure it isn't hepatitis. We'll help you with the ticket change fee."

It wasn't going to take much to convince me. MNS said America was messed up. Focusing on that had distracted me from how messed up I felt. But MNS had not given me back the joy and confidence I'd lost since leaving Good Shepherd. It hadn't given me anything like the relief I'd felt during this visit to Ethiopia. "I'll let Mark sleep until it's time to get up for the airport," I said. "He can be so stubborn."

I sat where Mark had been sitting all week, wrapped my cold feet in the bottom of my flannel nightgown, and rested my head on my arm along the bark of the couch. Inside, the baby woke. I rubbed my belly. Kick, baby, kick. In the kitchen, Mom buzzed the coffee beans in a blender and the percolator began to rumble.

When the sky had turned pink and the coffee smelled brewed, Mom shook me awake again. Outside, tall eucalyptus waved like black shadows in the dawn breeze. I tiptoed down the stairs and creaked open the rough-hewn door. Mark's shoulder under my hand was warm and moist. His skin smelled musky.

"Mm hmmm," he said, when I explained Mom's proposal. He was too sick even to lift his head off the pillow.

Mom and I made up the twin beds in an upstairs bedroom. With help from the bannister and me, Mark made it up the stairs. He didn't move again for hours. I unpacked, slid the suitcase under the bed, and put my books on the table between us.

What a miracle, staying in Ethiopia. I felt tender and thankful toward Mark, as though he had made a sacrifice for me, as though he had arranged to get sick because it would make me happy. As inexplicably, irrationally depressed as I'd been since I'd left Ethiopia, now I was just as irrationally happy. I folded back into the family as though I'd never left. Like the winter after the coup, I hung around Mom and Dad. Like then, I sewed, I read. Mark wasn't a husband any more. I wasn't a woman. I was a girl again, who'd been lonely and frightened, and was home.

It was ironic that, during this ultra-political time, I was so happy to be in Ethiopia. Ironic, but understandable. My place had always been in the cranny between my two cultures. I sank back gratefully, an American in the bosom of the Ethiopian Motherland, even as the army tightened control.

No one except the army trusted the army to run the country. Or as one historian wrote, everybody wanted a revolution, but no one wanted *this* revolution.

# CHAPTER 31

Soon after the beginning of 1977, EPRP sharp shooters began to pick off government officials. Men in positions of power felt the prickle of fear between their shoulders as they came and went from their offices, their homes, their cars.

Mengistu sent out the vans with the megaphones and organized another spontaneous show of support. There, he announced his own reign of terror for *adharies*, those who walk backward from the shining goals of the revolution. The Derg was not accused of Red Terror—Mengistu coined those words himself.

*"Kei Shibir!"* He shouted, over and over from the podium in Revolution Square.

*Kei*. Red. The approving faces of Lenin, Marx, and Engels watched approvingly.

*Shibir*. Terror. Enemies of the revolution, take note.

And in case anyone missed the point, Colonel Mengistu, at the end of this maniacal speech, shattered bottles of red liquid, possibly blood, on the asphalt.

The army threw itself into fighting White Terror with Red Terror. It was the modern version of Ethiopia's traditional fight-to-the-death that accompanied regime changes. Haile Selassie had held the empire together with bonds of charisma and the Solomonic mythology for almost sixty years. The amalgam of Cushitic, Semitic, Omotic and Nilotic peoples Emperor Menelik II had gathered into a nation otherwise had no common languages or cultures. Once the Derg delegitimized HIM, it had to substitute force to hold the country together.

Mandatory revolutionary discussions were held in every *kebelle* at ten on Sunday mornings. Churches objected and were ignored, being the opiate of the people. Anyone with a grievance now had an instrument of redress. *Adhari. Adhari*. That's all a person had to say. *Kebelle* leaders rewarded children who accused their parents. The merest whisper of *adhari* resulted in arrest and disappearance, imprisonment and torture.

Today, near where that billboard of European revolutionaries stared down on the faces of Ethiopians, just off Revolution Square which is The Square of the Cross again, survivors and relatives have created a Red Terror Museum. Thirty-six years after Mengistu's Kei-shebir speech, I followed a guide slowly past the displays.

The Derg's security forces boiled anti-revolutionaries in oil. They tore out fingernails. They touched electric prods to genitals. They thrust probes down throats. They hung people by the knees over eucalyptus poles, lashed their wrists and ankles together, and beat the bottoms of their feet. A student who pleaded innocent had to prove loyalty by raping, torturing, or assassinating another student. Preferably a girl.

The guide showed us the pincers and rods of torture. He led us through a door and stood in silence. The wall was pasted with hundreds of black and white photos of young adults. He warned us first, then led us into a room with a floor-to-ceiling glass bin full of glasses, shoes, bones, teeth, and the remnants of clothing pulled from mass grave sites. "They...they...they," he said of the victims.

Then he picked up a thermos and unscrewed the bottom. "We passed notes from prison to our families this way, when they brought us food," he said. The hair on my arm stood up. When had it shifted for him, from story to life?

A tome of over five hundred pages lay on the counter by the door: the names of those found guilty of crimes against humanity. They'd been given amnesty. Our guide repeated what the taxi driver had said when we told him where we were going: "The Red Terror is not over. We pass those who tortured us on the street. Our eyes meet. We can say nothing."

Every day during those early months of 1977, Dad went up by the compound gate to get his shoes shined. He sat in a row of men, all there for the same social and tonsorial reason. They talked softly about the disappeared from the night before, how many had died in the last dark urban battle. Sheep trotted by on the way to the meat department of the *mercato*. The men talked about the bodies of students, piled up on street corners. Donkey hoofs clip-clopped on the stony shoulders of the street. The men talked about lines at the morgues every morning.

The shoeshine boys brushed the men's shoes vigorously. The boys tapped with their wooden brush handles on their homemade polish boxes. The men switched from right to left foot on the boxes and talked on. The street smelled of farmyard and car exhaust. The men shook their heads. Wept. Told political jokes.

*What do the new Ethiopian clocks say?*
*I don't know. What?*
*Tikedem, tikedem, tikedem.*

Reporters from the *Washington Post* dropped by Dad's office to quiz him about who was who in the revolutionary alphabet soup: EPRP, EPRDA, EDU, POMOA, PMAC. Consular advisors from the embassy visited—officials, who knew that Dad and his missionary friends spoke local languages. They had friends in the communities. They heard things embassy folks would never hear.

Dad went out to find eggs, which had vanished from stores after the Derg set the price. Farmers weren't bothering to bring them into the city. "The chickens of the Derg have not yet started to lay," the man at the *souk* told Dad. They chucked together.

And Mark slept. He couldn't eat. He might keep down a few bites of oatmeal if I didn't add milk. To keep his glucose up, I supplied him with the Desta hard candies we'd loved in boarding school. He read his way through stacks of *Reader's Digest Condensed Books*. Some evenings I read out loud to him: *The Hobbit. A Wrinkle in Time.* Nothing heavy. Nothing existentially disturbing. Nothing that would remind us of the pain in the streets of Addis. Nothing that brought up our failed adult-hoods in the US. While Mark recovered, while I reveled in being home in Ethiopia, while death roamed the streets outside, there was nothing to do but wait for the fullness of time.

For once I had no illusion I should be doing something about—about anything. For once my work was clear and I could do it: gestate this baby. Finally, a job that didn't take huge effort. That was doing itself day by day. When the baby moved, I touched my belly. *I'm here.*

Good Shepherd School called and asked me to substitute for the French teacher, out on maternity leave. The kids whispered jokes about pregnant French teachers. I stood blushing, awkwardly sideways to the blackboard because of my belly, conjugating irregular verbs, pretending I didn't hear. Chalk dust tickled my nose.

The sound of evening shootings got more frequent. Some nights it came so near, we turned off lights and went to bed early to get safely below window level.

Mark's illness dragged on. It became obvious he would not be well before I went into my ninth month. We'd have to stay and have the baby in Ethiopia. That suited me just fine. More than just fine. What woman doesn't want her mother there when she's facing her first labor? The only worry was curfew.

One night, in the silence after curfew, a VW bug engine broke the evening silence, rattling down the street. I lifted my head from the hem I was putting in for Mom. The *kebelle* guard shouted. I suspended my needle over the plaid fabric. The bug didn't slow. At the explosion, I winced. Metal struck wood and shook the house.

We knew not to go out on the porch to see what had happened.

In the morning, the bug looked as though it had tried to climb a telephone pole. The *zebenya* said a military mucky-muck, drunk and grand, thought he could ignore curfew. The *kebelle* guard had been told to shoot first and ask questions later. His bullet pierced the car door and passed through the man's body.

The president of our *kebelle*, a friend and the director of the Presbyterian girls' school, came to our house. First, of course, there had to be food. Mom carried tea, steaming and fragrant, and a plate of cookies in from the kitchen. We chatted for the requisite time. Then our friend told us that military police had come to arrest the guard who'd shot the captain. "I stood right in front of that terrified boy," she said. "I told them he was following their orders."

At supper, Dad said it was only a matter of time before both the boy and she would be arrested. For the next couple of days Dad brooded. Then one afternoon he came through the door, arms hanging limp with relief. The US embassy had secreted our friend out to the States.

As my due date approached, Mom and I visited the famous fistula hospital, where an American doctor repaired the damage long labors at young ages do to women in Ethiopia. The doctor was happy for me to give birth there—but what about curfew? The uncertainty didn't disrupt my calm. Maybe I would go into labor during the day. Maybe a night labor would go on past dawn. Anyway, Mom had had seven babies, surely she'd know what to do.

Consciously I felt calm and fatalistic about my coming labor. But I had nightmares of blood, of angry men in black boots. When I first felt the baby's hiccups, rhythmic against my ribs, I joked that she'd developed a nervous tic. Even that gave me no regret. Ethiopia's sorrows and losses were tangible. Not like my slippery descent into darkness in the US, something I'd blamed on no one but myself. I was in a community again in Ethiopia. I was with family, the missionary aunties and uncles, and caring Ethiopians who worked for Dad in the office, for Mom in the kitchen. The balance was familiar. Faith in the inherent graciousness of the Ethiopian people had always rewarded us. In the US, I'd felt nothing resembling support.

On March twenty-third, the loud speakers cranked up again. The buzzing shout of fervor blared on the street. This time they were announcing a citywide search for illegal weapons. Dad brought the old hunting rifles of early missionaries down from the Crow's Nest. He wrapped them in burlap bags, and called the US Consul, who agreed to take possession if Dad could get them across town. One of the missionary aunties volunteered to drive—as an American woman, she was least likely to be stopped by military police. But she ran back to her office for herpurse, and Demissie, the driver who'd ferried us to Good Shepherd School every day, took the car to run office errands.

In no time, the news spread through the compound. My mind revved. *Demissie stopped by police. Demissie innocent of what he carried in the trunk. Police unwrapping the burlap. Demissie face down on the street. Like in the piassa that day. But this time, no return.*

When the *zebenya* opened the gate to Demissie at last, we poured out of homes and offices and surrounded the car. People clustered close, touching his arms, his back, as though to be sure he was real. Dad, dramatic as ever, leaned his head on Demissie's shoulder, weeping. He pulled the burlap bundle out of the trunk and unwrapped it. Demissie's face, baffled until that moment, went gray.

The search itself began. Soldiers and *kebelle* riffraff were ordered to administer revolutionary justice at will, and they rose to the occasion. We tracked their approach in our neighborhood by gunshot coming nearer. But when they came to the mission compound, they passed over. *Ferenj gid-yellem*, never mind the foreigners. We were guests and on-lookers, like boulders in the riverbed. People's lives eddied around us and went on.

# CHAPTER 32

Mark weighed 103 pounds in April, when he could eat again. I hugged him as he wobbled from the bedroom to the living room the first time, his pants pleating under a belt synched tight. I laughed, imagining the picture we made—me reaching over my huge belly to hold the adolescent-sized father of my child.

My due date was May first, International Labor Day—all Ethiopia might join me in celebrating the baby's birthday. We had arranged for me to deliver at the twenty-bed Mennonite mission hospital an hour's drive south. The last week of April, Mark and I packed our old gray suitcase and drove off the shoulder of the mountain, down past the volcanic lakes, to wait in the guest house there.

University students relentlessly mocked the veneer of socialism over Mengistu's dictatorship. They planned a huge demonstration to disrupt Labor Day celebrations. Socialist the government may not truly have been; well-armed it was. On May first, police gunned down students in the streets. Soldiers chased them into buildings and shot them there. They rounded up hundreds more, the brightest of the next generation from all over the country.

Troops crowded students into trucks and transported them to prison camps. When family members located them and brought food, they were told their children no longer needed to eat. Six hundred to a thousand young people were killed that weekend. The city was crisscrossed with funeral processions. Even Eastern Block countries joined the stunned silence we all felt.

Miriam was born on May fourth. As soon as we called to tell them, Mom and Dad drove down to get us.

I stroked Miriam's cheek, which was so soft I could hardly feel it. Dad cut her thin baby fingernails with his Swiss Army knife, taking the tiny curves carefully. Mark caught the white shavings in his palm.

They made a bed in the back of the station wagon for us. I cradled Miriam's molded head against my breast, and floated back to Addis, one day postpartum and dizzy with hormones and the milky smell of

Miriam's face and hair. The sky, the clouds, the top floors of buildings spun by backwards as we entered the city. White tents people erect for forty days of mourning spilled over the sidewalks and into the streets. Tears ran warm down my temples, but I didn't close my eyes. Life had never seemed so precious. So fragile.

We followed a bleating megaphone along the Ambo Road, past the Abuna Petros statue. Miriam stirred, and frowned in her sleep. I pressed a hand over one of her ears, pressed the other against me.

"Another search," Dad said, his head cocked to hear the distorted Amharic. This time, a twenty-four-hour city-wide curfew. The next morning, I woke to Miriam's whimper in a city strangely silent. No engines hummed. No horns honked. No one herded cattle or sheep past the compound gate. No donkeys laden with fine straw trotted by in their dogged, long-suffering way. Even the birds were silent, seeming to huddle in their nests, housebound like the rest of us, while the city was frisked.

Soldiers and *kebelle* thugs combed people's homes for the tools of revolution: guns and mimeograph machines. As we waited, our voices and even Miriam's cry seemed muted. Random bursts of gunshot startled us. But once again the angel of death passed over the mission compound.

After the search moved on, missionary aunties and uncles came knocking on the door. Mom ran into the kitchen to spread jam on left-over pancakes from breakfast. She cut homemade rolls into quarters and spread them with butter. The fragrance of Ethiopian coffee drifted through the living room. One auntie brought a cake made the Dutch way, with chocolate frosting hard as a shell around a soft center.

An uncle took pictures of our new family: Miriam frowning in her sleep; Mark thin, in a blue and purple striped t-shirt, sitting beside me on the piano bench. I look like a hippy, with my long straight hair. I smiled at my daughter, born in revolution, innocent and tiny, the purest, best thing I had ever done to make the world a better place.

A few days later, when I pulled Miriam's undershirt over her head, the fabric stuck to her skin. I peeled it carefully away, horrified. Miriam stirred. Whimpered. Under her arm, watery blisters had popped, and layers of baby skin slipped away from raw flesh underneath. I sobbed on Mark's shoulder. Mom ran to the cupboard for that dramatic but effective topical antibiotic, gentian violet.

She patted my back. "Impetigo isn't that serious."

"I can't protect her," I wailed. My hot face stung with the salt of a fresh outburst. "There will be so many things."

When Miriam was two weeks old, still curling like a fetus in her sleep, our visa extension ran out. The Socialist Republic of Ethiopia refused to renew. I braced myself for the shock of re-entry to the US. What I'd been through—in Chicago there would be no way to talk about it. Once again, my identification with Ethiopia would complicate my connecting with people in America.

But first I had to face the smell of dust and old urine in Haile Selassie International Airport. The stale air of the airplane. The narrow airplane seat that made nursing Miriam awkward—something we were both new at. In Chicago's O'Hare, I shuffled through the immigration line feeling slovenly. My clothes had wrinkled on the ten-hour flight from Paris. My hair stuck to my cheeks, full of static from the airplane head-rest. I leaked whenever Miriam whimpered. I could smell my own milk. Rolls of skin and fat jiggled at my waist when I walked.

Mark and I moved back into our room under the eaves in the house on Malden Street, but our hearts had already left Chicago. I admitted to myself, then to him, that I wasn't accomplishing any of my world-righting goals. The blind weren't receiving their sight, the poor weren't receiving justice. While I was away, I had gotten over the illusion that I was going to change the US education system. I wasn't capable (was I even interested?) in organizing demonstrations.

When people in Ethiopia had been starving, Americans had been moved to action. Now Ethiopia's problems had morphed. Crimes against humanity in someone else's nation—how can we stand up for each other? Whether Pinochet or Mengistu, whether in Ukraine or Myanmar, this is something we haven't figured out.

I told Mark I didn't see any point in raising our daughter in Uptown. I had also metabolized Avril and Roxanne's attacks, and the shame I'd felt—*These are not my people.* Being away had broken me loose.

Now, I couldn't tear open Mom's air form letters fast enough. Missions were being accused of tax evasion and assessed millions of dollars. The government had stopped renewing work permits. The socialist hounding-out of missionaries, as part of the crack-down on religion, was almost completed.

The aggrieved local peasant association in Dembi Dollo, where one of the earliest Presbyterian mission hospitals had been built, where Mark's dad had taught him about electricity and put him to work wiring the new wing, where they had taken the mission doctor hostage, where Dad had driven, facing the gauntlet of all those newly minted and armed *kebelle* guards—now Dembi Dollo activists had a new demand: the Presbyterian Church must pay them two million dollars to operate the hospital.

Ironically, that hospital was eventually run into the ground by its local administrators. They begged Presbyterians to take it back, and send missionary doctors again. But by then the wheel of history had been turning for almost two decades, and it was too late. PCUSA was divesting itself of hospitals all over the world.

Mom and my two youngest siblings came back to the States as soon as Good Shepherd School closed that June. Dad finished turning all the mission assets over to local church leaders, turned off the mission lights, and bought a ticket back to the States. But when he checked in at Haile Selassie I Airport, he was turned away. His name was still blacklisted over the doctor hostage in Dembi Dollo. The Republic would not let him leave the country until he had the signature of the Minister of Health.

That became another of Dad's favorite stories. He had felt sick with fear, standing there at the Ethiopian Airlines check-in counter. He thought his protection from God had finally run out. The government was going to keep him in Ethiopia long enough to figure out that the American Mission was no longer a legal entity with assets that could be extorted. Then he'd be the hostage.

He went down to the Ministry of Health the next day full of dread. But when the minister saw that he was Presbyterian, he asked Dad if he knew Dr. Carroll Loomis. Dad had supervised Uncle Carroll for years.

The Minister of Health had gone to medical school in Southern Illinois, he said. He had been lonely there, shocked as he faced racism for the first time. Dr. Loomis had heard there was an Ethiopian in the university and looked him up. The Loomises invited him to their home and befriended him. In gratitude for that human touch at a lonely time, the Minister took Dad's word that the situation in Dembi Dollo had been settled.

"But I didn't breathe easy until the plane wheels left the tarmac," Dad said, pretending to wipe the sweat from his forehead.

Dad's mission career of twenty-three years had ended in recrimination and violence, but he wasn't one to stew in regrets. Just as he always demanded we do, he pulled up his bootstraps and launched into a new career as pastor of a small Presbyterian church in North Portland.

My sisters and I had all married and scattered by then: Jane and Cathy in Southern Illinois, Joy in Minneapolis, me in Chicago. We didn't write letters. We never called. The out-of-sight-out-of-mind way of boarding school kids had kicked in. We had long ago extinguished the ability to miss each other.

Mark, eighteen-month-old Miriam, and I moved with Mom and Dad in a school bus and Volkswagen van caravan to Portland. We lived together for a few months, all of us getting started again. With Chris and Janice both still in high school, we were a three-generation family. Very Ethiopian. Chris and Janice adored Miriam, and lavished her with attention.

Over the next few years, gingerly, with lots of mixed feelings, Mark and I began to show up for church in Dad's small congregation. It helped that it was just up the street from our one-bedroom house. It helped that there were other young couples with toddlers Miriam's age. It helped when several couples from Miriam's preschool joined us there. My motives for attending church were as deeply social as they were spiritual.

But it also helped that Mom and Dad looked around and saw, for the first time, the injustices of the "land of the free" that they had defended so reactively while they were still strangers in the foreign land of Ethiopia, homesick on some level, for the culture they'd left in the middle of post-World War II idealism. Now Dad led the Portland Organizing Project. Mom and other church members went with him to demonstrate against police brutality and the real estate red-lining that was still keeping black families out of most neighborhoods in our supposedly liberal city.

This was the call to justice and mercy I'd read in Isaiah, Jeremiah, Amos, and Hosea when I couldn't understand the sermons in Maji. This is what I'd wanted from the house church in Malden—the church standing up for the people, for the neighborhoods, for the cities. Mark and I often had dinner at Mom and Dad's house after church. Just as when I was a teenager in Addis Ababa, I critiqued Dad's sermons over Sunday dinner. Janice and Chris, teenagers now, joined in. We challenged easy answers. Dad glowed with pride at our feistiness. Mom always had a witty and irreverent comment. We laughed a lot.

Over the next years, Mark built up a remodeling business. We added a son, Jesse, to our family. Four years later, another son. I named him Kenny for the brother who had died in Addis Ababa when I was five. I worked odd jobs: school bus driver, baby sitter, mini-mart cashier, term insurance sales. As the government under Reagan phased out the health care subsidy for Mark as a self-employed contractor, I took on more and more of our income. Just jobs that helped the budget. Not work that fed my drive for meaning.

I had chased that chimera in another life, in Chicago. Now we bought a home and played our parts as the mom and dad with three children, members of the church community. Mark preferred this world to the other. I was resigned.

*You should be grateful for this peaceful life,* I told myself. We'd seen Red Terror. What could be better than civil peace, evenhanded elections, clean supermarkets? On quiet neighborhood sidewalks, no one shouted at me, or noticed me at all, with my small children and their bikes and strollers. I could buy eggs, sugar, fuel—several brands of each—any time I needed them. The little news that leaked out of Ethiopia still sounded so grim. I should have felt relief to be shed of its dash toward self-destruction. I should have felt joy. Instead, I wandered through my days in a quiet fog of mild disappointment. Was this all? I'd grown up with so many more advantages than an Ethiopian peasant. I'd had so much potential. Shouldn't I be doing more with it?

# CHAPTER 33

In 1987, when Miriam was ten, Jesse was six, and Kenny was one, Mark got a call to paint the home of an elderly woman in the congregation. He ran over to bid the job and came home for lunch.

"Some siding just wants to blister," he said, over a sandwich. "I told her, 'Your house is a good candidate for vinyl.' But she wants me to paint."

Mark painted. The south side of her house baked that summer, so in the fall, Mark scraped and repainted, no charge. When it blistered again, the woman decided she should have bought vinyl siding. She asked Mark for all her money back.

Mark went over and sat with her. He explained how he'd spent money on paint, to say nothing of his time. He suggested they compromise. No, she said. She needed the money for vinyl siding.

An official letter arrived in the mail one day. I worried over it until Mark got home. He blanched, under his dark beard, when he opened it. The woman was taking him to small claims court.

Mark wrote a letter suggesting they ask elders in the church to mediate. She didn't answer. She was just as determined to sue as she had been to paint. People warned us that judges always side with the consumer.

Working for himself, Mark didn't have an employer to pay half his FICA and Social Security taxes. Money poured out as fast as he laboriously bailed it in but we were just barely paying our bills. Miriam qualified for subsidized breakfast and lunch at school. I was buying our cheese, milk, and Cheerios with WIC coupons. We never ate out. We never bought new clothes. All winter, we worried.

The court kept postponing. "Never mind," I told Mark. "This gives us time to save." I squirreled away every penny I could. I spent money on nothing but utilities and groceries. "We're going to write a check right outside the courtroom door and walk away," I said. I was going to walk away emotionally as well as financially.

Finally, during a warm spell in March of 1988, I put on a pleated corduroy skirt and sweater. Mark rushed home from a job, changed into clean jeans and a blue and red flannel shirt, and we went downtown. The courtroom smelled of floor wax and people. So many people with problems.

After he heard both sides, the judge had a few questions for the woman. Mark hadn't charged for repainting? No, she said.

He'd pressure washed her driveway? Yes, she said. He'd done a great job. She just wanted vinyl siding.

The judge shook his head and turned to Mark. "You did what she contracted for and more. Case dismissed. Can I have one of your business cards?" Everyone in the courtroom laughed.

My heart floated up like a helium balloon. I glanced secretly at the woman, afraid she'd be crying, or giving us the evil eye, but she was just looking down at the small, square purse in her lap.

I caught up on buying the shoes and clothes the kids had needed. Mark bought a used lawn mower with what was left over. I could have thought of a more exciting way to celebrate, but on balance, I was grateful to have a husband who mowed the lawn. If a better lawn mower was the reward he chose for himself, I could live with that.

Throughout the 1980s, as we had been putting down those roots in Portland and enjoying the benefits of a system that worked—street repairs, stop signs, polite drivers—the Derg in Ethiopia had been self-immolating. I found ways to support struggling people in Ethiopia and sent small donations every month.

The Eritrean People's Liberation Front (EPLF) had been fighting Ethiopia for decades already when Mengistu took over in 1978. Some generals had suggested that the new Socialist Republic of Ethiopia grant Eritrea autonomy. But Mengistu had blustered like King Solomon's son who said, when people pleaded for tax relief, "My father thrashed you with whips; I'll beat you with chains!"

We learned some things from charity newsletters, BBC sometimes had Ethiopia news, and Mom called me when she heard anything: Ethiopia's army grew to be Africa's largest, next to South Africa; Ethiopia was spending forty-two percent of its annual budget on arms; the army, to keep troop numbers up, swooped into villages on market days, cordoned off the center of town and conscripted all males over twelve; a tank cost as much as building a hospital; Mengistu's palace was guarded by thirty-two tanks.

In the middle of war in Eritrea, war also broke out with Somalia to the south. The US, always Ethiopia's ally, sided this time with Somalia so as not to support socialism—or communism—or dictatorship. No one was quite sure what to call it.

Millions of men were dying in Ethiopia, in the kind of war being waged all over Africa for complex reasons. For one, European men had drawn boundaries, like the line between Somalia and Ethiopia, to suit their colonial reasons, not for the good of Africans concerned. Sometimes people, like the Somalis, straddled two or even three nations; sometimes different peoples corralled within national boundaries carried centuries of memory, the lethal conflicts between them seemingly woven into their collective psyches. And sometimes African leaders thought like tribal big-men, now ruling over dozens of tribes as though they were all his own clan, beholden to him and obliged to feed his ambitions. All those wars for all those reasons enriched gun-runners from Russia and the West and took the lives of young Africans.

Domestic success in Ethiopia was as scarce as peace. The Derg announced land reform and nationalized rental property. City dwellers could only own one small home. To feed those city dwellers (and the army), the Derg set the price of grain below what the market would have borne, alienating peasants and depressing production.

Mengistu announced villagization, a ploy to break up opposition. Between 1980 and 1986, six hundred thousand families were moved off their homesteads and into villages. The Derg promised services that would compensate people for having to walk miles to their farms. Schools and clinics never materialized. A different kind of socialism ensued—people now shared marital fights, and their flocks passed around chicken diseases.

In densely populated northern areas, where another liberation group, the Tigrean People's Liberation Front (TPLF), was gaining strength, the government announced resettlement. Families were loaded into Soviet trucks and dropped off in wilderness areas hundreds of miles from their inherited hamlets. They were left to clear land, build homes and start new lives as best they could.

Where opposition resistance was strongest, the army blocked the roads, cutting off food transport. This turned a few dry years into a famine worse than Mother Nature had ever managed on her own. The West was horrified, once again, to see photographs of the starving people of Ethiopia. I told Mom I didn't want to hear the details. I increased our donations.

The aid concert was born. Americans and Europeans responded with open hearts. Charities like the supergroup Band Aid raised millions, and Mengistu, rewarded for plunging his own people into starvation, stepped up bombing raids, at $45,000 per sortie. Journalists reported seeing grain from the European Union being loaded directly onto Russian ships as payment for munitions. I felt sick.

But the morning after Mark's lawsuit was settled, I walked out to our yard feeling light and free. No matter what people do to each other, the earth turns. Morning follows night. Spring follows winter. The pear tree at the corner was covered with white popcorn blossoms and buzzing with bees, hungry, like I was, after a long winter.

I looked at our little brown bungalow. Mark and I had slept for years on the hide-a-bed in the living room. Kenny had been born in the one bedroom. We'd lived with plywood floors and unpainted drywall as we saved up money to buy materials and cover bills during the next phase of an endless remodel. Mark had jacked up the roof, built a stair-case and created a second story; he'd dug out and finished half of the basement. The hard part was almost done. The house was almost comfortable. At last.

And I was almost happy. I had a couple more years before Kenny started school. I was reading books like *Writing Down the Bones* and *On Becoming a Writer*. I was filling one loose leaf notebook each month with writing practice, dreaming of someday writing something real. That day, I breathed the stinky scent of those beautiful pear blossoms. I looked out from under the thick foam of them, from the corner of the yard. *Finally*, I thought. *Finally. Finally. I could live here forever and be content.*

Two days later, the shrilling phone interrupted lunch. I covered the mouthpiece. "It's Aunt Marcia. She wants us both on the line." Aunt Marcia was the missionary auntie who had run in to get her purse and left the rifles in burlap bags in the car that Demissie took and drove around town. Now she worked at Presbyterian Church headquarters.

Mark washed down a bite of his between-jobs sandwich with a swallow of coffee. He ran up to the bedroom extension.

*Would Mark and I consider going back to Ethiopia to work?*

Mark came down the stairs slowly. We stared at each other over Kenny's head as he chattered and chewed. His plate was littered with honey, peanut butter, and crusts. Fingerprints smeared a half-drunk glass of milk. Miriam was in her first year of middle school, an over-achiever and tiny for her age, just like her mother had been. Jesse had started first grade down the street.

Since figuring out in middle school that I couldn't live like the Ethiopians around me, I had never, ever planned to be a missionary.

I hadn't expected to see Ethiopia again after Miriam was born.

But Mark admitted he'd always quietly dreamed of going back overseas.

He admitted that he was exhausted, working for himself—hustling bids and estimates, doing the work, calculating the invoices, collecting payment, juggling past jobs, present jobs, and future jobs. "Maybe the call came from God," he said. I could hear his despair. "Why couldn't God use Aunt Marcia on the phone?"

"No dream?" I said. "No vision? No burning bush?"

So many bits had gone into my moment of hope under the pear tree. Not only the court case won. Not only the house almost finished. I finally had friends. Kenny would start preschool three mornings a week in the fall. I'd just been ordained an elder at the church. Mark was singing in the choir. Twenty years after graduating from Good Shepherd, I'd finally made it through the shock of moving to the States. *Why would I throw that away? Why would I ever want to start over again?* I didn't say a lot, though. I listened to Mark. I nodded. I felt paralyzed.

After a few weeks, I reassured myself that Ethiopia couldn't turn me into a misfit again in the two years they were asking for. Would they really send a Kurtz girl back to Ethiopia, where she'd be compared to beloved Mr. Kurr-tis, with his *tafach*, tasty Amharic? And how likely was it that we, who'd been fringe hippies, who'd lived in a commune, who'd left the church for so long, would be acceptable as missionaries?

I sweated over my statement of faith—how to be honest but not focus on doubts that would scuttle any chance of squeaking in. I wrote my essay about goals and dreams. I listed my work experiences.

As they've said in more recent controversies, PCUSA holds a wide umbrella. Certainly, a more conservative denomination would not have called us, but there were no uncomfortable questions in our interview at headquarters in Louisville, Kentucky. Aunt Marcia was honest about the challenges of living under the Derg. But we agreed that grinding incompetency was innocuous compared to the violence we'd seen.

"They want us more badly than we want them!" I said to Mark later.

When my work permit to teach arrived in Louisville, Aunt Marcia called us again, her smile audible. Since Mark didn't have an engineering degree, he couldn't get a work permit. He would be my dependent spouse, free to work wherever the Ethiopian partner needed someone who could do repairs, building, and logistics. Mark was a hard worker but he hated working on someone else's terms. He was thrilled to be a free agent.

Dad beamed at the news. He told of a church conference in West Africa, where someone had asked, *What is the best thing missionaries give to Africa?*

Dad teared up. His voice thinned. It broke. He cleared his throat. Just as when I was a child, tears stung my eyes as well. "An African church leader said, 'You missionaries never spoke our languages well. You never really understood our cultures. But your children grew up with us. When your children come back, they understand us.'"

We left for Ethiopia in the days when people could still see each other off. Jane was living in Colorado, Joy in Minnesota, but Cathy lived in Portland now. She was back from working for the UN in Togo, and our families picnicked in the summer, met over Sunday dinners at Mom and Dad's.

Cathy stood beside me at the gate. Her kids and ours ran in tight circles around the cart with our carry-ons. All of our voices were pitched a notch higher, Mom and Dad, Cathy, Mark and me. I felt dazed, as though we'd stepped unexpectedly onto some magical conveyor belt. Cathy's face looked haunted, the way mine felt whenever it had been someone else's trip.

# CHapTer 34

After the first ten-hour flight, from the gate at London Heathrow, I saw the green-yellow-red tail feathers of an Ethiopian Airlines jet on the tarmac. On board, I got the boys belted in, took out coloring books and magic markers. I ran my fingers over the Amharic *fidel* script etched into the backs of the food trays. I didn't understand the seat belt spiel in Amharic, but I held my breath, listening to the music of it. I turned to Mark and smiled when the stewardess switched to English, accented with the sounds we knew so well—"r" rolled, the short "a" softened, trouble with "th."

As we approached the airport, Mark pointed out the window. The flight pattern still ran over what had been Good Shepherd School. Below us, the octagonal dining hall spun as we circled. Baldy swung into view. My eyes stung. I didn't dare look at him.

We drove past the round Bank of Ethiopia and the French Lysee on Churchill Avenue. I had forgotten the rank smell of diesel exhaust from the buses and trucks on Addis Ababa streets. City Hall towered at the top of the avenue, decades old now. When it was newly built, Skins had used his fluent Amharic to charm the guard into letting four of us climb the tall, angular bell tower before it officially opened. The chimes had rung when we were up there, looking over the city. The music had floated my soul out over the rusty *korkoro* roofs of the slums, drifting with the sound, hanging midway between earth and heaven in the gray dusk air.

We drove on, past the statue of Abuna Petros. The gate of the former mission compound was still painted green. The sign now read Bethel Synods Coordinating Office. Addis Ababa was shabbier, more crowded, but Mark could have driven us from the airport straight home.

*Home*. Time warped. On the left sat our hostel for that first year of Good Shepherd School. I'd slept in the top bunk just to the left of that center window. On the right, the house where hepatitis had laid Mark low, where we'd brought day-old Miriam home. The office building where Dad had worked looked small and drab. Nothing sparkled like buildings, renovated, can sparkle in the States.

I had agreed to be the only foreign teacher at the Ethiopian girls' school. The house built for the school director had been held empty, waiting for an American teacher from PCUSA. It had been built before the shortages of socialism, lovely, with a fireplace, wood floors, and Ethiopian marble window sills. It was by far the nicest house we'd ever lived in. Exactly the kind of house I'd denied myself back when I was in middle school, so young and idealistic. Now, my self-imposed exile seemed to be over. Some days I felt queasy about our beautiful house: *Have I abandoned all my ideals?* Other days, gratitude washed over me.

Out the window of our bedroom, I woke to the huge, swaying eucalyptus trees in the forest across the street. Fire finches twittered softly and hopped from leaf to leaf of the sugar cane and Ethiopian cabbage in our neighbor's garden. Geranium and fuchsia shrubs grew tall as my shoulders, poinsettia into rangy trees. The nightjar sang its haunting song in the dark. Unlike the calm, maritime rain of Portland, rainy season at 8,000 feet in Addis Ababa announced itself with lightning and thunder, sometimes hail.

My euphoria about being in Ethiopia again was tempered by the challenges. No, they weren't lethal. Yes, they were annoying. Electricity went off several times a week, and we scrambled to find flashlights, candles, matches. We kept a bucket and pitcher by the toilet, and another in the kitchen for days when there was no running water. Pressure was so bad, I started calling the shower *the dribble*, and took baths instead.

The Derg hadn't learned anything from the egg-shortage days. Sugar, flour, and fuel took turns disappearing and showing up again on the black market. Soon after we arrived, someone figured out how to disappear all the rough, local toilet paper. I went to a souk and bought a pile of squares, put them on the back of the toilet, and told the kids, "Use what you need. But don't waste these. They cost more than all your allowances put together!"

"We don't get an allowance," Miriam said. "Remember?"

It was 1990, fifteen years after His Majesty had been deposed. Just as Dad had done, I got my news from BBC and over sweet cinnamon spiced tea with the Ethiopian staff in the office. The news was always grim for the Derg.

The Eritrean People's Liberation Force had already routed the Ethiopian army and occupied the main seaport.

Mengistu had retracted his most unpopular socialistic reforms.

Peasants were abandoning the villages and moving back to their homes. A few peasants' associations dismantled the cooperatives that had been forced on them, redistributing the land and tools among themselves. When *kebelle* leaders looked the other way, the wave spread, peasant associations grew bolder and evicted or even assassinated the government lackeys who had been their oppressors. *How quickly could incompetence and oppression turn, and the oppressed become violent?* But uneasiness could not extinguish the joy I felt to be back in Ethiopia.

The school semester opened and my new work life began. I taught school during the day. I lay awake at night and thought about things, just as I always had. What I'd seen as a child I saw in new ways. My life and the lives of people in Maji had differed in so much more than material comfort. While I was having a childhood, even in a remote corner of Ethiopia, children in rural Maji were learning how to do what their parents did. That's why we call them traditional cultures— tradition dictates from one generation to the next what life requires.

But those were the years when the modern, scientific, individualistic world created in the Northern Hemisphere was crashing into the traditional worlds of the Southern. And inexplicably, a few Ethiopian children my age, like the students at the mission school in Maji, had felt the change. They had jumped the rut of their fate as peasant farmers.

"My parents gave me to my grandmother," one of my friends said. We sat sipping tea. I breathed cinnamon and cloves and waited. "She was old, so I carried water for her, and gathered wood, and cooked. I was supposed to watch the goats, but I left them and ran to school. She beat me. But I went to school, anyway." Now this friend is the most highly educated woman of her clan. What inspired her? "I just wanted it," she said.

Children all over Africa were learning to read and write and think new thoughts in schools, many of them mission schools. Colonialism was about to fall apart. Europeans would no longer be the bureaucrats, politicians, and pastors of Africa. Those wayward children going to school would become the new African leaders—some of them noble, and some of them scalawags, just like human beings everywhere.

And I was back in that new Africa.

The girls' school had an Ethiopian name now, and an Ethiopian director. Class sizes had grown to over fifty. I'd agreed to come to Ethiopia to teach part time, but now my responsible self kicked in and I said yes to a full-time load.

I said yes to assisting the Ethiopian synod leader in the afternoon.

His office was a room I remembered from two previous iterations—our family had lived in that room during Mom and Dad's language study when I was five; it had been Dad's office during the Kei Shibir.

I also said yes to running the guesthouse in my free time. I felt willing to do anything, no matter how hard, to earn the right to stay.

For the next six years I taught pre-kindergarten through third grade English. I developed my own curriculum, because Oxford Press texts for Ethiopia had been burned in socialistic fervor. They'd been replaced with pamphlet sized texts on newsprint paper, full of grammar errors, evil landlords and stories of sacrifice for the Motherland.

I read easy-reader books to the girls and taught them songs—they could sing more complex English than they could speak. On Fridays, I took them outside to sing in the sun, on the dusty, trampled playground. Fifty girls in a circle is one huge circle.

The girls loved me. Of course they did. Their other classes ran on rote and copying things off the blackboard. But however they loved playing word games and singing with me, they would not behave for me.

"Remember the 'self-manager' button Miriam's school gave her?" I asked Mark. For a first-born, hard-working girl, it had been a coveted prize. She was small. It was huge, half covering her chest. "I don't think *self-manager* is even a concept here." The Ethiopian teachers yanked naughty girls' ears, smacked their palms or legs with lengths of garden hose, or made them kneel on the cement floors. The girls had been trained at home and at school to be punishment-managed. And I was a softie.

"T'cha, T'cha," they shouted, waving their hands, almost vaulting out of their seats. It took me months to realize they were shouting *Teacher*, not even hearing that American "r" that hangs in the air, mid-mouth. And all sixty girls wanted to be the special girl who got to choose the words for the next verse of our song.

Not learning Amharic as a child was a mistake I was not going to repeat. The sounds and music of Amharic had etched themselves into my brain, and now, being immersed at the school, I started pulling words out of the darkness.

Over summer break, I asked Etabez, the elementary science teacher, to tutor me for a couple of hours a day. Her guard opened her compound gate to a classic Ethiopian "villa"—the vicious guard dog chained up at the gate, the cobblestone drive, a few scraggly daisies and that low burgundy-leafed plant that bordered every flower garden of my childhood.

Etabez lived with her three children in the servants' quarters, three rooms that opened onto a cement veranda. Maroon velvet over-stuffed furniture, a coffee table, the dining room set, and a towering wardrobe crowded the living room so I could hardly turn around to take my coat off.

I had come ready to get to work (very American), but on the first day, Etabez had a different agenda. She'd spread fragrant grass and flower heads in the only open spot between the table and couches. She pointed me to the couch, her face a mixture of pride and shyness. Would I understand? She lit a chunk of frankincense in a broken saucer. The piney smoke twirled up and spread through the room. I was prob-ably her first American friend. She was my first real Ethiopian friend. I was ready to be pleased by anything she did.

She brought a brazier and lit the charcoal with a twist of paper and dried grass. She pulled up a three-legged stool. She settled her skirts around her knees in the graceful way Ethiopian women have. She spread a handful of green coffee beans on a small, concave metal plate. Patiently, hypnotically, she stirred with a metal rod bent over at the end. The room warmed. When the beans popped and turned glossy with coffee oils, she brought the tray to me and wafted the smoke in my direction. I breathed deeply. How many times had I soaked that smell into my lungs, as much as they could hold, when the school boys had roasted coffee over the wood stove in Maji?

Etabez pounded the hot beans into powder in a mortar. One of her daughters, my student, ran in and leaned against her mother's knee. She looked sideways at me, under thick lashes, through the haze of fragrant smoke. Etabez set the black clay *jebena* on the charcoal. She rolled a piece of scrap paper into a funnel and tapped the powder care-fully into the *jebena's* narrow neck. Every move was meditative. Her daughter ran back out, with a gust of chilly air from the door. Etabez and I visited softly, in her insecure English and my halting Amharic, waiting for the coffee to steep. We drank it sweet, blistering hot, from tulip shaped sinis, *Made in China* printed on the bottoms. I wondered again, *What did Ethiopians drink coffee from before they found sinis made in China?*

It was the deep rains, and Etabez's house had no heat, so as well as wearing a sweater, I brought a heavy, white, handwoven *gabi* and wrapped it around me, tucking it under my legs. Etabez gave me vocabulary lists—kitchen utensils, foods, and spices. One day she drilled me on parts of the body. She touched her head, neck, shoulders.

I imitated her and chanted the words after her. Moving on down, she clapped both hands vigorously onto her breasts. I felt that frisson of shock that accompanies a drop into the crevasse between cultures. I blushed. I waved my hands in the general direction of my own breasts, amused, unable to muster such boldness.

Etabez recorded sentences, with pauses for me to repeat as I drilled at home: *I ate; I will eat; I would have eaten.* Her girls ran in and out of the room, playing. Later, Etabez heard them in a new game. The younger girl said words in Amharic. Her sister repeated the words, mispronouncing them with my American accent.

The sun usually shone in the mornings, and I usually got home before the afternoon deluge. But sometimes rain pounded down on the *korkoro* roof and drowned out our voices. It splashed onto her veranda, turned the mud and gravel roadways off the main street into red rivers I splashed through as I drove home.

Etabez and I weren't totally disciplined as we worked on my Amharic, because we were both thrilled with our friendship. Etabez was short for Ehit Abeza, She-of-the-Plethora-of-Sisters. That should have been my name. After that summer, she treated me like a sister. When I said something clever, tried a new construction I'd picked up, or used an idiom at just the right time, she beamed. "You are my best student!" When I scrambled my syntax, something so easy for an American to do in Amharic, she said, "What has happened? You are so careless!"

Amharic had flowed around me like a river when I was a child. Now, between Etabez's help and my immersion at work, I quickly became semi-fluent. I still needed to simplify my sentences and find substitutes for the words I didn't know. I couldn't follow the high diction of radio or television Amharic, and I lost the train of quick, idiomatic gossip-diction my new friends used when they really got going. But I could swim for days at a time in the river of Amharic. I modeled Dad, proud of speaking good Amharic—a lovely language of pops and crackles, of lilting cadences.

My Oromo friends complained I was becoming Amhara. In many ways, they were right: learning their language is how we enter the hearts of another people. So I also repeated Dad's tangled, uncomfortable bifurcation of loyalty: his love of the beautiful and proud people from north central Ethiopia, and his identification with those minority peoples and cultures from southern Ethiopia, where we'd lived for so many years.

A middle school teacher found me one day slumped against the brick wall, grinding my teeth in frustration. I tried to maintain discipline in Amharic now—*Sit down! Don't disturb!* Ataweru! *Stop talking, stop talking, stop talking.* It didn't help much. That day I'd given up. Behind the closed door, first grade bedlam reverberated. Tears ran down my cheeks.

The Ethiopian teacher smiled. He shook his head—I was such a hopeless case. "Your job is not *mal-kes*, to cry," he said in Amharic. "Your job is *mas-lekes*, to cause crying!"

It was such an Ethiopian thing to say. In such a classic Amharic construction, with that causative prefix on the verb. Tears still dripping off my chin, I threw back my head and laughed. That I'd even understood what he said felt like a great victory. I wiped my face and opened the door. I marched back in to fight the battle before me, armed with humor and my cross-cultural prowess.

I joined Etabez and the other elementary teachers in the tea room, where walls painted in the days before the Derg were now smudged with grease and dirt. The smell of the day's snack greeted us at the door—suffocating oil haze from the samosas (*sambusas* in Amharic), nose tingling tomato, onion, garlic, and hot *berbere* spices smeared on Ethiopian style pizza rounds. I sipped spiced tea with my new girl-friends, and nibbled, and talked.

At first I mostly listened and faked understanding. I laughed, whether I understood all they said or not. But my Amharic improved. Another friend, Roman, was Oromo-Italian and light skinned—*kei*-red. Her fifth child and fourth daughter she named Amen. But when another son came a year later she named him Ebenezer. When God helped the Chosen People defeat the Philistine army, Samuel set up a memorial stone and called it Ebenezer, *stone of help*. He said, "Thus far the Lord has helped us." I loved the way Ethiopians named their children. *God help us! Another child!* Etabez and I called on Roman during her lying in.

These were the friendships that invited me in from he rim of the culture, where I'd been stuck as a child. The mix was exhilarating. It was also tricky. Later, when Roman was out sick, I was too busy with my three jobs and a family to visit her. She got back to school and reproached me: "Without your visiting me, I recovered." My mistakes felt like thorns tearing at my chronic desire to know what I was doing and always do it right.

# CHAPTER 35

When a sinus infection flared up into feverish exhaustion that fall, Etabez and Roman visited me every morning. They arrived with a thermos of *genfo*, hot buttered porridge, with a touch of *berbere*, thin enough for me to drink. *Genfo* is what women make for each other after childbirth. It's perfect for gaining back strength.

Back on my feet, I walked into the school office to get a new supply of chalk, frantic to get to the classroom before fifty-five unsupervised girls spun out of control. The school secretary, the beautiful and elegant Yadu, ignored my rushed request. She sat with her hands in her lap, smiling. "Are you well? How did you spend the night? Is there peace?"

Ah, how civilized. I took a deep breath and slowed down. "I am well," I said. "There is peace, thanks to God. And you? Your family?"

Yadu wore heels and pencil skirts, her nails long and impeccably polished. I'd never had such a sophisticated friend. The office, smelling of dust and typewriter ink, also held the sweet tang of her perfume.

"Why do you refuse to come have tea with me?" she said.

When had I ignored her invitation? Then I realized this was my invitation. I began to go Tuesday and Thursday to the office for tea with Yadu and her assistant, the other days to the tea room. Each set of friends acted offended—*you like them better than us!* I laughed it off and hoped I was doing the right thing. I counted on their grace to excuse me, because what does a foreigner know?

Six years later, after Mark and I were transferred to Nairobi, Kenya to work, I visited Ethiopia again. I made my way down to Yadu's office, and then to the tea room. Even the cleaning women along the path welcomed me back with hugs and kisses, first one cheek, then the other. Simple things like greeting them on the granite pathways or in the tiled hallways of the school had communicated warmth in spite of our status differences, in status-conscious Ethiopia.

I took a deep breath in the tea room. Steam condensing on the windows, fragrant tomatoes, ginger, cinnamon, onion and sugar like some exotic curry—it smelled so familiar. Etabez and Roman wouldn't hear of my buying my own tea and pizza. I practiced being a gracious guest, even though I had so much more than they.

We told each other the news of our children. They complained about the new school director. We fell into companionable silence. Then Etabez put her warm hand on mine. I looked up, into her eyes. "We don't write to you," she said. "It's not because we don't love you. It's because we miss you so much we can't write."

I knew exactly what she meant. I'd had and lost so many people, some temporarily, some permanently, in the comings and goings of my life: my sisters, my parents, Paul, friends like Jeanie Haspels. Mark. I had let them go. I had missed them too much to write.

I went back to Ethiopia after Mark died of esophageal cancer in 2013.

Etabez, Roman, and Yadu knocked on the guest house door early one morning to call on me. They were horrified to find me alone, and in tears. That Bethel Synods' compound held so many memories of Mark. Of my young children who had grown into adults and also left me.

The women crowded around me. They all started talking at once. *For shame! Pull yourself together! No, no, no!*

I bore their reproach as long as I could. But finally, I burst out, "You don't understand! You still have your husbands!" I hid my face in my hands. Silence surrounded me. When I mopped my eyes and looked out, they were crying with me.

Etabez invited me to spend the next weekend with her. She picked me up at the guesthouse in her car; her husband had come back from getting his PhD in Germany and she was a driving woman now. She surprised me with a trip to the spa—spas had come to Addis Ababa! The flower-growing industry had also come, and rose petals lay in drifts on the floor and across the lounge chairs.

Etabez took me home after our massages, and told me to rest. She fed me. And then she said, "You have your health. You have your children. You need to be strong for them. God's plan is good. You must not cry anymore."

Two years after Mark and I had arrived back in Ethiopia with our family, Kenny started first grade in the American-system mission school the next neighborhood over from us. Whenever I had a break, I volunteered in his classroom. One day, I set out for home a little late. Like everyone on foot in my neighborhood, I took a shortcut.

That area had been a eucalyptus forest when I was young, but now the tall trees crowded in, rustling, on one side, and mud-plaster houses with *korkoro* roofs crowded in just as closely on the other. Pulverized donkey droppings and eucalyptus oil scented the path. Dry season dust puffed up around my shoes. I walked down a steep hill and across a little stream that smelled of gray water.

On the other side of the stream sat the local elementary school, where usually I heard the children chanting their Amharic alphabet, just as the students had in Maji, while I filled out my workbooks. The Amharic *fidel's* letter-families have seven vowel markings each, hence the chanting: *luh-loo-lee-la-lay-**lih**-lo, muh-moo-mee-ma-may-**mih**-mo,* in endless singsong, with the lilt on the sixth form.

Government schools still ran morning and afternoon shifts. Even so, a hundred to one-fifty students were stuffed into classrooms that would have held thirty in the US. That day, the school bell rang just as I was passing. First shift flooded through the gate. Children swirled around me. I was suddenly a pied piper without a flute to make them dance.

"*Ferenj, ferenj,*" they shouted. "Geeve me money!"

They wouldn't have been able to hear a flute, anyway, in that din. With a population in the millions in Addis Ababa, and maybe a thousand foreigners, the children had probably never seen a white American in the flesh. I was sorry I hadn't taken the road. They wouldn't hurt me, but I would be shouted at all the way home. I tried smiling and nodding, *Please let me pass,* but five hundred children each wanted my attention.

A pebble landed by my feet. Something hit me in the back. I stopped and turned. Those crowding behind me swayed. Row after row bumped and tripped and pushed, getting stopped. The air throbbed with the silence.

I greeted them in Amharic, "Have you spent the morning well?"

Their answer rose up all around me. "*Dehena, yimesgen,*" we are well, thanks to God. The Ethiopian Orthodox Church worldview permeates Ethiopian culture with fasts, festivals, and a sense of God's inevitable will.

"Children," I said. "Is this how your parents teach you to treat a guest?"

"*Aydelem,*" a chorus of high voices answered. Of course not. Hospitality is all-important. The children surrounded me, faces turned up eagerly. The smell of wood smoke from their mothers' cooking fires rose from their ragged clothes. Those closest pressed against

197

me. Fingers lightly stroked the hairs on my arms. Little tugs pulled at the honey-brown ponytail hanging straight down my back. Hair that doesn't frizz up in the rain. Plastic hair, Etabez called it. I was an exotic animal.

"So why do you throw stones at me?" There was no answer for one long moment. Then someone called from far back in the crowd.

"*Sileminwedish.*"

"Yes, yes, it is because we love you," the others chorused. I laughed, struck dumb. But of course, it was true. They loved me. They wanted to get to know me. There were so many of them and only one of me. And I was acting shy. Any method would do to get a response.

"Do you speak Amharic?" asked a girl, maybe a third grader, at my elbow.

"*Tadias,*" I said. Literally it means *therefore*, but it's an idiom like *whatever*. We laughed together. A foreigner who said *tadias*!

I had dropped into the crack I'd grown up in, where I was insider and outsider at the same time. Where I was loved for how I belonged and how I didn't. I knew this place. It was richer and deeper than ever, now that I could speak to people. Zoo time was over, we had become just folks, standing in the sun in the middle of the road, smelling of smoke and dust.

"Go home now," I said. "*Ataschegrugn,*" don't hassle me, a whole sentence in one satisfying word. And they scattered, running ahead, running the other way, shouting their child business.

"*Ciao, ciao,*" we called to each other, a legacy from Italian days. When I turned to go, there were just six children left.

"Together let us go," a little girl said.

"I myself have three children," I told them as we walked along.

"*Way-way-way,*" the girl said, shaking her hand as though she had dipped it in hot water, as though to say how happy those three children must be. In high, fast Amharic they told me about their families —brothers and sisters by the dozens. When we crossed the stream and came to the densely traveled road to the *mercato*, people saw us coming and raised the usual cry.

"*Ferenj, ferenj!* Geeve me money!"

That day, my elbow-high bodyguards answered for me. "She is capable of our language. Don't bother her." And the waters parted and we passed through.

It was ironic, the way I took to living back in Ethiopia, after I had tried so hard to turn my face away. By the time we left Portland, our kids had had friends. My brother Chris's family lived around the corner from our eternally being-remodeled house. Scattered as we older sisters were, we gathered at Christmas, and brought our children for massive sleep-overs and stockings to Mom and Dad's house. What else does it take to feel at home?

But something deeply hidden gave a huge sigh when I got back. Sights and smells signaled to my unconscious that I was in a safe, belonging place again. Ethiopians gave me grace as a foreigner, something I never felt from my fellow Americans. It took so little: a bit of language, joining them in their spaces, pleasure in being included. Every effort I made was appreciated.

Mark and I visited Victoria Falls and rafted the Zambezi River during our sojourn back in Africa. Our Zimbabwean guide had us paddle around in the inflatable raft, practicing just above a rapid called the Boiling Pot, until he decided we were ready. The bright sunlight, our clothes already wet from spray, and the coming adventure raised goose-bumps on my arms.

The water of Vic Falls looked pristine as it fell from far above us, but it turned deep and opaque in the churning pool where the Middle Zambezi begins its run to the sea. High basalt walls, the drop to the ocean, and VW sized boulders littering the river bottom create class four and five rapids, one right after the other—the brochures advertise twenty-four in one day of rafting. The rapids have dramatic names: Overland-Truck Eater, The Mother, Terminator. I thought it was advertising hype. Surely no one would take a bunch of middle-aged novices like Mark and me out into real danger.

We approached a triple rapid called the Washing Machine—wash, rinse and spin—and the guide asked, "Easy or hard?"

"Hard!" we shouted. The raft headed for a huge swell of water.

"Left!" the guide shouted. "Right! Paddle!" On the back corner, I paddled for all I was worth. Going over a boulder, the raft recoiled like the tail of a whale and pitched me out. Gray-green water burned into my sinuses. It forced its way between my eyelids. Into my mouth. It tasted as earthy as it looked. It felt warmer than its spray. That was my first surprised thought. I kicked, to surface. Instead, I went deeper.

I was wearing the bright orange life jacket. I had on the royal blue helmet. I was going to drown anyway, in the suds cycle of the Washing Machine.

*The river doesn't even know I'm here*, I thought.

Then the current swirled me up. I shot over boulders, now facing forward, now spinning backwards, into the pool at the bottom of the rapid. I dog-paddled frantically.

Mark shouted as the raft, which had snagged on a rock, broke free and surged past. Behind it came one of the Zimbabwean rescue kayakers who skimmed down the river like water-skeeter bugs. He hovered, both of us paddling hard against the current. "Hold the rope," he shouted. "Wrap your feet up."

I grabbed the loop on the front of the kayak and locked my feet against each other over the nose. There was nothing to do but trust. All my life in Ethiopia, trust had worked. Dad had taught me that— use common sense, yes, but when events spin beyond the range of common sense, trust African generosity. Trust grace.

# CHAPTER 36

I went down the Zambizi river like a bow-sprite on the kayak. Whenever the guide nodded, I held my breath. The river washed over me. When I surfaced, water falling away from my head, he was concentrating. Round wet muscles pulled on the paddle.

As soon as we popped out of the rinse cycle, the river dragged us on. I'd fallen unharmed over one rapid in nothing but my fragile flesh and a helmet, and over another on the front of a kayak. I didn't want to test the Lord my God for a third miracle. The kayaker didn't either. He bent his back into paddling out of the current, to the shallows where the raft was waiting for us.

I opened my fingers, stiff from my desperate grip. I tried to stand, but my shaking legs couldn't lift my body out of the water. I crawled to the raft. I rolled over the edge into the watery bottom. Mark bent over me, his face tight with concern.

When we married, I had hoped that by clinging to Mark's kayak, I'd make it through the mother rapid of adulthood in the United States. I hoped to survive the ride. Yes, he was moody and often withdrawn. But he loved me.

Together we'd made it through the depths and darkness to the take-out. We had leaned on each other for the heart-bursting switchback climb, up the almost vertical walls of the gorge, seven hundred feet to the surface of the earth. Who else would have brought me back to Ethiopia? Twice.

My Ethiopian friends soon began to tell me, even when I knew I was slaughtering syntax, that my Amharic was perfect.

Now, traveling around the US, I meet Ethiopians who found refuge from their various waves of famine and war. They tell me what year they came to the US, and I know which team of brutes they were fleeing. They work in airports in Atlanta, Minneapolis, and Denver; they drive taxis in Washington DC; they process my credit card in parking lots in Portland. I speak to them, and they glow. *Your Amharic is perfect!* It's not. But I know they're saying my accent doesn't hurt their ears. We're both pleased.

When I travel back to Ethiopia, as I do a couple times a year, I speak in Amharic to the stewardesses on Ethiopian Airlines international flights, to waitresses and hotel bell-boys in Addis Ababa, to the taxi drivers there. They make the same delighted response. A chuckle. Appreciation that I can crackle the K, explode the T. "Ah, you speak perfectly!" And from then on, they watch out for me.

Putting my life back together after Mark's death, I decided to learn to read Amharic. Miriam watched in amazement as I drilled a five-inch-tall stack of flash cards—the thirty-three basic *fidel* letters and their six variations. "Why, Mom? At your age?" I didn't know why. Maybe it will keep my brain young.

Growing up I had watched Dad at feasts, or as he preached, or along the path greeting people. I saw how much people loved him for loving them. In between the Maji years and the Derg, Dad drove a group of visiting Americans to the palace for an audience with His Majesty. Panicked, the royal advisors realized no one had arranged for a translator. Someone whispered that Dad could speak Amharic, and he was pushed forward. Dad loved that story, how he translated for the emperor of Ethiopia.

In the US, I had looked like I should fit, but the fit rubbed. In Ethiopia, no one expected me to fit perfectly. I found, again, my cleft in the rock.

People who speak Amharic are proud of the language, complex and capable of great subtlety. They delight in word-play, their wax and gold with its treasured pun. They know we foreigners have a terrible time learning Amharic, and they feel a mixture of pride and sadness about that.

Ethiopians, actually, are proud of many things. For example, that theirs was the only African country Europe never colonized. Occupied, yes. Colonized, no. Theirs was also the only African army in the nineteenth century that routed Europeans, at Adwa.

They are proud of Mekeda, the Ethiopian Queen of Sheba.

"Of course the true ark of the covenant is in Axum," Etabez and Roman told me. They looked at me through the cloud of ginger, cinnamon, and *berbere* in the teacher's tea room as though I was crazy to question it.

Lucy, the mother of us all, lies in the museum in Addis Ababa. Her Amharic name is Dinkinish, You Are Awesome. Upstairs from Dinkinish's bones, stones carved with proto-Arabic script show evidence of the Arab-African mix of genes that gave the Semitic peoples of Ethiopia the aquiline noses they are also proud of. And the *fidel* is the oldest indigenous African alphabet.

Kings of the Solomonic dynasty boasted of their lineage, an unbroken line from Solomon and the Queen of Sheba, even if that line thinned out to a silken whisp over the centuries. Sahle Mariam, the son of a regional king, for example, took the name Emperor Menelik II to enhance the glow of that mythology, and rose to power as the inheritor of the Solomonic line on the male side, not the female side of his rival's claim.

When he was securely recognized as King of Kings, the armies of Menelik II marched out of the mountains of northern Ethiopia and extended the empire to its present borders.

Mom and Dad's generation of missionaries had worked in Ethiopia with Emperor Haile Selassie's permission. Another mixed-heritage nobleman using the banner of Amhara, and the last Solomonic ruler inheriting the male line, His Majesty Haile Selassie was intent on modernizing and unifying Ethiopia. There had to be an official language to bind together the eighty-some ethnic groups.

Canada, with only two language claimants, has struggled with this problem. India, Kenya—there is no easy solution. In Kenya now, there are urban children whose mother tongue is English, and they don't share a language with their grandparents. And how unlikely it was, anyway, that the proud Ethiopians would choose a European language to play the official role. And so, to this day, federal documents are written in Amharic and only then translated into English.

In Oromo areas, especially, there is resentment at having been dominated by the empire-building peoples from northern Ethiopia. Some passionately resisted what they then called Amharization, including the imposition of the Orthodox Church. An Oromo friend told me Orthodox priests threw holy water on the crowds and told them they'd been baptized. "The drops that fell on the ground baptized our land, so they took it next."

In the north, peasants had rights to their land. In the south of Ethiopia, Emperor Menelik II ruled that newly conquered land belonged to the throne. He gave huge land grants to his loyal commanders. Conquered peoples, like the Dizi in Maji, were pushed to the margins. Sophisticates in Addis Ababa still feel embarrassed by peoples who live along the margins of the country. They tell me it's good when the government makes naked people wear clothes, or takes away pastoralists' grazing land and forces them into agriculture. *They need to be civilized!*

They consider hunter-gatherer tribes like the Menja, who still live in the deep Southwestern forests, untouchable. The Menja bring large elephant-ear-shaped *godere* leaves with them to bars and coffee shops in town, and fold them into cups. If they drank from real cups, no one would ever use them again. "They will take our money, though," a Menja man tells me. But the Menja pay for their drinks by dropping their money from a height so flesh does not touch flesh.

"Of course they are unclean," a teenage city boy says. "They eat monkey. Monkeys have hands!" He's inherited centuries of teaching on clean and unclean foods by the Orthodox Church. He shudders.

The Semitic Ethiopian peoples' pride in their aquiline noses, thin lips, and *kei* skin translates into disdain for darker skin, wider noses, and thicker lips. *Those Africans*, they say. Mengistu Haile Mariam's mother was a servant or slave (depending on your sources) from one of the southern peoples. One historian speculates this is why he was so ruthless: the *barya*, slave, who overthrew the master.

As a child, I had nudged Mom and pointed, the Ethiopian way, with my chin, at a man's long pinky fingernail. It curled back toward his palm, yellow and horn-like. Mom whispered, "It proves he doesn't have to work with his hands." Through the centuries of feudalism and empire in Ethiopia, anyone who could afford a slave could avoid manual labor. This, many historians say, fed the appetite for the internal slave trade that persisted until Haile Selassie completely outlawed it in the 1940s.

I had learned about the slaving around Maji from Dad. On the Washa Wooha road, he stopped for a tour guide moment on one hairpin curve, overlooking those ridges of navy-blue mountains. He waved his arm over what he called the Sixty-Four-Million-Dollar View. He pointed out crumbling terraces faintly traced on the steep green mountainside. "The Maji people were so heavily slaved," he said in somber tones, "they lost the art of terracing."

What Dad knew, he had learned from the oral tradition holding the history of most of Africa. An old Dizi chief, speaking of his father and grandfather, told Dad, "We thought the common people were like *goon-don*, army ants. There would always be more of them. We sold them and destroyed ourselves." Those who were left lost their land and were introduced to hard liquor.

And Maji was conveniently situated on the escarpment overlooking the lowlands of Ethiopia, Kenya, and South Sudan. Slaves raided from those lowlands came funneling through Maji on the way inland.

Even still, web sites like Wikipedia and the Refugee Board of

Canada mention the Shankala, as though they are a distinct people of Ethiopia. But they are not. It's the term used by highland peoples for any of the Nilotic or Omotic peoples who live in the southern and western reaches of the country: the Dizi, the Me'en. The Nuer and Anua who straddle the borders, the Shilluk, the Suri, the Boma, the Majang, the Geleb. *Shankala* means the black people, people who are not the red, *kei* highlanders. The word *Shankala* groups these peoples, with all their different cultures and languages, into something that really meant black slave peoples. Urban Ethiopians these days use an abbreviation of the word as a term of affection for their darker skinned friends. But I've seen people from those darker people groups react to the S-word like American blacks react to the N-word. Somebody needs to explain this to Wikipedia.

I didn't put the pieces of this puzzle together as a child. Yes, Maji had a British consulate—I was simply proud that, so far from Addis, Maji rated. Huge rustling eucalyptus trees, planted a century before, marked the site. Whitewashed river stones sat in a pile there—so World War II planes could find it, Dad said. Ato Kulkai, Dad's foreman in the *megazen*, told of walking with the British over the mountains pushing a wheel. He didn't know what the wheel was for. Dad told him it was a click-wheel, to measure distance. Mapmakers used click-wheels in the days before the GPS.

As they set themselves up in Sudan and Kenya, the British tried to stifle the trade of slaves from their colonies that ran to and through Ethiopia—through Maji. The Dizi people are proud that their British consulate predates the consulate in Addis Ababa, but the reason for that is a dark one.

Various of the Ethiopian emperors banned slavery, without effect. There were terms and various price points for slaves of different skin tones and ages. Historians say Emperor Menelik II and Empress Taitu owned 70,000 slaves themselves. The Italians used the well-known slave trade in Ethiopia to justify invading. They, being so civilized, promised to eradicate slavery in Ethiopia once for all.

What drove the trans-Atlantic slave trade from West Africa was the need for men in the heavy work of sugar, tobacco and cotton plantations in the new world. Slaves from Ethiopia were not trekked across the forty-six hundred mile wide bulge of Africa. When they were exported, they were traded up to Egypt and from there into the Arabian Peninsula and as far away as India and China. The East wasn't looking for men, but for the beautiful Ethiopian women. Arabian harems also needed eunuchs. For that, Arabs paid a premium for young Ethiopian boys, castrated locally or after purchase. Because the Orthodox Church forbade Christians from selling slaves, or from owning other Christians, all this activity was run by Muslim Ethiopians, and it preyed on other Muslims or traditional religionists.

Now that I know these things, I wish I didn't. At the same time, I wish I could learn more. There is one book, written by Major Darley, an unapologetic British elephant poacher: *Slaves and Ivory in Abyssinia: A Record of Adventure and Exploration Among the Ethiopian Slave-Raiders.* Amazingly, Darley was transiting in Maji in 1913, when word of Emperor Menelik II's death came by runner. Soldiers and government functionaries faced "early retirement" in the chaos that would ensue in the battle for the throne. They took their pensions in their own hands—literally.

Babies were taken from their enslaved mothers and laid in rows on the floor of a hut in the British Consulate in Maji. The horrified Darley bought a cow. He took rags, dipped them in milk, and dripped it into the mouths of tiny babies, keeping them alive until their mothers could identify and claim them. He walked out of Maji under the imperial soldiers' protection, such as it was. On the single-file trails, pressed on every side by forests that wanted to erase all signs of human passing, counter raiding parties struck. Spear-armed warriors killed the slavers. Children, wives, and neighbors slipped away free, back into the forests.

When Darley reached Jimma, site of the largest Ethiopian slave market, he set up camp where all the foot paths from Kaffa, Maji, and Boma regions came together like tributaries into a delta. He threw down a stick for every hundred slaves he counted. When he couldn't stomach watching any longer, he moved camp. He bundled the sticks and counted them: sixty in two days. Clearly Ethiopian psychology has been scarred by its own unique slaving history.

Though none of the Europeans succeeded in colonizing Ethiopia, all this while they were around, scratching at the door, looking for a way to break in. Portuguese explorers arrived when they were a great maritime power in the mid 1400s. They brought the classic combination of military might and Catholic missions. Both were ineffective. Catholic teachings ran into the wall of the Ethiopian Orthodox Church, founded eleven hundred years before. And the real uses of colonization—cheap resources and cheap (or free) labor—couldn't yet be put to work in Europe. Still, when a Muslim sultan invaded from what is now Somalia, the Ethiopian emperor sent for help from his friends in Portugal. A fleet carrying Vasco Da Gama's brother Christovao and four hundred musketeers sailed into the Red Sea and helped the Ethiopians defeat the sultan.

Two hundred years later, a few Portuguese Jesuits were still in Ethiopia, still trying to plant the Catholic faith. They won over the emperor. Feminist historians have found evidence that the queen herself joined those who rose up in defense of the true church—the Ethiopian Orthodox Church—expelled the Portuguese, and forced their friend, the Ethiopian emperor, to abdicate.

In the 1880s, African colonization picked up momentum. European jackals circled Ethiopia, gobbling up the more accessible lowlands around the borders: French Somaliland, Eritrea, and Italian Somaliland. The British hovered from their colonies in Sudan and Kenya, which cradle Ethiopia's curving western backbone. But the mountains and plateaux of Ethiopia, rising to eight, ten, fourteen thousand feet were effective shields. Ethiopian emperors held the Europeans off.

This is one reason that in Addis Ababa, the hovels of poor people lean against the walls of rich people's villas. Addis Ababa was only an apartheid city like Nairobi or Johannesburg for a short time under the Italians, who expelled tens of thousands of Ethiopians from city limits. Before and since, rich and poor in Addis Ababa have lived together in symbiotic relationships unrelated to race.

But the difficult truth for Mom and Dad was that they were agents of the empire. They had to accept the status quo of Ethiopian politics —their careers as missionaries depended on work permits issued by His Majesty. They must have bargained that what they could bring to the people of Maji offset the dark history of the government they worked under.

# CHAPTER 37

Mom and Dad's compromise with the power structure of Ethiopia played out in practical ways: they became good friends with the governor. Our families visited back and forth, being the only two families in Maji that lived in houses with corners, with living rooms and dining rooms for entertaining. Dad kept the governor's and police Land Rovers running. There they sat, on blocks on the mission compound for weeks on end, as though proclaiming Dad's political alignment, while he waited for parts to be ordered and sent from Addis.

Meanwhile, the Dizi people Mom and Dad had gone to serve had been pushed out of the valleys and onto the steep mountainsides (which they no longer knew how to terrace) by the predecessors of the very people Dad was helping.

"They call the landlords *neftegna*," Dad told me, an apologetic look wrinkling his forehead. *Neftegna* was originally the name for troops carrying rifles, as compared to flintlock guns. It got generalized to mean *those who conquered with rifles and stayed to rule*. When I read of England under kings and lords who sent men to the gallows for poaching deer in the forests that had once been part of the commons, I think of the way southern Ethiopians use *neftegna*, and how any history of violence and oppression stains human relationships. How the dominated hang onto their resentment; how disdain can creep into the oppressor's heart to justify his inhuman treatment of his fellow human.

There were also things Mom and Dad never did know. When the missionaries asked the names of non-Semitic peoples, government officials gave the derogatory names they used. I was shocked to go back in 1990 to an Ethiopia where the tribal names I knew as a child couldn't be spoken in polite society.

So Dad and I became speakers of the language used by the *neftegna*. I hold a tangle of feelings in my heart: joy, that speaking Amharic gives me a path to people's hearts even in Maji, where still no one speaks English well; delight in the musical, tonal, unwritten Dizi language, and sorrow that in Maji, the spirit of the Dizi people was thoroughly broken by those they called the *neftegna*.

In other parts of the country, the Oromo people were not so bowed. The missionaries who worked in Oromo areas picked up some of their language, absorbed some of their resentment, and felt less comfortable living between oppressor and oppressed. A boarding school roommate spoke once about the Amharas in a tone of Oromo resentment, and I felt horrified. I was only ten, I had already absorbed what was called the Amharization of Ethiopia, and the divine right of His Majesty to rule.

And look more closely at the soldiers who poured back into Addis Ababa in 1913, when Emperor Menelik II died. Out of a job, sweeping up slaves by the thousands. Many of them were Oromos, who so resent domination by the Ethiopian emperor, but who filled the emperor's armies.

Ethiopia was never colonized by Europe, so foreigners in the fifties and sixties were not viewed as any threat to the dignity or freedom of Ethiopians. Instead, Ethiopians make their uneasy peace with each other. *Ferenj gid yellem*, never mind the white folks. They stumble over tiers of oppression and suffering at each other's hands.

The missionaries who had opened the Ethiopian girls' school in Addis Ababa in 1926 also built the Bethel Church down the street. It sat, with mud stucco walls and thatched roof, in the middle of a plot of land as big as a city block, if Addis Ababa had city blocks. Without cooking fires to provide creosote from the inside out, thatch absorbs rain. Damp thatch invites insects, and has to be frequently replaced. The termites and their frass in the roof gave the Bethel Church's musty smell a rank undertone.

Like all the mission churches, the Bethel Church services were an awkward amalgam of cultures—Protestant Reformation meeting 1950s USA meeting African traditions of the numinous. Which the missionaries had no knowledge of. With their Ethiopian language tutors, missionaries translated the hymns of people like Fanny Crosby and John Wesley into Amharic. A missionary auntie played a pump-organ for the services at the Bethel Church. The pump organ wailed and wheezed. The little congregation, raised to sing in unison using Ethiopia's Japanese-sounding pentatonic scale, valiantly tried to manage the octave-based tunes. The whining, sliding results made me wince, even as a child.

In the late 1960s, the Ethiopian elders of Bethel Church decided to build. They designed a huge cement church in the shape of a cross, similar to the Beta Giorgis church of Lalibella, carved out of bedrock in northern Ethiopia. Dad and the other missionaries recommended the church elders build a smaller church, one that matched the size of their congregation. They politely declined the missionaries' advice. The missionaries believed in self-led indigenous churches, so they had to hold their tongues. Among themselves they referred to the plan as the Bethel White Elephant.

Then the country wandered into the dark tunnel of the Derg.

For the first time in the Ethiopian Orthodox Church's 1600-year history, the Abuna, the Archbishop, was chosen not by bishops, but by the government. People in the streets referred to him as *Comrade Abuna*. The Orthodox Church, imbedded as it was in Ethiopian culture, was protected from most Marxist attacks. Protestants, however, were a minority. *Kebelles* made experimental attacks on mission churches. When the security forces of the Derg looked away, religious persecution spread.

The downtown headquarter building of the Presbyterian-Lutheran denomination was nationalized. The Good Shepherd School compound was confiscated. In Maji, the rough eucalyptus cross that had been pressed into wet mud on the little church was pulled off and the hole plastered over. The sanctuary became a vet clinic where the mules now got their shots.

A few members of the straggly congregation in Maji, those who didn't become comrades, still gathered secretly to pray. One of them later pointed out to me how the plaster patch on the front of the church made a negative-space cross that had sat, like a shadowy promise, on the front of the vet clinic through the dark Derg years.

Thousands of people were locked up for crimes against the revolution, including prayer. In some places religious leaders—imams, priests, pastors and shamans—were imprisoned and sometimes tortured. One of the Lutheran pastors died of his injuries in prison and is still honored as a martyr.

Dad and the others despaired, sure their frail churches, led by a few Ethiopian pastors who didn't even have high school educations, would not survive. The churches were disappearing underground as Dad turned out the lights of the mission. Had Colonel Mengistu and the *kebelle* thugs not read that martyrs' blood is the seed of the faith? Did the missionaries forget?

When I got back to Ethiopia to teach, I heard the stories of those years. As communism ripped through families, communities, neighborhoods, as the peasant's relationship to the land was torn, as traditions of respect and honor were shredded, people suffered. They grieved. They turned to faith.

Because of curfews, people who met for evening vigils and prayer meetings now prayed all night. Youth group leaders, warned that police were coming for them, ate their membership lists. Pastors, thrown into the squalid prisons, sent word out that parishioners should stop praying for their release. They quoted the words of Joseph, sold by his brothers as a slave: "They meant this for evil, God has used it for good." They said, *God has given me a new ministry. I am planting a church here.*

People poured into the big cement Bethel White Elephant that had once echoed, mostly empty.

Back in Addis Ababa to live, I ventured down the street to Bethel with a retired-and-still-working missionary auntie. Ushers led us slowly down the aisles and finally tucked us into a perceived space on one of the benches. Dry season was in its warm, dusty height, but the building felt cool and smelled damp, of stones and cement. We stood for the first hymn—an Ethiopian melody, with a chorus that we sang over and over, swaying and clapping. Behind me and to each side, the joy cry trilled. A young man with a guitar accompanied us—the wheezy pump organ was long gone. Another boy, on a synthesizer, made a rollicking rumba beat sound like it belonged in church and was perfectly attuned to the pentatonic melody.

Sitting again, we all silently renegotiated our seats, sitting forward-back-forward-back to fit onto the bench. Late-comers, now that no more bodies could be squeezed in, leaned in the windows. The familiar smells of cotton clothing worn many days, of sweat, wood smoke, kerosene exhaust, and *berbere* spices took me back decades to church in the Maji school hall.

After a few months, elders announced they were going to break the congregation into two services. Surprisingly, the crowding seemed the same for a couple of weeks. Then one Sunday, I found myself being herded out of first service through the side doors. The ushers swept through the sanctuary cajoling everyone to their feet.

As my auntie and I walked around to the front, we saw that the doors were still locked. Pressed against them was the kind of crowd that gathers in the US for opening night at a movie, a concert, a football game. Some of the worshippers who came out the side doors with us were jostling their way into the crowd. They had been filling the church for first service and staying put for second. People were willing to sit in church all morning if there was going to be singing and prayer.

Song-writing had spread like the wind through the persecuted church. Choir members brought in their compositions, written on the pulpy pages of blue exercise books. Choirs discussed the theology of the lyrics and sent songs back for revision. Every church had several choirs, and the best choirs traveled. New songs, taped, spread within weeks to every corner of the country.

A friend from Maji gave me a tape of songs his brother had written in the Dizi style of music—less Arab in sound, more contrapuntal, accompanied by the soft plucking on the gut strings of a *krar*. What had happened long ago in Europe exploded in Ethiopia: new expressions of faith in local languages. Then, in German, Dutch, English instead of Latin. Now, in Amharic, Afan Oromo, Dizin instead of Ge'ez.

The anthropologist in me was fascinated to learn, to observe. However, when it came to our own family, going to Ethiopia to be missionaries threw us back, ironically, into churchlessness. After just one experience at Bethel, Mark and the kids had said *imbi*, a word that means *Refusal!* Mark couldn't understand Amharic. The hundreds of parishioners had hundreds of children, and my kids were not about to leave my side and brave the floods of children who might pinch them, feel their hair, and taunt them in a language they couldn't understand. If I wanted to attend Bethel, I had to attend with my auntie, not my family.

Soon enough, my fascination with the transformed Ethiopian church wore off. I could sometimes lose myself in the repetitive, almost hypnotic choruses, and sometimes the Amharic lyrics sank in. I thought I was at least clapping and swaying appropriately until a friend visiting from the States whispered, "Too white?" and winked at me. I'm a Scots Calvinist in heart and body.

But what I really came to dislike was the shouting. As my own spiritual practices grew more quiet, the Bethel microphones were being turned as high as they could go. They buzzed the speakers. Preachers started modestly. Eyes downcast. Reverent. By the time they were finished with hour-long sermons, they were fiery eyed and shouting. I put bits of Kleenex in my ears.

Did Ethiopian pastors think God would hear them better if they shouted? Did they believe their fervor would prove that they were inspired by the Holy Spirit? Or was the shouting imported from traditional spirit worship—those ceremonies that had been carefully hidden from the missionaries when I was a child? I don't know the answer. But I couldn't consider my spiritual state under the verbal onslaught. I spent the worship hours chiding myself: *Value cultural differences; God is listening, why should you mind?* It took a while for me to admit I just didn't like being shouted at. Not in any language.

I gave up on Bethel and we searched for a church where we all felt comfortable. For a while we attended the International Evangelical Church, led by the mission that ran the kids' school. I braced myself against its pietistic, male-dominated theology. I chided myself again: *Don't be so prickly.*

The kids liked seeing their friends there. Ever since high school, I'd loved singing hymns beside Mark, my alto blending with his bass. But a series of sermons from Daniel and Revelation, sermons taking wildly fantastical metaphor and turning it into predictions about the immanent end-times, put me over the top.

I reassured myself that the kids were getting plenty of Christian teaching in their school chapels and Bible classes. But because their school was conservative, my kids ended up more conservative than we were. They were horrified as they got old enough to figure out that we'd lived together before we married. They were appalled that we'd smoked pot. For a while, they were uncomfortable thinking that their mother might be a feminist, something very suspect in those denominations that taught the headship of Jesus over the world, the headship of men over the church, and the headship of husbands over their wives.

When I was stretched too thin by my work to struggle with church, too, we all stayed home and read a Bible story together. A missionary who didn't go to church. I had found yet another way to be a misfit.

It was such a relief—our family alone, without workers, without anyone observing every move. As I stood over the toasted cheese sandwiches, Mark came in, leaned over my shoulder and wrapped his arms around my waist. I leaned back into him. His breath was warm on my scalp. The thick smell of butter and toasting bread filled the kitchen. In Ethiopia, same-gender friends hold hands or walk arm in arm, but public affection between sexual partners was taboo, so we generally avoided the daily affections we had shared in our little being-remodeled house in Portland.

Lunch over, Mark herded the boys into their shared room. "You don't have to sleep. But you have to get along," I heard him say, closing their door. They pawed through the Lego bins, and plastic bits made a brittle rustling. Miriam read in her room.

Mark closed our curtains and the light shone rose-colored through the fabric from the States I'd hung on clips. Flies buzzed and bumped against the window on the other side of the curtains. Birds chuckled softly in the bushes outside. We quietly made love. I drifted to sleep with my head in that hollow between Mark's chest and his shoulder. Sunday could always be a day of rest.

# CHapTer 38

It was clear from the beginning of our new life in Ethiopia that Mengistu's government was on borrowed time. It's amazing how long dysfunction can wander on—the Derg substituted zeal, divisiveness, and strong-arm tactics for effectiveness for fourteen years. No one can hold their breath indefinitely. We breathed and kept going with no idea when the collapse would finally come.

On February 23, 1991, a guerrilla coalition of the Tigray, northern Amharas, and Oromos swept southward. In two weeks, they pushed the Ethiopian army back a hundred miles. BBC newsmen did quick research and told us that the leaders, the Tigrean People's Liberation Front, trained by the Eritrean People's Liberation Army (EPLA), celebrated Albanian Socialism. It was hard to take anyone seriously who proposed to solve Ethiopia's dysfunctional socialism with a harsher form of the same.

The US charge d'affairs, Robert Houdek, called Americans together for a briefing (the US had pulled its ambassador long ago in protest). I asked Mark if he wanted to go.

"Nah," Mark said. "You'll tell me everything." We laughed. Crowds were not his thing.

Ethiopian guards frisked me at the gate of the embassy compound. The woman soldier's hands bump over my underwires. I smelled the garlic and ginger on her breath. Feeling small, I slipped through the gate between ten-foot walls topped by loops of evil looking razor wire.

The embassy grounds were lush and shaded. Walkways, lined by low growing flowers, wound like granite rivers through eye-shocking grass, which had been watered and mowed. Roses bloomed in circular gardens sunk into the lawns. I breathed deeply and caught their faint sweetness.

In the ambassador's gilt and cream living room, folding chairs sat in rows.

"The guerrillas pushed on the door to see whether it might swing open," Houdek said. "To everyone's surprise, it didn't swing open. It fell in." Colonel Mengistu was more vulnerable than anyone realized. The

Ethiopian army had given no resistance in the far north of Ethiopia. Houdek didn't think we would see it anywhere else. "You need to start evacuating non-essential personnel. Women and children."

After the meeting, we scattered back out into the shade-dappled grounds, a hardship post on the world's most beautiful compound. I could pick out the other missionaries. Like mine, their clothes had faded on clotheslines in the tropical sun. Americans on official assignment, (official Americans), went to the States during the summer rains and shopped in the malls. They dried their brightly colored latest fashions in clothes dryers.

"Shannon and her mom are being evacuated to Kenya," Miriam said. "She cried all weekend. She's afraid something will happen to her dad."

I gathered up the supper plates. "Whatever we decide, we'll stick together."

Proud our mission would let us make our own decision, Miriam's smile lit up the dimming dining room. I carried the plates to the kitchen and left them, scraped and stacked, for Zewde to wash in the morning. I went back to the table, where Mark was drawing plans for new wiring in the guest house.

The downside of getting to make our own decision was making it. The school building next door cast our house into shade even though the sun was only now setting. Kenny and Jesse piled into the living room and set up their Lego castles among green towel hills. Gray playing-card roads netted the red and blue rug. I was glad the boys seemed so unaffected by the political drama. I didn't consider that the wars of their Lego knights might mirror the war approaching on the horizon.

The smell of Zewde's gratin potatoes, warmed up in the oven, still filled the dining room. I brushed at crumbs. Mark put aside his sketch and leaned on his elbows on our tablecloth embroidered with Ethiopian crosses that weave and loop, looking Celtic.

"I have the work permit," I said. "I'm not non-essential."

"We can't just abandon everybody," Mark said.

But in the Red Terror, association with us foreigners was sometimes enough for an accusation. *Adhari.* What would Albanian socialism bring? Eventually we settled on a matrix for evacuation: we'd leave if the school closed. We'd go, not to the US but to Nairobi. We'd come back to our jobs as soon as the city was peaceful again.

February ended. The small rains began. The Woyani, as Etabez called them, pushed south again. Radio airwaves lit up and the city of Addis Ababa grew still every evening to listen to the BBC News. Some of our American colleagues panicked. I marveled at their fear, because I didn't feel it. The Woyani were advancing like a slow mudslide, not an avalanche. My strongest feeling was impatience to turn the page and see how it would all work out.

Again, the Woyani pulled up and regrouped. Again, they advanced. Again, Houdek called us to his ornate living room cluttered with folding chairs. The crowd was a little smaller, but not enough to reassure him. He gave us a brief history lesson—soldiers raping and looting as the war went on and on in Congo/Zaire; forty years of civil war in Sudan so far; lethal ethnic riots in Kenya every election year; slaughter in the streets of Mogadishu when the government fell. "We live in a rough neighborhood," he said. "I sure wish I could convince you missionaries to leave."

Everyone in the crowd laughed. An odd envy flows both ways between official and unofficial Americans in countries like Ethiopia. Americans on assignment get hardship-post bonuses. The rest of us make long-term commitments, we speak local languages, we work in the communities. We take our chances. These things are admired, even by people who don't do it. Houdek knew we would make our evacuation decisions based on our local advisors, not on orders from the embassy. But he also knew we'd turn to him in panic if we got in trouble.

Through March and April, Mark and I listened to the news. We tested our decision, checking in with each other over and over. Our matrix held.

One evening in May, Miriam asked to be excused from the table. Her plate looked untouched. "I'm going to bed," she said. It was only 6:30. I turned her shoulder and laid a hand on her forehead. Her face was pale, but her skin was cool.

Cleaning up in the kitchen, I picked up her lunchbox. The yeasty smell of bread that had sat warm all day wafted out—a sandwich with one bite gone, limp carrot sticks, and two broken cookies. I stood, frowning. No appetite. Fatigue. The mystery cleared. Hepatitis. I knew, just as Mom had known with Mark a dozen years before.

The city of Addis has no sewer system for its millions of citizens. Villas have septic tanks, but the clay soil retards percolation and they overflow. The middle-poor, like Zewde, share latrines that get emptied long after they need it. (When she had us to her house, she always reminded me to use the bathroom at home before leaving.) The really poor use the gutters and the median strips. If rains didn't flush the city twice a year, we would all die of water-borne diseases like hepatitis and cholera.

The next morning Mark took Miriam to the clinic.

I walked over to school between two craggy-barked pines that towered over my ferns and begonia. I breathed the piney compost deeply, and gathered the energy to face my three hundred restless Ethiopian girls.

I hit a few guitar chords and the girls joined, *Good morning to you! We're all in our places with smiles on our faces.*

In second grade: *Mary wore her red dress.*

In third grade, the girls almost catapulted themselves out of their seats, as always, wanting to choose bread, pasta, banana for the food song. They shouted, *T'cha, T'cha,* and waved their hands wildly.

Miriam went straight to bed again when she got home, as though she'd walked twenty miles in the snow that day.

In the morning, she insisted she was going to school if her bilirubin test was normal. She and Mark headed out to get her results.

I came home after teaching, to the smell of my hot lunch. It was the civic duty of the wealthy to share their resources by hiring the less fortunate. That had always been Ethiopia's trickle-down economics. Foreigners who didn't hire help were considered incomprehensibly selfish. Zewde had shared her good fortune at having a job by taking in a poor relatives' teenage daughter, who watched the baby and cooked for her while Zewde cooked for me. In the past year, Zewde had also become like a sister who corrected my Amharic and told me, *Don't wear those shoes with that dress.* Or, *That skirt has gotten too faded,* before I walked out the door to teach.

The clatter of her cleaning in the kitchen and the laughter of my students on the playground next door covered the silence of eating alone that day. I was savoring a Zewde fruit salad—papaya, mango, oranges and banana—when a ruckus rose up next door. We rushed to the schoolyard. Little girls cheered. Older girls trilled the joy cry. Zewde grabbed my hand. The hair on my arms rose up. A radio buzzed high-diction Amharic. I strained but couldn't understand a word.

"*Sheshe,*" Zewde shouted. Water welled up around her black irises. He fled. I didn't need to ask who. It sank in slowly. The Woyani were still miles out of Addis. Civil chaos had arrived.

Little girls in their blue skirt-red sweater uniforms were mobbing the school gate. High school girls in black skirts and blue sweaters ran among them, pulling sisters' arms, waving down taxis. Parents were showing up in cars, honking. Zewde said something, but I couldn't hear over the cacophony and I couldn't read lips in Amharic.

We drifted back to the house. I was excited, smack in the middle of history. I was scared. Being foreign had given me a safe neutral space during the coup and the Red Terror—*ferenj gid-yellem*—never mind the foreigner. Would that hold again?

Mark and Miriam ran into the house a half hour later. "Bilirubin normal," Mark said. "But she does have a bladder infection." They'd been on their way to school when shots exploded from the crowded slums near the *mercato*. People in the streets began to shout and whistle. Mark made a u-turn and came home.

Miriam's eyes looked filmy and unfocused. She waited only to hear me say that Mengistu had abdicated before she kicked off her shoes and crawled into bed fully dressed. She left her bedroom door open, as though nothing would keep her from sleeping. As though she didn't want to be alone. I looked in on her from time to time. Hours later she didn't seem to have moved.

A lot of international pushing and pulling had been going on with Mengistu, the world worried about how it would end between him and the Woyani. From BBC that night we learned that he had flown south, refueled in Nairobi, and ended up in Zimbabwe. Later, we found out he'd not only been given refuge, but a 25,000-acre ranch in a country that seized land from white farmers but didn't redistribute it to the peasants. Some Africans are more equal than others.

I clung to what Julian of Norwich had said so long ago—and surely the Middle Ages were as tumultuous as anything we were about to go through—*All will be well, all things will be well, all manner of things will be well.*

Zewde called the next day. She shouted over the static. I struggled with phone Amharic, but I figured it out. She couldn't get across town to work. I told her not to worry, but she fussed and fumed. She liked thinking I couldn't get along without her. She never did believe I cooked for my own family in America, that Promised Land.

For breakfast, I cooked up some of the wheat Zewde had toasted and cracked in the blender, as fragrant in the cooking as it had been in the toasting, with a gritty popcorn-like smell. I unsuccessfully tried to get Miriam to eat. Mark ran off to some project he had going. I compulsively guessed at the future, one scenario after another, as though hitting on the right one would give me some power over it.

Three piles of battered blue exercise books sat on the buffet. I moved one pile to the table and sat down to start correcting the weekly quizzes. The exercise books smelled of *berbere*, from all those lunches eaten with fingers in the dusty sunshine of the school yard. My eyes bleared over. One stack done, I stretched. Folded some towels, crispy from the Addis sun and wind on the clothesline. Sat down to the next pile of exercise books, cheap paper soft as fabric, staples pulling through on the covers.

I was distracting myself, waiting for Miriam to feel better, waiting, with the seven million citizens of Addis, for someone to govern us. Mengistu evacuating himself hadn't been on anyone's list of probable eventualities—a creative new option in Africa's list of methods for transfer of power. What about our matrix? But the thought of evacuating was followed instantaneously by the queasiness I'd lived with all my life in Ethiopia: no one would even consider airlifting Zewde, Etabez or my students out of danger.

After lunch, I crawled in bed to read to Miriam. The boys snuggled around us like warm puppies.

# CHAPTER 39

I'm not good at waiting. In Portland one year, rain and snowmelt swelled the Willamette River, threatening hundred-year flood status. The river rose slowly. Inch by inch. Would it over-top the flood-walls and engulf downtown? I couldn't turn the radio off. The river rolled relentlessly toward us, swelling as every tributary and mountain spring dumped its water in. That's how I felt, waiting.

The flood of deserting government soldiers drifting into Addis grew, pushed by the Woyani advances, now coming from both north and west. Government functionaries fled the country. Prison guards left their posts. Political prisoners and criminals walked out of the jails. There was still an uneasy calm; still much abiding by law in spite of enforcement breaking down.

My school director, Ato Girma, stopped by the house in his director's outfit—sport jacket, trousers and Nikes. Thin, dark, full of controlled energy, he spoke a mixture of English and Amharic almost too fast to follow. "The soldiers stand in the *mercato* and look at their feet in shame," he said. "They haven't been paid for months."

I checked in on Miriam, unmoving and silent in her bed. I cooked, and Mark and I did dishes. He played Legos with the boys. Like the audience in a theatre, we were part of the event, but not the actors.

A brisk trade began—Kalashnikovs for food money. As dusk fell, householders warned off looters with the weapons they were picking up in the *mercato*. "A bullet fired into the air sounds different," Ato Girma assured me. "Different from..." we looked at the boys, playing on the living room floor. Ato Girma's voice trailed off.

Mark looked up at breakfast the next morning. A bullet slug had come through our roof and petered out with its tip through the ceiling. Four-year-old Kenny pounced on the white ceiling disk that had popped onto the floor. Mark lifted him up by the legs to pry the slug out. Jesse jiggled his thin body with impatience, head slung back. As soon as Kenny's feet landed, Jesse nationalized the slug and added it to his collection.

What were the boys feeling? I wondered, but I didn't ask. What would I do if I asked and they said they were scared? I had risen to the demands of my intrepid dad. Now I was silently asking my kids to do the same. They appeared calm, mirroring Mark's and my fatalism. They tell me now that there were some things that scared them, but mostly they watched and saw that we trusted our friends, trusted Ethiopia, trusted God. So they trusted us.

And what about Miriam, so pale, in bed? The clinic had said to drink a lot. I brought her an orange Fanta, which filled her warm room with a chemical tang. She took a sip, slumped back on her pillow, and closed her eyes. Until she was better, how could we travel?

Colleagues from down country came into Addis, pushed along by the Woyani. They flew out to the US. We inherited their dog. One day another bullet came through the guesthouse roof, so spent by piercing the roof and ceiling that it landed on the glass-covered desk and didn't even raise a chip. I seized on the omen: the danger would spend itself out.

During the BBC News Hour, activity all over the city stopped. The Woyani had marched to within thirty miles of Addis. The Oromo Liberation Front had joined Trigreans. Coalition forces were circling in from three directions. Ethiopians from the diaspora of Derg exiles were meeting in London to work out an interim, inter-ethnic, power-sharing government.

Day after day, Miriam slept. Ato Girma came one evening with elders from the Bethel Church. "Miriam, they want to pray for you," I whispered, smoothing her hair off her forehead. She shook her head.

"She's sleeping," I lied apologetically to the men in their suit coats, arms on their thighs, hands clasped. "We can pray here." Mark was building a fire in the fireplace, and the smell of a match and burning paper still hung faintly in the warm air. I bowed my head with the men and let myself be carried by prayers in Amharic, the cadences so familiar, ornate and rich with the attributes of God—grace, mercy, all-powerful creator—and sparkling with explosives.

Street news reported that Ethiopian Air Force jets had taken off and flown in formation to Yemen. Gunmen had rounded up the head-master of the British School with his family in the middle of the night, and, faces covered, threatened to shoot their dog. Ato Girma shook his head in disbelief. "They've been watching American movies."

The Woyani advanced again. Ten miles out, now. On Thursday, Ato Girma said he was going to open school again on Monday. I now find that fantastic, but accepted it without question at the time.

For Mark, there was always something to do. The boys followed him around. He made them little bows and arrows, and they sat on their knees at the dining room table all morning coloring paper targets. I mopped the floors. Miriam slept. Ato Girma visited, whip-lashing in his staccato mix of Amharic and English, between euphoria and anxiety.

Stories of more lawlessness came in. The volume of nightly shooting increased. "Bullets can go through our cement block walls," Girma said. "But not through mud walls." So the poor were safer than we were in our villas. That seemed like an apt irony to me, *The last shall be first.* I hoped people would keep their AK-47s aimed to the sky.

On Friday evening, the phone rang. Mark mouthed *Embassy* to me as he nodded and said his *um-hums* into the mouthpiece. When he hung up, he turned with his eyebrows up and his hands open in a what-do-we-do-now gesture. "There's one more flight out. Lufthansa to Frankfurt. Then they close the airport."

"Frankfurt!" I said. Frankfurt was an eight-hour flight. "Miriam can't even sit up in bed." And where would we go from Frankfurt? The Nairobi option, two hours away with mission guest houses, had slipped away without our knowing it. It was a shock: our matrix, which had felt so smart, so reassuring, was completely irrelevant in the end.

At supper, Kenny and Jesse chattered to each other. Mark and I were silent, wrapped in our struggle to sort out what had happened. By bedtime I was completely tangled in threads that wound this way and that way in my mind. None of them led out of the maze. "What are we going to do?" I asked as we climbed into bed. I snuggled up. Tentatively put my feet against Mark's warm calves. Mark didn't pull away. He also didn't answer.

"I'm listening," I said. He rubbed his foot against mine. We'd been married almost thirty years. I knew what he was saying. That he wasn't falling asleep. That he was gathering his thoughts. That I should wait.

His sister, a physical therapist, told me that while people have different processing speeds, "Mark is the slowest processor I've ever known."

I wasn't sure why I felt so calm about the possibility that we would let that flight go without us. What I wanted was reassurance that it was okay to feel the way I did. "The thing is," I said, "if we stay here out of some twisted sense of adventure or martyrdom, I could never forgive myself. You know. If something happened." My thoughts weren't the kind I wanted to say out loud. *If something awful happened.*

*After all the grief had passed. It would be easier to forgive God. Easier than forgiving each other. Easier than forgiving myself.*

Mark still didn't speak. I nudged him. He took a deep pull of air. "I think we should pray that God will tell us in a dream what to do."

I laughed out loud. "Do you think we're Gideon? Or Jacob?" He'd said it so sincerely. I hugged him so I didn't sound harsh. "What if God wants to tell us some other way?" I turned out the lamp and slid down so my head rested on his shoulder. The baked-bread scent of his skin was tinged with hard-work sweat.

Mark nuzzled my hair. Then he prayed out loud for us. That God would give us wisdom. However he wished to do it.

When Mark woke up the next morning, he found me waiting. "I had your dream," I said. "We were at the airport. An announcement came over the loud speakers—people with odd numbered tickets needed to start boarding. People with even numbers should stay. Our tickets all ended in two."

Mark raised his eyes in an amused thank-you to God.

American friends don't know what to think of my dream. We natter on about economic forces, political forces, but spiritual forces? They make us squirm. My own intuitive wisdom sent up a message, maybe. Misdirected denial about getting my family to safety. I don't say what I think about my dream, because that goes to a place where I feel privately delighted by my faith, but mystified and unable to talk about it.

Ato Girma just smiled and nodded. Ethiopians live in a world richly populated by spirits. God still speaks to Ethiopians in visions, still heals and performs miracles, still answers prayers. It seemed only right to Ato Girma that I be directed by God himself.

Lufthansa took off. The airport closed. As far as I know, we were the only American family in Addis Ababa during what became known as the Time of Change. But Mark and I were at peace. With our Ethiopian friends, we were relieved that the Mengistu era was over. With them, we were scared about what would happen next.

Almost immediately Miriam's skin and eyes turned yellow and her urine turned brown—hepatitis. I was so thankful that we'd stayed, that we hadn't stressed Miriam's out-of-commission liver, that we hadn't gotten quarantined in Germany, where the only word I knew was my last name. I held onto faith—I was Gideon. I was Jacob. I was the Wise Men, warned in a dream to return another way.

And how strange and right it felt to be in Addis for the fall of the regime we had watched begin. How symmetrical: Mark sick and Mariam born; now Miriam sick. Another revolution a la hepatitis.

I didn't assume the dream meant none of us would get hurt. It just reassured me that God would be present. There would be grace. A light would shine, whatever the darkness we were walking into.

That's really all the promise we ever have.

We moved Miriam's bed to the living room. I took my hard-currency checkbook and ran to the one supermarket with imported food—one week, shelf after shelf of pickles from Bulgaria, another week not a pickle in sight but Romanian jam in gold and ruby, rows upon rows. Recently I'd bought a six-month supply of powdered milk. Now I bought a quintal of sugar and two of flour.

Zewde and I looked like dusty millers by the time we finished bagging it up and sharing it out with Etabez, Roman, Yadu and Ato Girma. We could all make bread if the city shut down. Bread, sweet tea, and friends. It would see us through.

On Monday, BBC announced that the US Under Secretary for Africa had scuttled the coalition peace conference in London in favor of the Albanian-admiring Woyani. Who then announced on Radio Ethiopia that they would march into the city the next day. They asked the citizens of Addis Ababa not to resist.

Life can seem cheap in Ethiopia, even though people grieve dramatically and passionately. A high infant mortality rate brings the average life span down to about forty-five. And war brutalizes. So as Mark and the boys made a false bottom in one of the closets to hide our laptop, he told them that if soldiers came to our house, Miriam and I would hide in the attic and he would pretend not to know where we were. I signaled cut with my hands. Mark stopped there. Jesse nodded, solemn.

The Ethiopian church elders came again: Ato Girma, Yadu's husband, and our neighbor, grizzled and thin, who had been a young church leader in Dad's era. They laid hands on the door posts of the compound houses and prayed for God's protection.

Blue dusk turned to night. The crescendo of gunfire didn't sound like a warm welcome for the Woyani, but I hoped it was still just citizens warning off looters. Mark pulled Miriam's mattress off the bed and I sat with her below window level. In front of the fireplace, Jesse snuggled up with a giant bear he called Jesse Junior. Mark threw another piece of firewood on. The fire crackled and flared up. The faint smell of smoke seemed homey. Mark pulled Kenny against his chest. I opened Jesse's latest Redwall book and started reading aloud—another story about good mice and squirrels battling weasels and stoats.

I was in mid-sentence when the lights went out. Mark and I looked at each other's flickering faces. I closed the book. None of the kids said a word.

# CHAPTER 40

I fumbled my way to the kitchen, lit candles, and brought out my afternoon's experiment—homemade marshmallows. To our disappointment, they jiggled, foamy, not something you could push onto a stick and toast. Kenny sniffed at his and licked it cautiously. Miriam could have all she wanted, to keep her blood sugar up.

Mark took one of the candles back to the kitchen. In a minute, popcorn kernels rang against the lid of a pan and then thudded into each other's soft sides. The smell of comfort food wafted out to us.

Salt on our tongues. Flickering yellow and orange on our eyes. Silence in the living room.

When the popcorn was gone, Mark flopped the boys' foam mattresses onto the floor of the windowless hallway in the middle of the house. We dragged Miriam's mattress from the living room with her on it. The boys jumped on, squealing, for a ride. Mark and I settled on either side of Kenny in the darkness. The shooting sounded muted and distant from our little cave.

I pictured bullets falling through the air. I hoped all the city's children were safely indoors. Jesse's body on the other side of me relaxed. Kenny finally stopped his restless thrashing.

Mark shook my shoulder. "I want to sleep in my own bed." I lay and stared into the pitch darkness. *A stray shell hits our house. We die in rubble. The boys wake up screaming. The noise. The dust. The smoke. Miriam is all they have left.*

Mark pulled on my hand. I held tight. Prayed an inchoate prayer— *Please.* I tucked the *gabi* back around Kenny, already moist and musky in sleep.

In early dawn, I woke. Rosy light came through the curtain. Thud.

Guns at the palace at dawn. My whole body remembered the sound: every year, celebrating the Ethiopian army turning back the Italians; in the dark during the coup; Mengistu killing off his rivals in 1977. Mark turned over and pulled me close. We listened, half asleep. The only danger for us would be a misfire in fighting at this end of town.

The city fell silent around eight o'clock. Mark got up and hopefully opened the doors and curtains. The light woke up the kids. A little later, Ato Girma burst in the front door, his dark face alight. "The Woyani are coming."

We left Mark's special-order animal pancakes soaking up home-made syrup and ran up to the gate. Jesse, on tiptoes, stuck his face between the bars. Mark and I passed Kenny back and forth so he could see. We were the only white faces in the crowd. It didn't matter. The soldiers never turned their heads.

Some of the men wore black jellies. Some wore tire sandals, others, traditional untanned leather sandals. Bandoliers crisscrossed their chests. Their Afros were as long as their military green shorts were short. Their mules pulled anti-aircraft guns on carts.

A soldier with a radio transmitter shouted a guttural command. It was the first time I'd heard the Tigrinya language. The column of soldiers stopped. They faced forward. They did not speak. All morning we stood watching, millions of us completely silent, along the streets. Just as silently, the Woyani took the city.

Ethiopia had ricocheted from feudalism into communism. Now what? For a country with over eighty ethnic groups, and languages from four different language families, power-sharing had sounded like a good idea to me. But the US had undercut the process in London and backed the might-makes-right of the Woyani—what was the rush? We had taken eleven years to write our first constitution.

Thousands of Ethiopians felt the same. The day after the Woyani entered, people demonstrated in front of the US Embassy. It isn't negotiation skills guerrilla armies practice in the bush: soldiers shot into the crowd. Around the city that day, they killed six or eight people.

Our family stayed inside the school compound for two weeks until Ethiopian resignation set in again, and the sun that rose was their sun again. One day, I decided it was okay to go out; a single American on the streets wouldn't stir up resentment.

"Swedish?" a souk-keeper asked. I felt pleased to be taken for a Swede. From what people told me, Swedish has sounds and syntax like Amharic, so Swedes speak good Amharic. I was tempted. But I shook my head and made apologetic eyes.

"Amerr-ican," I said.

The shopkeeper laughed in hospitable delight. He thrust his hand forward to shake mine. He lowered his voice. "Don't be troubled. Your government we protest. But you, we love. America is our mother. All we hope is that America will take us once again and suckle us at her breast."

I smiled. I doubted our State Department understood the intense loyalty that came with the African world view, where community is the cushion between life and death. But I was sure Houdek wasn't thinking, *Let America suckle you at her breast.*

I pretended to study the collection of old Orthodox crosses under the glass of the *souk's* tiny counter. I pointed to a small one with heavy, round arms. Someone had worn it on a string around their neck for years. The ring was rubbed almost through. I offered five birr, though I didn't really need one more cross.

His eyes went bright. "Ten," he said.

Bargaining in Ethiopia is only tangentially about economics. "Seven-fifty," I countered, and gave the coins to my new friend.

Abuna Petros had stood so patiently through the decades, chained to his marble machine gun. Now he stood guard over Woyani soldiers. Street news said the Ethiopian Air Force in Yemen was going to attack, so anti-aircraft guns stood among the roses in the traffic circle, pointing at the sky. The soldiers hung their camo shirts on them, and on the points of the wrought iron fence, to crisp dry in the sun. Young men who could sleep wherever they laid their heads, they draped their lean bodies across the tank or sprawled in its shadow. Within the month, they were issued long camo pants to replace their mini shorts. They cut their hair. And Addis Ababa picked up where it had left off.

Jesse turned yellow. The next week, Kenny did. We made the living room into a sick ward. The boys had light cases and felt better before Miriam.

Our PCUSA bosses had told us in orientation not to talk politics in our host countries, but there wasn't any way to get away from politics in June 1991 in Addis Ababa. The Woyani had slipped between Oromos and Amharas, the two biggest people groups. Amharas were gloomy. Oromos were ecstatic because the Woyani were talking power sharing and ethnic sovereignty. The Oromos were to become bitterly disappointed in this, but for now, they thought they would finally have the power their position as largest ethnic group deserved. Our Oromo friends in the church were deeply involved with the Oromo Liberation Front. They wouldn't greet us in Amharic any more.

"*Fai-yada,*" we said to them now. "*Garida.*" And we bumped shoulders instead of kissing cheeks.

Addis Ababa wasn't Addis Ababa any more, they told us. The city needed to go back to the name of the Oromo village that was here, which they said Emperor Menelik had invaded and Queen Taitu had renamed. Overnight, a century of writing Afan Oromo in Amharic script was over. Afan Oromo in Roman script popped up on signs— huge words with double vowels and double consonants, x for the explosive t and q for explosive k, a dizzying new language.

Mark took sodas to a meeting in Oromo country and they sat untouched in the middle of the table. Someone whispered to him later that no one would drink from a bottle that still said *ko-ka ko-la* in the Amharic *fidel* on the bottle.

A month later, Ato Girma invited us to his apartment. Miriam, still weak and yellow, couldn't walk that far, so Mark got a wheelbarrow. It wobbled down the cinder gravel path. Miriam held both sides with whitened knuckles. She alternately laughed and screamed.

"Don't worry," Jesse said. He trotted on one side, sure he could catch his sister if she tipped. Mark carried her up the stairs.

Ato Girma's living room, smaller than our bedroom and furnished with just a couch and coffee table, was fragrant with onions, garlic, cumin, and ginger. The cinder block walls were smudged and chipped. "Your house says spice-spice," I said to his wife, Mulu Shewa. We kissed the air, cheek on cheek, first one side and then the other. Mulu Shewa wouldn't speak English, but she laughed at the boys' silliness, so we knew she understood some. Kenny sat close beside her on the couch, and she sneaked extra sugar into his milky tea. Years later he told us that he ran up to visit her when Mark and I were busy. She gave him warm milk with as much sugar as he wanted. Our lonely little boy had found another shy soul. And who needs to talk?

That day, Ato Girma was full of gloom. The Tigreans would be insufferable, he said.

"But the Woyani are talking about power sharing," I said.

"You don't know the hearts of these Africans." Girma's face rested on his hands, his elbows on his knees above a sweet glass of Addis Tea. "And you must stop calling them Woyani."

I was surprised. That's all I had ever heard them called.

"When they're the government, you can't call them guerrillas anymore. Even if they are," he said, and laughed.

Girma got out the Uno cards. Mark, Mulu, and I shook our heads, we would watch. Mark slipped his arm behind my back on the foam cushion of the couch. Politics faded. The game went on and on.

It could go on forever. My cheeks forgot how not to smile. I had, in that simple room, all that I'd come to Ethiopia for. Not to make the world a better place. Not to support the partner church. Not to teach English. Not really. I hadn't come to save anyone's soul. I'd come back to feed my own.

When the school year ended in 1977, the Derg had laid claim to Good Shepherd School. Soldiers frisked everyone and confiscated students' books, trumpets, basketballs. No one argued with the Derg soldiers and their Kalashnikovs.

Fourteen years later, after the Derg fell, I drove out there. I'd chosen the perfect moment: the new guerrilla government was still making soft reassuring noises to keep everyone calm. I made my own soft reassuring noises, chatting with the soldiers in Amharic. They let me in and gave me a tour. The Derg had turned the dorms and classrooms into a rehabilitation center for soldiers wounded in their misbegotten wars with Somalia, Eritrea and Ethiopia's own liberation armies. We kids had thronged with the agility of kids along the uneven sidewalks, sculpted out of granite by the workmen with their sharp little hammers. But how rough they looked to me now, as I thought of men on crutches and in wheelchairs.

The Derg had tried to legislate reforestation, and had done its part at Good Shepherd. Dozens of eucalyptus trees, now as big around as a man's thigh, swayed and rustled on the field where Chester Wenger had dodged in our games of pom-pom-pull-away in the dusk after supper. Dozens more crowded what had been the softball diamond where Mark had shouted, *That's my girl!* More between the dorm and the dining hall, where the boys had chased Jeanie Haspels and me as we played Black Stallion, and the light was blue gray just before dark.

All the buildings looked old now. Rust streaked their roofs where galvanizing had worn off the *korkoro*. Paint had chipped off the cement block walls, leaving them speckled with gray. As long as I talked and laughed with the soldiers in Amharic, they kept their Kalashnikovs hitched on their shoulders and let me keep walking. The dry season sun burned down on my head.

"Don't go there," they said, when I started up to where the big swing had stood, where the fifth grader swung with Slinger as high as she could go and let the boys look up under her dress. "There was a latrine. *Feneda.*" It exploded? A big bowl-shaped depression in the grass convinced me I had heard correctly.

The asphalt up at the basketball court had buckled. Grass pushed through cracks, and the free throw line was faint as a shadow under rusting rims, hanging crooked, bare of nets. Exactly in that spot, right under that basket was where I had first seen Mark twenty-five years before.

Only the Baldie, Crew Cut, and Moglie hills looked the same. Crew Cut would get a buzz when they next harvested the eucalyptus. Then its hair would grow again. The fields beyond Good Shepherd ran up Baldie, the fields that were so wet with clay soil when we hiked up the year the prince died that mud stuck to our shoes and made us taller by two inches. We had kicked, and clods of black mud flew up and landed in someone else's hair. Then Benny Gamber kicked and his whole shoe came off and we collapsed in the mud, weak with laughter.

The fields would turn brown and gold in the dry season, chartreuse with teff in the rains. The hills would be there forever, come empire, come communism, come guerrillas. The hills and fields were the things that would never change.

A group of us put in a petition to the new government to take Good Shepherd back. I became president of the once and future Good Shepherd School Board. But a few months later our case fizzled. The government wasn't going to be that accommodating. When I drove by and tried to peer in the gate one more time, the soldiers waved me on with their Kalashnikovs. They didn't smile or speak.

# CHAPTER 41

When Miriam was sixteen and Jesse twelve, we visited Maji. Ethiopian Airlines didn't fly into Washa Wooha anymore. The old workhorse C-47s had been retired, and EAL flew turbo props now, carrying sixteen people and no freight, into an airstrip that had been leveled on the other side of the ridge. A town called Tum had grown up as the government center there, several thousand feet lower than Maji.

There was a new mission station in Tum, too. Mark had gone down and helped build one of the houses. Now, as he toured me around, I fell in love. A huge window opened over the dining room table and looked out at the setting sun. I wanted to live within the cozy mud walls, under the *korkoro* roof, and be the Dizi translation advisor.

"What would I do here?" Mark asked, before blowing out the candle in our guest bedroom. "Do you really want to put the kids in boarding school?" His calm practicality cooled my fever. I took a deep breath and snuggled up, laying aside again what had felt like my destiny as a child—being the only white person to speak Dizin.

The road from Tum to Maji wound seventeen miles up to Maji. We took Miriam and Jesse and set out to walk the short cut, up the back and along the ridge.

Ato Kulkai guided us. He had seemed old when he was Dad's foreman. He was still lean and tall. Ethiopians gray slowly, but his hair and whiskers were almost white around his dignified, deeply wrinkled face. His walking stick stood seven feet tall, knobby and polished with wax and oil, like the ones Dad had bought for us to break in and gallop around on. Legal tender then was tin cans, precious as gold to people who otherwise had only clay pots and gourds.

Miriam and Jesse ran ahead, out of sight. Just as I had once been, they were the middle of a gang of curious children they couldn't speak to.

We walked across the fields to the base of an almost vertical climb: *YeKir Demozay Dagut*—Forget My Wages Cliff. It may have been half a mile straight up. It seemed an unending climb. My oxygen-starved lungs burned. My knees ached.

Ato Kulkai told us a story: a city boy, straight out of university, had been assigned to teach in the Maji government school, on the mission compound during the Derg, with offices in the house Dad and Grandpa built for us. Halfway up the cliff, the new teacher said, "*Yekir demozay.*" He turned around and went back to Addis Ababa.

It was more than his wages he left behind on the cliff, it was his whole career. It wasn't easy to qualify for a spot in the university. And then, in their first semester, a quarter of the freshmen flunked out and went home in shame. In that ironic Ethiopian way, they called it December Graduation. But this young man had made it through. On *Yekir Demozay*, he gave up a job for life in the government school system. Ato Kulkai laughed with me, and watched Mark's face with anticipation as I translated the story. Just as when I was a child, the rugged beauty of Maji was a thing of pride for its people.

Stones cropped out of the side of the cliff like rungs on Jacob's ladder. Where there weren't stones, depressions in the clay showed where people before me had placed their feet going up and coming down. Half the time I was pulling myself along with my hands, grabbing bushes or saplings for balance. At a switchback, Mark, Ato Kulkai, and I stepped aside to catch our breath. My heart was pounding so hard it rattled my head and chest as it tried to get the scant highland oxygen to my muscles. My legs trembled. I wasn't the mountain goat I'd been as a child. My body told me without a doubt I was older, and climbing to nine thousand feet.

A woman, going up fast, passed. She balanced a huge gourd of honey on her head. Her neck muscles connected in wide cords to her shoulders. Strands from the thick grass plug in the neck of the gourd bounced with her every step. She touched the gourd with the fingertips of one hand. Under her upraised arm, her earth-brown dress was split at the seam and showed the smooth skin over her ribs. Sweat beaded on her top lip. She turned only her eyes to look at me, then dropped them as though to nod a greeting. She couldn't look down to see where to step, but intuitively she knew. She climbed precisely from stone to stone, her perfect posture taught, not with a book, but with the family livelihood in a gourd.

"*Jeshi,*" I said, proud that I could remember the Dizi greeting.

"*Jesha,*" she whispered.

The next time we stopped to rest, a man from the Suri people, who used to come naked from lowland areas to the Maji clinic, caught up and joined our little party. He was not naked. He wore a jacket and a rifle. As when I was a child, he was completely uninhibited. I was the one embarrassed, keeping my eyes at shoulder height.

Up the *dagut*, across the ridge, we came to the base of the big waterfall. There was only a flat grassy spot left to show where the shed had sat when Ato Kulkai ran the mission grist mill. In 1978, high school boys in Maji had been seized with the passion infecting the whole country. They were drunk with the need to march, to riot, to be the broad masses and throw off the yoke of oppression. Americans— the missionaries—had left by then. The mission compound had been nationalized. But the boys worked themselves into a frenzy and ran down to the mill shouting, "Capitalist puppy dogs!" They pounded the pelton wheel into brass shards.

Women paid the price for that political fervor—for the next twenty years, the boys' sisters and mothers went back to grinding grain by hand. I felt a surge of my old feminist anger rise with my sadness.

Ato Kulkai pushed the grass aside with his walking stick. He pried out a piece of brass for me, from the tangle of roots and stems. Heavy in my pocket, it pulled down one side of my faded denim skirt as I walked.

The children waited for us on the flat spot where the long, low thatched school building had sat. The local kids sprawled on close cropped grass, rough housing and teasing. Jesse and Miriam talked softly in the center.

We walked with them up the hill, to the former mission com-pound, through the spot where the gate had stood. It was a shock to see the compound without the live *korch* fence enclosing it. The land fell steeply away on three sides. The mission homes, clustered on the knoll, looked vulnerable, unprotected. They looked decrepit.

I walked to where Jane had said we were lifting our eyes to the hills. A stunted Shasta daisy still held out against the vigorous African crab grass. The twin *gojos* were no more, those huge mushroom-like huts. Not a trace remained, not even bare earth where workers had tramped the ground and covered it with woven *selains*. No rushes, no stucco rubble. Whatever debris the *gojos* left behind had composted back into the soil. I squinted at their ghostly presence.

"Is this all?" Jesse said.

"That was my house when I was your age," I said, and pointed. Most of the windows were broken and covered with cardboard. One corner post had been eaten through by termites and the porch sagged now, like the cheek of a stroke victim.

"Well, duh. Can we go now?" Miriam said. They ran off with the amoeba mass of children. There was only one road, and it led to town.

After our 1960 furlough in Boise, in my infinite 10-year-old wisdom, I had told Jane that someday the Washa Wooha road would be lined with billboards like those on the freeways out the open windows of the family station wagon. We both wept for the future desecration of Maji's beauty. I didn't imagine it would look like this in 1993; that progress might run backwards, not forward, in places like Maji.

Africa would stay poor, I thought, as Mark and I followed the kids to town. As long as it was restricted to fueling the industrial world with cheap resources and labor.

We ducked into the one restaurant in Maji, with a rusted *korkoro* roof and glassless windows, the wooden shutters swung open. The hostess hollered at the chattering crowd of Ethiopian kids. They ran off. Our benches and table rocked on the lumpy earth floor. The air smelled of spices and dust. A cool breeze blew in on the back of my neck.

For a few dollars-worth of *birr* we ordered the gray down-country *injera*. The *wat*, without city spices like cumin, ginger, and cardamom to soften the sting of red peppers, made my lips burn and my nose run. Chickens cackled on the dirt floor under our table. They clustered at Jesse's feet.

"Stop feeding the wildlife," I said.

"Busted," Miriam said, and Jesse giggled.

By the time of that visit to Maji, I had spent three of the six years I'd be in Ethiopia teaching English. I chronically carried on a silent mental fight with the more conservative missionaries. Surely, they were looking askance at me, asking themselves how I, a member of liberal PCUSA, could call myself a missionary. For my part, I wasn't even sure I wanted to be known as one. I would never be the true believer that everyone assumes a missionary is, the deeply convicted person with no questions about vocation and calling. Instead, I'd always be the woman who'd been the girl who'd cried about a God who would condemn the Dizi people to hell even if it wasn't their fault they hadn't heard about Jesus.

In those dark, ambivalent missionary nights, I understood more and more deeply what I was there for. Not speaking Amharic had left a hole in my childhood experience. Now I was making an exchange—my teaching gifts for healing. By learning Amharic, I was filling what had been left empty, making the people of Ethiopia mine, not just their hospitality, their beautiful landscapes, and bracing highland climate.

Beginning when I was eighteen, leaving Ethiopia for college, I had said to myself at the end of every visit, "Look! Listen! Remember everything! This is the last time you will see Ethiopia!"

Since 2001 I've had a consulting job that takes me back to Ethiopia once or twice a year. I've been back so often I don't tell myself to say goodbye like that anymore. Now I'm in danger of not looking, not listening, not holding Ethiopia in a final embrace. Now I'm in danger of finding one day that the last time I saw Ethiopia passed me by without notice.

Why do the small ways I fit in Ethiopia still mean so much more to me than all the thousand ways I am thoroughly and completely American? My bond with Ethiopia is mostly mysterious. Maybe spiritual bonds always are. I can see shadowy outlines, though. When our family went as strangers to Ethiopia, we were welcomed and loved. In the US, the strange, hybrid self I'd turned into was rejected. I made my way the best I could in Pasadena, in college, in Chicago. When I went back to Ethiopia to work, the school and church communities opened and took me in again. Why wouldn't that warmth draw me back over and over?

Dr. Yshak, a friend who came through the Maji mission school after the Kurtzes left, used to travel with me sometimes. In the car, he told stories and jokes. I think his English was better than my Amharic, but we used Amharic, so even the driver can join in.

Leaving Maji one time, as we drove down the dirt track past where the shaggy, thatched mission school had sat, I was feeling teary. "Those were such wonderful years for me," I said, seeing the wispy image of little girls running with teddy bears.

"It was the golden age for all of Maji, when the missionaries were with us," Dr. Yshak said.

I hadn't known that. Didn't expect it. But of course. Ethiopians believe a house says warm-warm when a guest arrives.

"Now we are abandoned," he said. "No one wants to help us. When will you come back to live with us?"

My friend Etabez takes my hand and says the same thing. "You've learned our language. Build a house! Come for vacations! When you retire, grow old with us."

I feel grateful for their love. My visits are some of the happiest times of my year. I thanked Dr. Yshak. I thank Etabez. I agree it would be right, it would be wonderful to live with them again.

But in the end, I know I won't. I would miss my children if I moved back to Ethiopia. My grandchildren would grow up, stage by stage, without me. My sisters and brother would talk about interesting things without me. I have American friends. Real friends, finally.

But wait. My daughter lived for eight years in Malawi and Kenya. Her daughter was born in Malawi. She loves to travel! My son taught for three years in Abu Dhabi; his daughter was born there; he wants to teach overseas again! We have an international family! And I would come back every year, during Ethiopia's rainy season, for Oregon's delightful summers. Wouldn't I?

It's no use, that lovely fantasy. I am a foreigner on a visa in Ethiopia. My Amharic is adequate, but I can't share my deepest feelings when my mind is scrambling to figure out the simple way to say things, and the words still don't fall easily into the right order. I will always return to the United States, and resume my lifelong struggle. The exact contours of my dual loyalties burrow deeply, hidden even to me. No matter where I live, the other half of my heart will fill with longing.

I know the part of this to say to my Ethiopian friends. I know how to say no and also let them know they are not second-class citizens in my life. "My grandchildren..." I say, and shake my head in regret.

They nod thoughtfully, bowing to the primacy of grandchildren.

And we let go of each others' hands, silently hoping it isn't yet the last time.


On that family visit to Maji, as Jesse and Miriam ran off toward town, Mark and I walked up the little rise to the house Dad and Grandpa Kurtz had built for us. The cedar trees that arced away from it, that moaned in the night wind, where we tried to monkey-jump from limb to limb, had grown dark and shaggy. The one at the kitchen corner had lost all its limbs. It towered, a twenty-foot-tall stump.

Mark's arm bumped my shoulder. "You okay?"

I wasn't sure. At what had been our dining room window, I cupped my hands around my face to see through the reflections. One leaning bookcase, left from the Derg occupation, held a book missing its cover. A broken chair lay on its side with three legs helplessly in the air like a beetle upended. Maybe we shouldn't have come. Maybe it would have been better just to remember.

I straightened up and turned. There, spread before me was the valley, bright in the midday sun. Red Rock and the Sleeping Giant flanked it on either side. Across, the Ridge. The Gap. The hazy golden lowlands beyond. A raptor floated on some invisible current. The view from our dining room window, with the *gojos* gone, was as beautiful as Mom had always said it would be.

# Glossary of Amharic Words

**Adhari**  A counter-revolutionary, from the Ge'ez word to walk backwards

**Ato**  Mister

**Bait**  House (the same in Arabic and Hebrew, an example of the Semitic inheritance)

**Berchee**  Be brave (the command form for a female.) Amharic has four forms for "you"—male, female, plural and polite.

**Buna**  There is both tradition and scientific evidence that coffee originated in Ethiopia. One of the southern provinces, and a people group, are called Kaffa.

**Caio**  Imported from the Italian, in Ethiopia *Caio* means good-bye

**Korkoro**  Corrugated iron sheeting

**Fidel**  The *Ge'ez* alphabet, actually a syllabary, with a verbal marking attached to each consonant. The oldest indigenous written alphabet of Africa.

**Gabi**  A heavy cotton blanket/shawl Ethiopians wrap themselves in against the cold

**Ge'ez**  The dead source language of the Semitic languages of Ethiopia.

**Gojo**  A traditional, round thatched hut

**Goon-don**  Army ant

**Goom**  Fog

**Kei**  The color red

**Kiremt**  The heavy rains, usually occurring between mid-June and mid-September

**Megazen**  Shop, warehouse (imported from Italian)

**Netella**  A gauzy white cotton shawl, with a brightly colored, geometric border

**Teff**  The indigenous and endemic food grain of Ethiopia (the T is the explosive form)

**Zebenya**  Guard

# for furTHer reaDinG

While I am not a historian, I am a lover of history. And I have been a lover of Ethiopian history since my early teen years, during which I waded my way into Jay Williams' book on Solomon and Sheba, and tried to read my parents' copy of *Wax and Gold*, about Ethiopian culture and language. The following are some of the historical resources I have absorbed through the years, in addition to snippets from US newspapers when news of Ethiopia was available, and clippings from Ethiopian newspapers, which Mom sent home in her letters. I offer this resource list for the curious.

- Barker, A.J. (1971). *The Rape of Ethiopia 1936*. New York: Ballantine Books Inc. A history of the Italian invasion of Ethiopia.
- Bulatovich, Alexander, translated & edited by Richard Seltzer (2000). *Ethiopia Through Russian Eyes; Country in Transition 1896–1898*. Trenton, NJ: Red Sea Press. A Russian officer, linguist, cartographer, astronomer and historian accompanied one of Menelik's generals into SW Ethiopia.
- Clapham, Christopher (1969). *Haile Selassie's Government*. London: Longmans, Green and Co. Ltd. A rather scholarly view of His Majesty's reign.
- Cotterell, Peter (1988). *Cry Ethiopia*. Sussex, England: Richard Clay Ltd. The first-hand experience of a missionary living in Ethiopia during the fall of His Majesty's regime and the brutal early years of Mengistu. He weaves history in as I have.
- Darley, Major Henry (1935). *Slaves and Ivory in Abyssinia: A record of adventure and exploration among the Ethiopian Slave-raiders*. New York: Robert M McBride & Co. The first-hand account of years at the British Consul in Maji, and the trip out to Jimma by foot after Menelik's death.
- Hancock, Graham (1992). *The Sign and the Seal: The Quest for the Lost Ark of the Covenant*. New York: Simon & Schuster, Inc. A deep investigation into all the oral myths about the location of the Ark. Spoiler—he concludes it is in Ethiopia!

- Kapuscinski, Ryszard (author) and William R. Brand (translator) (1978). *The Emperor: Downfall of an Autocrat*. New York: Random House. Fascinating and first-hand report on Haile Selassie by a Polish journalist.

- Markakis, John and Nega Ayele (1986) *Class and Revolution in Ethiopia*. Trenton, NJ: The Red Sea Press. There was widespread euphoria about the Ethiopian "bloodless revolution" in the socialist world—until the revolution turned bloody.

- Salvadori, Cynthia (2010). *Slaves and Ivory Continued: Letters of RCR Whalley British Consul, Maji, SW Ethiopia 1930-1935*. Addis Ababa, Ethiopia: Shama Books. More first-hand writing about the situation in deep SW Ethiopia during the early years of the 20th century.

- Tola, Abera (2014). *Ethiopia: Dark side of Oromo expansions and Menelik conquests. ECADF: Ethiopian News and Views*, web article. An article calling for balance between Oromo and Amhara, given that both were brutal in their stages of expansion.

- Vivo, Raul Valdes (1977) *Ethiopia: the unknown revolution*. Ciudad de La Habana, Cuba: Editorial de Ciencias Sociales. Another view of the Ethiopian revolution from the Socialist point of view.

- Williams, Jay (1959). *Solomon and Sheba*. New York: Random House. A rendition of the stories of Solomon and Sheba.

CPSIA information can be obtained
at www.ICGtesting.com
Printed in the USA
LVHW041448220719
624851LV00002B/2

9 781946 395153